Edward Spencer, Thomas Francis Bayard

An Outline of the Public Life and Services of Thomas F. Bayard

Senator of the United States from the State of Delaware, 1869-1880

Edward Spencer, Thomas Francis Bayard

An Outline of the Public Life and Services of Thomas F. Bayard
Senator of the United States from the State of Delaware, 1869-1880

ISBN/EAN: 9783337157784

Printed in Europe, USA, Canada, Australia, Japan

Cover: Foto ©ninafisch / pixelio.de

More available books at **www.hansebooks.com**

AN OUTLINE

OF THE

PUBLIC LIFE AND SERVICES

OF

THOMAS F. BAYARD,

SENATOR OF THE UNITED STATES FROM THE STATE OF DELAWARE,
1869-1880.

WITH EXTRACTS FROM HIS SPEECHES AND THE DEBATES OF CONGRESS.

BY

EDWARD SPENCER.

NEW YORK:
D. APPLETON AND COMPANY,
1, 3, AND 5 BOND STREET.
1880.

COPYRIGHT BY
D. APPLETON AND COMPANY.
1880.

THIS OUTLINE

OF THE PUBLIC LIFE AND SERVICES

OF

THOMAS F. BAYARD

IS DEDICATED TO

THE YOUNG MEN OF THE UNITED STATES.

THE LIVES OF THE FATHERS

ARE OFTEN HELD UP TO THEM AS EXAMPLES:

THE LIFE OF ONE OF THEIR CONTEMPORARIES

SHOWS

HOW THOSE EXAMPLES SHOULD BE FOLLOWED.

Self-reverence, self-knowledge, self-control,
These three alone lead life to sovereign power,
Yet not for power (power of herself
Would come uncalled for), but to live by law,
Acting the law we live by without fear;
And because right is right, to follow right
Were wisdom in the scorn of consequence.
TENNYSON: "Œnone."

[Quoted by Mr. Bayard in his Phi Beta Kappa Oration, Harvard University, June 28, 1877.]

CONTENTS.

CHAPTER I.
	PAGE
ANCESTRY OF MR. BAYARD	1

CHAPTER II.
EARLY LIFE OF MR. BAYARD	13

CHAPTER III.
STATE OF POLITICS—1869-'70	26

CHAPTER IV.
OUTLINE OF MR. BAYARD'S POLITICAL SERVICES . .	47

CHAPTER V.
LEADING QUESTIONS.—MR. BAYARD'S VIEWS . . .	57

CHAPTER VI.
THE UNION AND THE CONSTITUTION . . .	80

CHAPTER VII.
FINANCE AND THE CURRENCY . . .	101

CHAPTER VIII.
TARIFF AND REVENUE REFORM .	133

CHAPTER IX.

"This is a Government of Laws" . . 159

CHAPTER X.

Defense of the South . 185

CHAPTER XI.

The Battle against Centralization 212

CHAPTER XII.

Economy and Reform in Government 231

CHAPTER XIII.

The Electoral Commission 251

CHAPTER XIV.

Mr. Bayard in the Senate . . . 273

LIFE

OF

THOMAS F. BAYARD.

CHAPTER I.

ANCESTRY OF MR. BAYARD.

The family to which Mr. Bayard belongs is a numerous one, and its members are widely distributed in both the Old World and the New. Those who take an interest in antiquarian investigations have traced back its origin to the province of Dauphiné, now the department of the Isère, in the southeast of France, where, about six leagues from Grenoble, the ruins of the Château Bayard, crowning a hill which commands one of the noblest prospects in that romantic region, mark what is regarded as the cradle of the race. From the earliest times the Bayards were distinguished for courage in war and fidelity to their sovereign. A Seigneur de Bayard, the head of the house, was slain at the battle of Poitiers in the vain attempt to prevent the capture of King John the Good by the English. His son fell in combat with the same enemy at Azincourt, and his grandson at Montlhéry. But the second in descent from this last was more widely known than either, and, joining to the hereditary prowess and constancy of his race a purity and nobility of character peculiarly his own, has furnished to history and romance the ideal of a perfect knight. Pierre du Terrail, Seigneur de Bayard,* "the knight without fear and without reproach," was the famous captain of Charles VIII, Louis XII, and Francis I, the latter of whom, after the battle of Marignano, would receive the honor of knighthood from no hand but that of Bayard. In 1503 he, single-handed, kept the bridge of the Garigliano against the Spaniards, and saved the whole French army. In the wars between Francis and the Emperor Charles V, he was the most trusted French leader, and fell by an arquebuse-shot while conducting the retreat at the passage of the Sesia, April 30, 1524. As he left no heirs, his estates and rank descended to the next of kin, and the family name, Du Terrail, was merged in the territorial name Bayard.

Among the descendants of these Bayards were three brothers, Jacques, Thomas, and Philippe, who had embraced the Reformed or Huguenot faith. During the persecutions which followed the Massacre of St. Bartholomew, they, with thousands of their fellow-believers, fled from France, and took refuge in Holland, where their descendants still exist. One of these, Samuel Bayard, early in the seventeenth century, married Anneke, or Anna,

---

* Bayard was not married. Says Jean Cohen, his secretary: "Mais il eu avoir contracté verbalement et par lettres l'engagement avec une belle et noble demoiselle de la maison de Trèque dans le Milanez, de laquelle il avoit eu une fille naturelle, nommée Jeanne Terrail, digne fille du plus vertueux de tous les pères. Elle fut mariée, un an après la mort de son père, à François de Bocsozel, seigneur de Chastelart."

But the records attesting this marriage exist in the church attached to the Château Bayard, in Dauphiny, and were lately exhibited by the curé of the parish, then custodian, to Miss Anderson, the daughter of the gallant General Robert Anderson, of Fort Sumter fame, and who is herself related to the Bayards.

daughter of Balthazar Stuyvesant, and sister of Peter Stuyvesant, governor of New Amsterdam. Anna Bayard, being a widow at the time of her brother's appointment, with her three sons, Balthazar, Nicholas, and Petrus, and a daughter, Catherine, embarked with him for the New World, landing at New Amsterdam, May 11, 1647. From these three brothers all the Bayards in the United States are descended.

Balthazar and Nicholas married in New Amsterdam, and their descendants are still living in New York.* Petrus, the youngest son, also married, established himself in business as a hatter, and was on the road to substantial prosperity, when an event occurred which changed the whole course of his life. This event was his meeting with Dankers and Sluyter, the Labadist emissaries or commissioners.

As the story of the Labadist colony in America is comparatively little known, a few words about it may not be out of place. Jean de Labadie, a man of singular gifts and eloquence, a sort of Protestant Savonarola, with all the enthusiasm and mysticism and the power of swaying the people which distinguished the famous Florentine, had been a shining light of the Jesuit order, but quitted in discontent both it and the Church of Rome, and, after trying various forms of faith and finding none to his mind, resolved as a last resort to found a church of his own. He soon gathered about him a band of devoted followers. Their doctrines differed not greatly from those of the Dutch Reformed Church, but they laid claim

---

* Balthazar married Maritjie Loockermans, and left children who intermarried with the Jays and Stuyvesants. Nicholas was appointed Receiver-General of the New Netherlands in 1673. He was a strong opposer of the seizure of power by Leisler in 1689, and was imprisoned by order of the latter for more than a year.

to a much higher spirituality, and in some respects seem to have resembled the Moravians, in others the Shakers. Certain features of their discipline were so objectionable to the Dutch authorities that they were expelled from one town after another, until at last they found a quiet resting-place at Wiewerd, in Friesland. But here, too, they became straitened both for means and room, and so determined to plant a colony in America.

Two of their leading members, Jasper Dankers and Peter Sluyter, were sent across the Atlantic on a tour of exploration, who, after various wanderings and adventures, pitched upon a tract of land in Cecil County, Maryland, between the Elk and Bohemia rivers, forming part of the great Bohemia Manor grant of Augustine Herrmann, the magnate of that region, and a conspicuous personage in the early history of Maryland. To this choice they were led partly by the fertility of the soil and mildness of the climate, but chiefly by the persuasions of Ephraim Herrmann, son and heir of Augustine, of whom they had made a convert during their stay in New York, and who made them lavish promises of land if they would plant their proposed colony within his father's territory.

The prospect seeming an inviting one to the mother-church in Friesland, Dankers and Sluyter were sent out again to found the settlement as proposed. Ephraim was as good as his word; and through his influence a tract of land between the Elk and Bohemia rivers, and containing about 3,750 acres, was conveyed in August, 1684, to Dankers, Sluyter, and three others, one of whom was Petrus Bayard.

Petrus, like Ephraim, had been made a convert by the missionaries during their stay in New York, and he now resolved to renounce his prospects there, and cast his lot with the Labadists. He was naturalized by the Maryland Assembly on September 26, 1684, and appears to have passed nearly all the rest of his life in the community. The Labadists left no annals or records by which their history can be traced after this settlement; but Petrus is favorably mentioned by name in the sketch of the colony published in 1692 by Dittelbach, a deserter from the sect, who speaks in strong terms of the arbitrary and oppressive rule of Sluyter and his wife. In 1688 the parent-church at Wieword was dissolved, and the property divided among the members; and ten years later the same course was taken by the community at Bohemia Manor. In July, 1698, a partition of the land took place, Samuel Bayard, the eldest son of Petrus, receiving a considerable tract as his share. Petrus himself had probably by this time withdrawn from the community, as he died in New York in 1699. Sluyter reserved the lion's share of the land for himself, and kept up some semblance of a church for several years, but at his death the sect became extinct in Maryland, and the remains of the mother-church in Friesland ceased to exist at about the same time.

Of Samuel, the son of Petrus (or Peter, as he was called after his naturalization in Maryland), we have but little record. He seems to have lived on his Bohemia Manor farm in the ease and abundance which characterized the open-handed life of the Maryland country gentleman of those times. Luxuries were rarer then in the colony than they were fifty years later, and rarer still in those far up-country plantations; but the soil, the forest, and the water furnished plenty for all and for all comers; and Samuel, among his neighbors, passed for a rich man. He built himself a large brick house, in which he and his descendants lived till 1789. He died in 1721, leaving three sons, Samuel, Peter, and James, and one daughter, Mary Anne.

James, the third son, married Mary Asheton, of Virginia, and of this marriage were born two sons, John and James Asheton. John Bayard lived in Philadelphia, and took an active part on the patriotic side at the outbreak of the Revolution. He was chairman of the Committee of Inspection for the county of Philadelphia, and Bancroft pronounces him "a patriot of singular purity of character and disinterestedness; personally brave, pensive, earnest, and devout." *

His brother, James Asheton Bayard, died in 1769, leaving two sons, John, and James Asheton the second, the latter an infant but two years old. John Bayard held the rank of colonel in the American army during the war of the Revolution, in which he distinguished himself by his courage and conduct. He commanded the artillery at the battle of Brandywine.

James Asheton Bayard, the second, was born in Philadelphia, but, after his graduation at Princeton College, removed to Delaware, where he married Anne, daughter of Governor Richard Bassett.† His talents and character soon won for him the esteem of his fellow citizens, who shortly after he had attained his majority elected him one of their representatives in Congress. Here he soon showed his ability as chairman of the committee that conducted

---

* "History of the United States," viii, 385.

† Judith Bassett, the mother of Governor Bassett, was a niece of Augustine Herrmann, and in this way the original Bohemia Manor house came into the Bayard family. Bassett had served with distinction in the Revolutionary war, and commanded a troop of light horse, which was attached to Washington's headquarters at the time of Arnold's treason.

the impeachment of Senator Blount, and particularly distinguished himself by his statesmanlike treatment of the difficult constitutional questions that arose during the progress of that important case. President Adams, who had from the first noted Mr. Bayard's ability, nominated him as Minister to France. The nomination was confirmed by the Senate, and he was commissioned, but declined the appointment. His reasons for this are stated in a characteristic letter:

"WASHINGTON, *February* 22, 1801.

". . . You are right in your conjecture as to the office offered me. I have since been nominated Minister to France, concurred in *nem con.*, commissioned, and resigned. Under proper circumstances, the acceptance would have been complete gratification; but, under the existing, I thought the resignation most honorable. To have taken $18,000 out of the public treasury, with a knowledge that no service could be rendered by me, as the French Government would have waited for a man who represented the existing feelings and views of this Government, would have been disgraceful.

"Another consideration of great weight arose from the part I took in the Presidential election. As I had given the *turn* to the election, it was impossible for me to accept an office which would be held on the tenure of Mr. Jefferson's pleasure. My ambition shall never be gratified at the expense of a suspicion.

"I shall never lose sight of the motto of the great original of our name."

In the House he was one of the leaders of the Federal party; but, far from being a violent partisan, he was conspicuous for wise moderation, forbearance, and constant recognition of the great truth, so often forgotten, that parties are not ends in themselves, but only means to an end; and he never hesitated between the success of his party and the welfare of his country. This he signally displayed in the memorable contest between Jefferson and Burr, where, perceiving that the peace of the country was in danger, he prevailed upon his political allies to sacrifice their party preferences for the general good.

After serving in the House for two terms with an ability, integrity, and patriotism that won the admiration of his political opponents, he was elected to the Senate. In 1812 he was selected by President Madison as one of the commissioners to treat for peace with Great Britain, and it was largely due to his firmness and tact that the treaty of Ghent was signed. While still in Europe he was chosen by the President as envoy to St. Petersburg, but, being seized with a mortal illness, returned to America only to die.

He died in August, 1815, leaving four sons: Richard H., James Asheton, Edward, and Henry M. Bayard, and two daughters.

Richard, the eldest son, was the first mayor of Wilmington. He afterward twice represented Delaware in the United States Senate, from 1836 to 1839, and from 1841 to 1845, and was Minister to Belgium from 1849 to 1852.

James Asheton, the second son, also represented his native State in the Senate, to which body he was elected in 1850, 1856, and 1862. This remarkable proof of the abiding confidence of his fellow citizens was not obtained by any of the arts of the demagogue, which he despised so heartily as almost to err on the other side. He was a consistent constitutional Democrat throughout, devotedly attached to the Union and the Constitution, in his fidelity to which he never swerved; though those who were ready to shift their position with every phase of party exigency, or who held, with Senator Morton, that "definitions advance," in measuring his distance from the new idols which they had set up, imagined that he had moved because they had themselves drifted.

The ties which bound Delaware to her sister States of the South were strong and close, and there were not wanting fiery spirits who would gladly have seen the State swept away on the wave of the secession movement, had not her wisest and most trusted leaders resisted it to the utmost. The whole influence and constant teaching of the Bayards, father and son, were at all times strongly in favor of the Union, and in opposition to secession. The action of the Delaware Legislature in promptly rejecting the proposition of the Mississippi commissioner to induce Delaware to join the new confederacy was wholly in accord with their views and earnest counsels. In fact, the only disunion sentiments ever uttered in Delaware were heard from the ranks of their political and personal opponents; and such sentiments never found favor in the heart of that ancient and patriotic little commonwealth.

As a lawyer he stood in the first rank; and it is hardly an exaggeration to say that his was, perhaps, the finest legal mind that Delaware, in her long line of eminent lawyers, had ever produced. His great strength lay in the depth and singular clearness of his intellect. He possessed but few of the graces of popular oratory, and none of the arts that win popularity; indeed, what gave him eminence as a lawyer was perhaps somewhat injurious to him as a pleader and public speaker. He was apt to forget his hearers and the impression he was making or desired to make upon them, and, following closely the line of thought once started, was utterly, and sometimes amusingly, forgetful of the passage of time, and unconscious of what was going on around him.

This habit of absorbing thought made him sometimes absent-minded to an extent which often surprised, and even annoyed, those who did not know his peculiarities. He would pass acquaintances and even intimate friends on the street without a sign of recognition, and by this apparent discourtesy often gave serious offense, until the cause was explained. Being, however, a man of remarkable simplicity and frankness of character, wholly free from affectation or insincerity, he had the thorough confidence of all who knew him. Spotless integrity, and a lofty independence and straightforwardness that despised all subterfuges, finesse, and crooked ways to ends however desirable, marked his whole career, professional, political, and social.

Not only did these qualities secure him the unbroken confidence of his friends and political allies, as was testified by his re-elections to the Senate, but they were candidly admitted by his political opponents, who more than once paid manly tributes to his worth. An instance of this occurred in the wretched business of the Credit Mobilier, from which more than one once fair reputation issued sadly besmirched. In their report to the House of Representatives, the Republican committee of investigation, after reflecting severely upon the conduct of some of their associates, remarked: "We commend to them, and to all men, the letter of the venerable Senator Bayard, in response to an offer of some of this stock." The letter referred to was written in 1868, before the true character of that complex web of fraud had been exposed, and in it Mr. Bayard had said: "I take it for granted that the corporation has no application to make to Congress on which I shall be called upon to act officially, as I could not, consistently with my views of duty, vote upon a question in which I had a pecuniary interest."

It is almost superfluous to add that while the investigation was in progress, and no one could say on whom next the plague-spot of corruption would be detected, no friend of Senator Bayard felt a moment's uneasiness lest he should for one weak moment have dallied with the temptation.

Mr. Bayard entered political life as a Democrat, and was a candidate for Congress in 1828 as a "Jackson man." From the constitutional principles of that party he has never wavered, nor shrunk from the open avowal of his convictions, in war or in peace. Under the administration of Van Buren he held the position of United States Attorney for Delaware. His three terms in the Senate have already been mentioned.

When, after his election to the Senate in 1862, the unconstitutional "iron-clad" oath was offered to him, the statesman who had grown gray in his country's service, he felt it as an insult as well as an outrage. After an impressive argument and protest, he took the oath, and resigned his seat. Mr. George R. Riddle was then elected to fill the vacancy, but, this gentleman dying not long after, Mr. Bayard was prevailed upon to return and serve out the unexpired term resulting from his own resignation.

While in the Senate he filled many important positions, and on the death of Judge Butler, of South Carolina, became the chairman of the Committee on the Judiciary. His reports and arguments upon constitutional questions always had great weight, and are still cited as authority.

On the same day on which Mr. Bayard was elected to

fill his own unexpired term, his son, Thomas F. Bayard, was also elected for the full succeeding term; and on March 4, 1869, both father and son were senators, the term of the latter beginning at noon of the day when that of the former expired.

Since his retirement Mr. Bayard has lived, with his family, in Wilmington, where he still survives at the age of eighty-one, much enfeebled in body, but cheered by the knowledge that his place is filled by no unworthy successor to his name, his honors, and his principles.

CHAPTER II.

EARLY LIFE OF MR. BAYARD.

THOMAS FRANCIS BAYARD, the second and only surviving son of James Asheton Bayard and Anne Francis,* was born in Wilmington, Delaware, October 29, 1828.

His great-grandfather, Richard Bassett, had joined the Methodist Church under the ministration of Bishop Francis Asbury, and his houses in Dover, Wilmington, and Bohemia Manor were always the homes of the itinerant ministers of that denomination. Mr. Bassett was, in various ways, a leading member of that church, and its historian has had frequent occasion to mention him in terms of gratitude and eulogy.† His descendants continued the hospitable practice of entertaining at their homes the ministers during the conference; and the venerable Ezekiel Cooper always made his home in Wilmington at the house of James A. Bayard. Born of a family connected with Methodism almost from its establishment in this country, Thomas Francis Bayard received the rite of Christian baptism in that church.

Young Bayard's boyhood was spent in Delaware until he reached the age of thirteen, when he went to the

---

* Granddaughter of Captain Tench Francis, of Philadelphia, who was captain of a troop in the American forces in the Revolution.

† Stevens, "History of the Methodist Episcopal Church," i, 316–318; iii, 405; iv, 502.

school of Dr. Francis L. Hawks, at Flushing, on Long Island, a clergyman distinguished for his literary attainments as well as ripe scholarship, with whom he remained until the establishment was broken up.

His father removed to New York in 1843, as a wider field for the practice of his profession—the law—where also he had a daughter married to August Van Cortlandt Schermerhorn. This lady, however, dying, and Mr. Bayard's health beginning to fail, he returned to Delaware. During the residence of his father in New York, young Bayard entered the mercantile house of his brother-in-law, Mr. Schermerhorn, and, applying himself to his duties with zeal and intelligence, laid the foundation of that sound and thorough knowledge of business and that clear, practical grasp of all subjects connected with trade and finance which have been so marked a feature in his career as a statesman. His business training was afterward continued in the house of S. Morris Waln, in Philadelphia, where he remained until he reached the age of twenty.

At this time the death of his elder and only brother drew him back to his parents in Delaware, where he entered upon the study of the law, and was admitted to the bar in 1851, assisting his father in his practice.

An incident of this period of his life has been related to us by a personal friend, in whose words we relate it: "When Mr. Bayard was a young man, and not troubled with a great number of cases, he was called upon to defend a young employee in one of the machine shops who had been accused of stealing tools. Mr. Bayard was successful in his defense, and the young man was acquitted. In consideration of his services, the apprentices and others working in the shop made up a sum of money by general subscription, and brought it to Mr. Bayard, who refused to take it, telling them to give the money to the young man, who would need it to help him to set up for himself and make a start in life. They did so; and to-day that man is a respectable citizen of Wilmington, owning a small homestead, and quite prosperous in business."

Young as he was, Mr. Bayard's marked ability was promptly recognized, and in 1853 he was appointed United States Attorney for Delaware, but resigned the office in 1854. Some of his friends jocosely said, in allusion to his father's high reputation, that "Tom didn't like to hear it said, whenever the firm won a suit, 'Oh, that's the old man.' He wanted to go where he could get the credit of what he did." However this may have been, after resigning the attorneyship, he removed to Philadelphia, and associated himself in legal practice with his friend William Shippen.

Here he remained until 1858, when, Mr. Shippen dying and Mr. Bayard's father being much occupied with the duties of his public office, he returned to Wilmington, and devoted himself laboriously to his profession, in which he rapidly attained eminence.

Besides his regular professional business, his ability and character caused him to be selected by many of his numerous kindred for trusts, executorships, and the management of involved estates; and in this way a great mass of business which he could not delegate to others has been thrown upon him. Both before and after his entrance upon public life, he has been one of the hardest-worked of hard-worked men.

Early in 1861, when war was seen to be imminent, and no one could tell what perils or troubles were ahead, the people of Wilmington, like those of most towns at or near the border, began devising means for self-protection in case of any disorders. The old militia laws had fallen into disuse, and there was really no military arm to support the civil authority in case of any necessity. A militia company was therefore organized under the law, with Mr. W. Thatcher as captain, and Mr. Bayard as first lieutenant. Some time later it virtually ceased to exist, so large a number of its members having enlisted into the United States Army as to make it not worth while to continue the organization, though it was never disbanded. During the excited times which followed, an officer of the Federal army, whose zeal outran his discretion, demanded the arms of the company, which Mr. Bayard refused to surrender without an order from Gen. Du Pont, commanding the militia of Delaware, or from the Governor of the State, as the muskets were the State's property. The officer broke open the door of the armory and carried off the muskets, and the United States Government afterward paid the State of Delaware for them. The matter would not be worth mentioning, had it not given rise long after to a silly story that Mr. Bayard was once "captain of a rebel company."

In June, 1861, while hopes were still entertained by many of a peaceful accommodation, a peace meeting of citizens, without distinction of party, was held in Dover. Mr. Bayard was one of the speakers. While some of those who spoke were passionate in their remarks, he was calm and temperate. He reminded his hearers that "with this secession, or revolution, or rebellion, or by whatever name it may be called, the State of Delaware has naught to do. To our constitutional duties toward each and every member of this Union we have been faithful in all times. Never has a word, a thought, an act of ours, been unfaithful to the Union of our fathers; in letter and in spirit it has been faithfully kept by us."

But he adverted to the horrors of a fratricidal war on so gigantic a scale, the ruin that would be wrought, and the danger that, whatever might be the issue, which no man then could certainly foresee, constitutional liberty might perish in the struggle. Better, he thought, "while deeply deploring the revolution which has severed eleven States from the Union," if a peaceful accommodation was impossible, that the discontented States should be allowed to withdraw than run the awful risk of such a war. His calm and earnest eloquence had great weight, and the meeting resolved "that there was no necessity for convening the Legislature."

This speech, it was alleged by many, saved Delaware from secession. Whether this was so or not, it certainly calmed down a state of excitement in which some unwise action might have been taken. "It brought to men's minds," as a leading Delawarian said, "the fact that they were in the Union—had no part in the rebellion, and that it was their duty to remain as they were, and keep Delaware as one of the United States." In this, as ever, he approved himself faithful to the Constitution and the Union under it, his devotion to which has never wavered, as witness his public record, from first to last.

There was, it is true, a secession speech made at that meeting (at least, such is the statement of a newspaper), but it was made by a gentleman now an office-holder of the Republican party. Nor do we mean to imply that this gentleman was insincere either then or now: it was a time when many men were thrown off their balance, and viewed things distorted under the all-prevailing excitement. Not all had the calm, steady mind that stood like a rock amid the storm.

Though always much interested in political matters, he had scarcely taken any prominent part in them until his election to succeed his father in the Senate, as has been already mentioned. At once he became one of the most active and laborious members of that body. Of course, the small conservative minority could do little in controlling legislation, but there was much effective work he could do on committees; and, on matters not of a party character, his voice was often heard with effect, as it always was with attention. His moderation, urbanity, dignity of manner, and personal character won him the esteem of his political opponents; and even the overbearing Morton and passionate Logan treated him with respect. They recognized in him an antagonist that always fought fair; that never willfully misrepresented an opponent, never lost his temper, and never struck a foul blow. And his earnest presentation of facts, his manly appeals to their better judgment, often carried more weight than the most fiery and vehement eloquence could have done. And as he would not condescend to tricks in debate, so he earnestly opposed all irregular strategy in party action, such as placing political riders on appropriation bills, defeating objectionable legislation by withholding supplies from any department of the Government, and similar indirect tactics.

Notwithstanding his robust frame, the excessive labor he has undergone has sometimes taxed him to the utmost, and in 1872 he was quite broken down by hard work on the New York Custom-House and Southern committees of investigation. However, he won a great triumph in the repeal of the moiety laws, and those permitting the seizure of merchants' books and papers under "general warrant"; for, at that time, the Democrats had but fifteen votes in the Senate, and not only the custom-house officers but the whole administration bitterly opposed the repeal.

In 1875, when President Grant was urging the passage of the "force bills," and a struggle of sheer endurance in debate was imminent, as it was evident the revolutionary programme could only be defeated by steady and prolonged resistance, Mr. Bayard, in his absence, was chosen by his associates as their leader in the coming contest.

In the year 1877 he received the honorary degree of LL. D. of Harvard College, and delivered an eloquent address before the Phi Beta Kappa Society, of which he is an honorary member, the subject being "Unwritten Law." Indeed, so general has been the admiration of his character among young men, who are so quick to recognize true chivalry, that he has been made honorary member of nearly half the literary societies in the country.

In the Senate he is now Chairman of the Committee on Finance, and member of the Committee on the Judiciary.

On November 11, 1879, on the occasion of his return from Europe, he was welcomed by his fellow citizens with a public reception, which called together perhaps the largest assemblage ever collected in Wilmington. Men of all parties joined in welcoming him, and testifying their personal respect and their appreciation of his services to his country. He made a brief address, full of feeling and gratitude, such as the occasion and circumstances might well excite. "This," he said, "is the town where I was born, as was my father before me; and in this room is many a face well known to me from childhood. In full view of those who now surround me, my life has been lived, and my incomings and outgoings all known. When, therefore, the judgment of such a court comes to be passed after a full half century of trial and experience in private life and in public service, and it is rendered in sentences so full of generous approbation, affection, and respect as your worthy and venerable chairman [Dr. L. P. Bush] has addressed to me, what must be my emotions, and how full to overflowing my cup of blessings and of honor!"

After adverting to what he had observed in Europe, he contrasts that country with this, not to make the usual vainglorious boast, but to draw a lesson of admonition.

"This summer I have been looking across the Atlantic, thinking of the country I could not see; contrasting what I did see of the daily lives of men and women in other lands with that of my own, and when so often I heard 'Labor with a groan and not a voice,' and realized the abuses and injustice of class privilege, whereby the bar of humble birth was kept and fastened on men from the cradle to the grave, I turned, as if for purer air, to the American States, where the noble equities of humanity are acknowledged and respected, and where the one great essential equality, *the equality of opportunity*, is secured to all. And experience and reflection, with increased opportunities for comparison with other countries and systems of government, bring me only to a higher appreciation of the generosity, justice, and moral grandeur of the principles upon which our own was founded.

"But my admiration for our system of government was accompanied by an apprehensive realization of the conditions under which only it can be practically and permanently maintained.

"And the conviction grows stronger and clearer daily that such a government can only be maintained by the exercise and employment of the higher and better qualities of human nature.

"It is a government of laws emanating from popular will, but that will must be for honest and worthy ends, accomplished by honorable means. It is controlled by public opinion, but that opinion must be the intelligent result of knowledge carefully acquired, and deliberation, and not the unstable froth of tumult and gusty passion. And, to make public principles secure, they must be engrafted on private honor; the wishes of an intelligent and upright constituency must be reflected by intelligent and upright representatives.

"A faithful representative should rather displease his constituents than consent to that which injures them. It is his duty fully and freely to account to them, but not to conceal his true opinions for fear of their displeasure, for his enlightened conscience can not be disregarded without injury to them and his entire loss of usefulness.

"To maintain this government of ours, such are some of the conditions, and it is upon the self-protecting elements of society that we must rely."

In October, 1856, Mr. Bayard married Louisa, daughter of Josiah Lee, a well-known banker of Baltimore, and has three sons and six daughters living.

In his family life Mr. Bayard is exceedingly plain and

domestic, living in summer in Wilmington, and in Washington in the winter.

A newspaper correspondent thus describes his home, and, in part, the host: "His summer home is a fine old-fashioned mansion, situated in the outskirts of Wilmington (on Clayton Street), which was once the property of S B. Davis, the guardian of Myra Clark, now known to fame as Myra Clark Gaines. It is a roomy house, furnished with a view solely to comfortable living. Mr. Bayard's 'den,' or library, has all the marks of the working room of a man of literary tastes. The walls are lined with book-shelves, and the table is always covered with books and papers, which are confusion itself to anybody but himself. The floor, too, is strewed with books and newspapers. The visitor always finds the host at work, but never too busy to talk. For Tom Bayard is not only the soul of hospitality, but one of the most fluent talkers you ever saw. When he gets very much interested, he is apt to walk up and down the room with his hands in his pockets and indulge in a monologue. His words flow like water from the mouth of a pitcher, and if taken down in shorthand they will be found to make perfect sentences and notable for the display of a rich vocabulary.

"No one is more popular in Washington society than Mr. Bayard, and, adding to his genial, manly qualities a thorough acquaintance with French, he is one of the most sought-after of our public men at the dinners and receptions of the diplomatists who make their residence here. He lives, however, the life of a very simple republican gentleman, with good taste and unostentatiously. He gives his hospitality to his friends, and never turns his home into a place for the intrusion of vulgar politics, where he may advance his interests by entertaining a horde of people in whom he has no interest save as they may advance his own."

Yet Mr. Bayard is not one of those expansive souls who open every chamber of their hearts to every comer. There is a delicate reserve about him, a sort of shrinking from anything like effusiveness, which has been sometimes mistaken for pride. This quality is well characterized in a private letter from a gentleman, eminent for his knowledge of men and fine reading of character, who has known him for twenty-five years, and who had been applied to by the writer for some personal reminiscences.

"Our ideas and feelings," he writes, "not to say fancies, have run a great deal in the same grooves, and there has been a sort of *rapport* between us, which has been established, naturally enough, no doubt, but I can hardly tell you how. He is very fond of poetry, and very much alive to its influences in all ways. His sensibilities are quick; his feelings are tender; he has a great deal of sentiment, and before he took to finance and statesmanship in general was of a decidedly imaginative turn. In social and private life he is absolutely simple, natural, and unaffected, with a boyishness that would be boyish, if it were not, like everything else in his character, thoroughly manly. It is very, very attractive to me, that perfect genuineness of life, thought, and conversation, in any man who has seen the world and knows it; but in a public man, who has breathed the malarious air of the capital for so many years, with all its moral sinks and undrained political sewers, it is positively marvelous.

"But all this is *talk*, which you have more than enough of. I have not one reminiscence to give you; nor do I believe you can get many from those who know Bayard best and see him most. He belongs to that thoroughly healthy class who exhibit no symptoms—much less phenomena. You would not notice a manly, or kind, or gentle thing in him, because you associate the idea of nothing else with him. If I wanted him to try a case for a poor client for nothing, and do his best, I would send the case to him without asking, and he would do it as a matter of course. He lives his life so naturally that you can not write it unless you write the whole of it."

But, if we have failed to depict the character of Mr. Bayard, we can at least give his own idea of what an American statesman should be, as told in his speech before the Phi Beta Kappa Society, and leave those who know him to judge how far his own life corresponds to his ideal.

"It is in our power to create a standard of American character and manhood as lofty as that of any age or nation, and to compel our representatives at home and abroad to conform their conduct to it.

"The spirit of true chivalry in all its gentleness and unselfishness, showing tenderness to the feeble and resistance to the overbearing, mercy to whom mercy is due, and honor to whom honor, can and does exist in America to-day, under the 'hodden gray' of the laborer and mechanic, the threadbare coat of the clerk, or the grave garb of the hard-worked merchant or man of the professions as truly as it ever did under the helmet and chain-armor of any knight-errant in the olden time.

"The American people can justly demand from those who are delegated to represent them abroad or at home a punctilious observance of honor and delicate pride in their private and public conduct, and the moral influence to be obtained by dignified self-respect, intelligence, and high personal integrity will far outweigh any attempted competition with the show and glitter of the representatives of other governments, not based upon the principle of voluntary and orderly self-control."

And we may close this chapter with the closing words of his address to the students of the University of Virginia, as the echo of the inmost feeling of his nature:

>"Who misses or who wins the prize,
> Go, lose or conquer as you can;
> But if you fall, or if you rise,
> Be each, pray God, a GENTLEMAN."

CHAPTER III.

STATE OF POLITICS.—1869–'70.

THOMAS FRANCIS BAYARD entered the Senate of the United States at the first session of the Forty-first Congress. He came into public life at the same time that General Grant first took the presidency. The Presidential election of the preceding year had been a most exciting one, because so many conflicting hopes were risked upon it. One side of those whose political convictions were ardent and active thought that all that had been accomplished during and since the civil war was staked upon the result; the other side conceived that it involved the safety of all that remained of constitutional government. Probably much the larger majority of voters did not hold either of these admittedly partisan views, but they were tired and worn out with the excitements and evil effects of a long and violent struggle, which, after the losses and bloodshed of four years of frightful strife, had been continued during four more years upon the floors of Congress. They wanted a settlement, scarcely caring upon what terms it was made, so that it was conclusive and promised to be final. They wanted civil peace as well as military truce; they wanted a restoration of social harmony, and a permanent renewal of general business on the basis of fiscal reform and financial regeneration.

The canvass of 1868 was made by the Democratic

party under the leadership of Horatio Seymour, of New York, a statesman whose ability and patriotism were conceded even by those who were inclined to deplore his irresoluteness, not to say vacillation, in making up his mind to action; but his force, his popularity, and his winning eloquence were heavily handicapped by the widespread mistrust inspired by the nomination of Francis P. Blair, Jr., as the second person on the ticket—a mistrust which ripened into open revolt after the publication of General Blair's "Brodhead letter," practically asserting his belief that the constitutional amendments had no validity. The platform on which Mr. Seymour, an avowed "hard-money man," had been nominated, was utterly sophisticated and made distasteful to the business community by having injected into it the greenback heresies of the Ohio politicians. On the other hand, both the candidates and the platform of the Republicans were strong and positive. Those who objected to the latter had at least the satisfaction of understanding it. It pledged the party and the candidates under it to the enforcement of the constitutional amendments. It favored the resumption of specie payments and the inviolability of the public debt. The candidate for the vice-presidency on this ticket was Schuyler Colfax, an active and popular politician, the Speaker of the House of Representatives, whose hopes of a career had not yet been blighted by the disclosure of his connection with the Pacific Railroad Credit Mobilier. Ulysses S. Grant, the nominee for the presidency, was stronger in those days than either his party or its platform. He was the successful military chieftain who had conducted a great war to its end. In the immediate hour of victory he had been modest in regard to himself, magnanimous toward his enemies. He was not a politician, and he had seemed anxious to eschew a party nomination, expressing his wish to be the candidate of and to be elected "by the whole people." He had administered the War Department frugally and prudently, and it was not then known that he was incapable of true statesmanship, and had not a jot of respect for the reservations and limitations of a Constitution whose text and whose principles he knew surprisingly little about. Indeed, very little was known of him besides his military history, but that little was generally in his favor. The persistent silence of such a man did not seem to be either perverse or vacuous, when the few rifts in it revealed such words as, "Let us have peace."

The country desired peace as ardently in 1868 as it does in 1880, and people who were not politicians nor eager in regard to the exact drawing of political lines and political distinctions, really believed and hoped that peace would be obtained by supporting the candidature of Grant. In the election of November 3, 1868, Grant and Colfax received 214 electoral votes to 80 for Seymour and Blair. Delaware's vote was given to the latter, and Mr. Bayard entered the Senate to become the steadfast opponent of the Republican party, and of the acts and tendencies of President Grant's administration.

This opposition was not the outgrowth of a factious temper, nor of a partisan spirit. Mr. Bayard, though always a party man, was never a mere partisan. But his close observation of the acts and debates of the Thirty-ninth and Fortieth Congresses had given him the worst opinion of the designs of the Republican majority in Congress, and he knew that even so strong a man as Grant, if he refused to lead, would be compelled to follow in the pathway of extreme radicalism. He knew that the

Forty-first Congress was the political executor of its immediate predecessors, and that to complete and "perfect" the "policy of reconstruction" according to the plan which had been mapped out would require the Republican party to take still longer strides toward centralization, and to make still more serious encroachments upon the Constitution. Mr. Bayard entered Congress with the one leading idea, one polar star of intent, which every vote cast, every word uttered by him in his senatorial service, has served to disclose: it was to restore the Union in reality and bind the hearts of his countrymen in the common cause of national pride, honor, and welfare. To this end he has denounced and opposed everything tainted with sectional animosity, or tending to the injury or discredit of the Union. His guide has been the Constitution and the equality of each and every member of the great "family of States" and their inhabitants.

The Thirty-ninth Congress, in seeking what it chose to consider "security for the future," had in effect remodeled the Constitution to suit the extreme views of the overwhelming majority which directed its legislation. It had passed a great variety of measures, such as the Freedman's Bureau Bill, the Civil Rights Bill, the Reconstruction Act, the Tenure of Office Act, etc., which President Johnson regarded as being unconstitutional. When he vetoed them, the bills were passed over his objections, and the House, in retaliation for his disagreements with Congress, adopted articles of impeachment against him, which the Fortieth Congress pressed with a vehemence very nearly successful. Mr. Bayard knew that President Grant would not risk exposing himself to any such collisions with Congress as those which President Johnson was forced to bear the brunt of, and consequently he felt satisfied that the reconstruction policy would be pushed forward to the bitter end.

That policy inspired every one holding Mr. Bayard's views about the Constitution with the most gloomy forebodings. The power claimed for Congress to enforce, by "appropriate legislation," the new amendments to the Constitution, was practically unlimited, except in so far as that body was amenable to the pressure of public opinion effectively awakened. The opposition in Congress could do nothing but protest—so long as the majority had a two thirds vote in both Houses and so long as they proved their determination to maintain this controlling preponderance of force by admitting new communities like Colorado and Nebraska into the family of States, even while keeping out Virginia and Georgia and Louisiana. It was natural to suppose that General Grant would not be particularly hostile to the indefinite maintenance of military government in the South, nor to the "enforcement acts" which practically gave to commanders, personally appointed by him from among his favorites, entire control of the machinery of elections in that section. His ambition, though not at that time known, was suspected, and, anyhow, he was a man who needed to be curbed by explicit laws, rather than to be given free rein and the impetus of new powers and new authority created expressly for him to exercise.

The Forty-first Congress was not composed of members likely to inspire a strict constructionist with confidence in their moderation or their power of abstention from injurious law-making. In many respects it was worse than its predecessors. It is true that James H. Lane and Benjamin Wade were no longer there, and Thaddeus Stevens had succumbed. But Simon Cameron and John Scott sat in the seats of Cowan and Buckalew, and Oliver P. Morton had entered the Senate; Daniel Pratt had replaced Thomas A. Hendricks; Conkling had succeeded Ira Harris, and the successors of Collamer and Fessenden were much more extreme than they had been. The Democrats had secured an immense gain in the person of Allen G. Thurman, but it grieved them and mortified even their opponents to see the vacant seats of senators from the Southern States filled so generally by the class of men called "carpet-baggers." These adventurers, in a body, voted with the Radicals on political issues, and (with some few exceptions) put their votes where they would "do them the most good" in indifferent questions. They were the source of a great deal of corruption, and eventually of great injury to the Republican party, but their votes were indispensable in working out "the policy of reconstruction," and for the sake of these votes the drill-masters of their party, such as Morton and Conkling, graciously condoned their "evil communications," and cherished their association.

But it was simply a caricature upon representative government to find the seats of Houston and Wigfall filled by men like Flanagan and Hamilton; to see "Parson" Brownlow seated where John Bell and Andrew Johnson had sat; to see Florida represented by Gilbert and Osborn, and George E. Spencer and Willard Warner coming up to Washington with their credentials as "senators from Alabama" stuffed in their carpet-bags. Louisiana was represented by such men as John S. Harris, William Pitt Kellogg, and J. Rodman West. Mississippi was admitted with Hiram Revells (colored man) and Adelbert Ames for its senators (a *coup de théâtre* which soon ended). South Carolina had for its senators T. J. Robertson and T. J. Sawyer. There were certain men, named Abbott and Pool, who had been admitted as senators from North Carolina. When Clayton and Dorsey came in from Arkansas, the carpet-bagger *coterie* was quite made up.

In spite of its incongruous elements, and its diverse and unequal composition, however, the Senate of the Forty-first Congress was an able body, and a picturesque one also. Schuyler Colfax, Vice-President and the presiding officer, was remarkably well fitted for the performance of the routine and physical duties devolving upon him. He was quick, alert, and fair in his rulings. He had great experience as a Congressman, and had served as Speaker for three successive Congresses, passing, indeed, direct from the Speaker's chair to the Vice-President's. The Chaplain of the Senate, Rev. J. P. Newman, D. D., was a leading divine of the Methodist Church, and a particular friend of Grant, to whom he delighted to minister. The Secretary was George C. Gorham, of California, esteemed then and now to be the astutest "whip" and the most skillful "wire-puller" in the Republican party; while conspicuous among the lesser officials was the venerable and white-headed Isaac Bassett, from time immemorial assistant door-keeper of the Senate.

The *habitués* of the reporters' gallery knew all those "good gray heads" below them (but the Forty-first Congress had, perhaps, more than its proportion of men whose locks did not indicate the pale cast of thought), and even the most transient spectator in the strangers' gallery would understand that senators sat right or left of the Vice-President's desk, according to their party affiliations. The irony of the arrangement was to crowd the entire body of conservative members upon "the extreme left," and to give them seats upon "the mountain" rather than on the equable plain where their thoughts were wont to exercise.

Front seat, middle aisle, left-hand side, one of the best seats in the chamber, was occupied by Oliver P. Morton, the "great war governor" of Indiana, one of the clearest heads, the ablest minds who ever came into the Senate. If Morton had been in Congress earlier, the radical party could have done without Thaddeus Stevens, for Morton was the Mirabeau, the Marat, and the Danton of his party. An intense and earnest man, the logical texture of his intellect was so fine that it was only equaled by the convenient pliancy of his convictions. He was equally intrepid in declaring his opinions, and in abandoning them when they became inconvenient. It did not trouble him to see the *reductio ad absurdum* at the end of the vista of his argument, and his "platform" was arranged upon the principle of the ferry-boat piers in New York, so as to rise and fall in proportion to the height of every tide. Morton's head was fully as clear as the general tone of his intellect was somber. He had what is called a "legal mind," and his mental vision was seldom obscured by those clouds of hesitancy and doubt which breed irresolution in persons of more fastidious conscience. He was seldom surpassed in the faculty of stripping off the veils in which men are wont to cloak a dubious statement, and of presenting it in all its rude, naked, brutal force. He was a born leader, full of ambition. He wreaked his bitterness upon his political associates only less than upon his political enemies. Oliver P. Morton was the type, and the ablest exemplar of a class of politicians which has come to the surface since and in consequence of the civil war. It is to be hoped that they will entirely disappear with the influences which gave them conspicuousness and the generation in which they lived and have been tolerated.

George F. Edmunds had an equally good seat on the same row, and four desks off from Morton. Like the Senator from Indiana, Mr. Edmunds had clean hands and a clear head, but, while Morton was an impetuous leader, the instinct of Edmunds is not formative, but destructive. He is a critic and a detective, with a much keener eye for flaws and blemishes than for beauties. His intellect, like his wit, is mordant; he is better at setting pitfalls for others than in mapping out broad pathways for himself. He conducts politics as some men play whist, expecting to profit more by watching the play and surprising the errors of his opponents than by his own superior skill. He ventures less upon finesse of his own than upon exposing the maladroitness of others. It is currently believed among the attachés of the Senate that Edmunds has eyes in the back of his head, and that his ears are never confused, no matter what bedlam of sounds may be rife. He is a very serviceable Senator, especially to his party; and it is probably not a bad thing for a seat in the Senate to be constantly occupied by a man who is at once the bane of fools and the terror of adventurers and jobbers.

Not far back of Mr. Edmunds sat Roscoe Conkling, who already then, as he still continues to do, contemplated himself as *the* Senator from New York. The Senator has the advantages which considerable culture, great abilities as a lawyer and a politician, and great adroitness in threading both the broader and narrower ways of party "management," have secured to him. Mr.

Conkling was the rival of Senator Morton in the " cabal " which conducted most of the political business of ex-President Grant during his two terms in office, and it is likely that Conkling reaped many more personal benefits from this alliance than fell to Morton's share. But he has not Morton's political courage, much less his moral and physical courage.

William Pitt Fessenden, of Maine, was chairman of the Committee on Finance in March, 1869, a man of singular ability and fairness. His vote against the impeachment of Andrew Johnson had not been forgiven by his party, but he was allowed to hold his place at the head of the Committee on Finance. He died, however, during the recess of Congress, and at the beginning of the ensuing session the chairmanship of this committee fell to John Sherman, of Ohio, the present Secretary of the Treasury. Sherman sat on the left, near the main aisle. Careful, laborious, astute, and watchful, Mr. Sherman was the embodiment of calculation. It is possible that he has convictions in regard to finance, to the tariff, and political affairs generally; it is certain, however, that he has always held to these by a cable which he could slip whenever the breeze seemed either to favor or to threaten. In relation to the currency, Mr. Sherman has shifted his helm quite as often as Morton; but what Morton did for the good of the party, Mr. Sherman did for the good of John Sherman. He probably knew more about banking than any other man in Congress; and in his present position it must not be denied that he has done the country substantial service.

The three seats on the extreme right of the Senate Chamber were occupied by a rare group. In front was William G. Brownlow; behind him Hiram R. Revells, the comfortable-looking mulatto selected to succeed Jefferson Davis; while the upper seat was filled by Mr. J. W. Flanagan, of Flanagan's Mills, Texas, whose like the Senate will not soon look upon again. This Senator, whose orthography was practically, if not theoretically, phonetic, and who regarded all syntax as an open question, if not an impertinence, was always conspicuous in the discussions of educational subjects. When the Republicans in 1873 displaced Charles Sumner from his post as Chairman of the Committee on Foreign Relations, putting Simon Cameron in his stead, they assigned Sumner to the foot of Flanagan's class, the Committee on "Education and Labor," of which he was chairman, and his son, who on his visiting cards described his office as "Cleark," was clerk.

On the rear seat, behind Mr. Edmunds, sat Charles Sumner, and in front of him Henry Wilson, his colleague from Massachusetts. Carl Schurz, present Secretary of the Interior, was in the front row on the left side of the Chamber, his colleague, Charles D. Drake, whose efficient services to Republicanism were paid with the Chief Judgeship of the Court of Claims, occupying an outside desk on the right of the main aisle. On the right of Edmunds sat Henry B. Anthony, of Rhode Island, one of the oldest, shrewdest, and most capable Senators in the whole body, looking much more like a "cotton lord" than his colleague, William Sprague. On Mr. Anthony's right sat a "studious-looking, stoop-shouldered gentleman"—Mr. Justin S. Morrill, late Chairman of the Ways and Means Committee of the House, and author and framer of the successive bills which have saddled the country with the protective-tariff system. Mr. Morrill seized his opportunity early, in March, 1861, in fact, as soon as the members whose States had seceded were outside the doors of Congress, and he probably knows more about "woolens" than any other man in Washington.

In the front row sat Simon Cameron, between John Pool and Justin Morrill, his small eyes twinkling cannily beneath the gray pent-house brows. On Mr. Edmunds's left, stout, oleaginous, Pecksniffy, was Samuel C. Pomeroy,* one of Kansas's senators, and behind him Hannibal Hamlin, of Maine, a fossiliferous remnant of ante-bellum days in look, but modern enough and wise enough in ways if you came to deal with him. Reuben E. Fenton, the Greeleyite Senator from New York, sat in the middle row on the far right, and behind him Matthew H. Carpenter, of Wisconsin, a man whose appearance and whose address are equally fascinating, a clever lawyer, and the most ready debater on constitutional questions in the Senate, whose mind is as clear as a bell, who argues one way and votes another, and continually takes retainers in causes which he despises. Not far from Sumner sat James W. Nye, of Nevada, whose vulgar wit must have been particularly distasteful to the fastidious Senator from Beacon Street. Jacob M. Howard, of Michigan, a plodding, laborious Senator, but a good lawyer, sat on Nye's right, and on Mr. Howard's right again was Zachariah Chandler, Howard's uproarious colleague, gaunt, harsh, boisterous, repulsive, purse-proud, but prompt, resolute, energetic, full of daring, full of business training and resourceful mother-wit, and utterly unscrupulous in regard to any question of ways and means. Chandler knew both men and things thoroughly well. His success as a merchant was easy to understand. One of his speeches in the Senate in 1870, on the decline of American ship-

---

* Senator Dilworthy, of the "Golden Age."

ping, made after a visit to the British iron-ship yards on the Clyde and the Mersey, is quite the best speech on that subject.

Lyman Trumbull, one of the ablest lawyers and most conscientious men in the Senate, sat beside Timothy O. Howe, Carpenter's colleague, not a bad lawyer himself, but a wretched speaker. James Harlan, of Iowa, who became Grant's Secretary of the Interior, and George H. Williams, of Oregon, afterward Grant's Attorney General, did not sit together, but were " tarred with the same stick." If they had come from Southern States, they would have earned the title of carpet-baggers. Both notoriously unscrupulous, Harlan found in the Indian Bureau what Williams sought in the department of justice, and both are thought to have worked their placers pretty well.

The Democratic phalanx in the Senate when Mr. Bayard came to reinforce it was not strong, neither was it compact. The two oldest members, George Vickers, of Maryland, and Garrett Davis, of Kentucky, happened to be, both of them, uncompromising, old-line, Henry Clay Whigs, and devoted and "unconditional Union men," whose war fevers and war fervor had been suddenly quenched by Mr. Lincoln's emancipation proclamation and by the anti-slavery amendment. Both these estimable old gentlemen had had "hay on their horns" for some years at the very idea of an enforced negro equality; and the zeal with which they now fought for the reserved rights of the States was as amusing as it was sincere. It recalls an anecdote which that eminent Knickerbocker, James W. Gerard, used to tell of the famous "Doctors' Riot" in New York. Among those who went out with the Mayor and the troops was Baron von Steuben, the Revolutionary general, who, when the military

were about to fire, lifted his hands in horrified protest.
"For God's sake, do not—" he began, when a well-aimed
missile struck him in the forehead and felled him to the
ground. As soon as he could be picked up, he shouted, in
quite a different tone: "Shoodt the taint schoundrels,
Mayor, shoodt dem!"

Mr. Vickers was a small, quiet, unobtrusive gentleman,
of very estimable life. He had grown gray as a family
lawyer in a country town, and was not used to the turmoil
of politics. He was sound and stanch, however, delivered
long, solid constitutional arguments, that were a bit prosy,
perhaps, but he could and did sit it out with the best of
them in those frequent all-night sessions in which argument was hopeless, and filibustering became a disagreeable
party duty. Mr. Garrett Davis, on the contrary, was a
salamander in the fire of politics, his natural element. He
was the most peppery of senators, always quarreling, and
never letting the sun go down upon his wrath. The sun
often went down, and sometimes rose, upon his speeches,
however, which were the longest of the period, dry as
stubble, and seldom exhilarating in their style. Mr. Davis
was a sterling old gentleman, as courteous and high-
minded as he was garrulous, and as ready to joke as any
of his opponents were about "the short gentleman's long
speeches."

On some of the questions arising in the Senate, then
and later, the Democrats were aided by the voices and
votes of Lyman Trumbull, of Boreman and Willey, the
two senators from West Virginia, of Hamilton, of Texas,
Norton, of Minnesota, Fenton, of New York, and Tipton,
of Nebraska, the latter, together with Fowler, of Tennessee, and Robertson, of South Carolina, becoming more
and more liberal as their experience grew. But the Dem-

ocratic names which could be depended upon on all occasions were few indeed when Mr. Bayard came first to the Senate. Eugene Casserly, of California, was one of the best and strongest of these—a man who always stood by Mr. Bayard's side. In the New York Custom-House Investigations Mr. Casserly and Senator Bayard were in steady coöperation. William T. Hamilton, of Maryland, the present Governor of that State, was a clear, logical speaker, a strict State-rights Democrat, and a pronounced and most uncompromising believer in hard money. Large, portly, yet active in person, plain, homely, farmer-like in dress and manners, with an emphatic style of direct speech, and in conversation a proclivity for expletives and round, Jacksonian oaths, few who did not know him were able to detect under this exterior the wealthy capitalist and banker, the experienced politician, and a Congressman of three successive terms. Mr. Hamilton's seat was about midway of the middle row of desks upon the left. The farthest seat upon the outer row on the left was occupied by John W. Johnston, then as now Senator from Virginia, a safe, unassuming man, business-like rather than brilliant, but looking after the concerns of his constituents with steadfast, unflagging solicitude.

In the same row, in the rear of Mr. Hamilton, sat Thomas C. McCreery, of Kentucky, whose confessed laziness did not prevent him from being one of the most original and striking "characters" of the Senate. He probably thought—at any rate, acted as if he thought—that Garrett Davis had superfluous energy enough for two senators. He seldom spoke, seldom made a motion, or offered a resolution, or indulged in incidental remarks (the index of Senate proceedings gives ten times as much space to Sherman or Sumner, or Pomeroy, as to

McCreery), yet, whenever he did speak, he was sure of a large and delighted audience, for he was an orator such as only Kentucky has produced, elegant, ornate, imaginative. He had the appearance and wore the dress of the "old school," but in a sort of negligé withal. His round figure, bald head, encinctured as with the priestly tonsure, and his somnolent manner, were charmingly conspicuous from the galleries.

Mr. Bayard's desk was immediately in front of that of Mr. John P. Stockton, Democratic Senator from New Jersey. Mr. Stockton, son of Commodore Stockton, the distinguished millionaire diplomatist and Senator, was himself marked with many traits inherited from his father. He had the look, the aplomb, and the manners of a resident at foreign courts, as he had been, and was withal a most able Senator and a thoroughly capable man in every way. His thoughtful face and incisive address were sharpened and intensified by the consciousness that he had been made to suffer unworthily for opinion's sake. He was unquestionably turned out of the Senate by a majority vote on March 27, 1866, in order to give the Republicans a two thirds majority in that body. Mr. Stockton was a Democrat by education and conviction, and he and Mr. Bayard worked together with perfect unanimity on many momentous occasions. He looked, dressed, and had the manners of a high-bred man of the world, was a clever debater, and never missed the chance to make a point against his political opponents.

Willard Saulsbury, who sat next to Mr. McCreery and was Mr. Bayard's colleague, as he had been the colleague of James Asheton Bayard, was not a ready debater, though a frequent one. But he was a good lawyer, having served for five years as Attorney General of Delaware, and he was the last surviving Democrat of the old régime left in the Senate. The wave which swept Jesse D. Bright away had failed to remove Mr. Saulsbury, who was an inveterate peace Democrat, always ready, in season and out of season, to raise his voice in protest against the revolutionary acts which he could not arrest. Mr. Saulsbury, who originally came into the Senate in 1859, was perhaps a "Bourbon," but he had in a very high degree the courage of his opinions, and all through the period from 1860 to 1870 he never ceased to denounce what he found to be contrary to the principles he held and flagitious in his views of the sanctity of the Constitution. His speeches were elaborate, long, heavy, but downright and direct. The Republicans tried to avoid replying to him, but very often his stalwart accusations irritated them to make fierce retorts. An indomitable stickler for precedent, restless, impatient, often pacing the carpet in the rear of the senators' seats, Mr. Saulsbury never concealed that half his affection for Delaware consisted in admiration of her old ways. "I say, as one of the representatives of Delaware on this floor," he remarked when the Freedman's Bureau Bill was under discussion in the Thirty-ninth Congress, "that she has the proud and noble character of being the first to enter the Federal Union under a Constitution formed by equals. She has been the very last to obey a mandate, legislative or executive, for abolishing slavery. She has been the last slave-holding State, thank God, in America, and I am one of the last slave-holders in America."

Next to Senator Johnston sat Allen G. Thurman, of Ohio, one of the best and readiest debaters, ablest lawyers, and clearest-headed men who ever came to the Senate. No one can note his square, sturdy figure, his firm face, not without the illumination of a sort of grim humor twinkling in it, and the inimitable flourish of his red bandanna handkerchief as he takes snuff, without recognizing at once the mental gladiator filled with *certaminis gaudia*. A Virginian by birth, brought up among plain Ohio folks, a judge and a lawyer deep read in the principles and versed in all the practical rules of his profession, an ardent politician of the Jacksonian school, with amendments made to conform systems to his own original thought, Senator Thurman came to the Senate fortified with a store of unusual resources, which he is always willing and even eager to draw upon at sight in an unlimited way. Critical as Edmunds, he has that sort of constructive ability in which Edmunds is conspicuously lacking. His services on the Judiciary Committee have been important and valuable, and his power of work is simply prodigious. Edmunds can pick to pieces a bill, a charter, or a proposition, but Thurman can amend it so as to remove its evils, and give vitality and usefulness to what was before noxious and injurious. He is full of ambition, wants to be President, likes the sound of his own voice. He would have been a still more serviceable Senator, a more prominent and a more consistent statesman, had he chanced to represent some other State than Ohio. The turbid condition of politics there, the conflict of interest and faction, the winds of party favor blowing from so many different quarters, have not always enabled this learned and astute Senator to sail as directly on one course as plain men desire. He has had to steer between Scylla and Charybdis, and his keel has been abraded by the deadly rocks upon both larboard and starboard. The Democratic party and the country, however, owe a debt of recognizance to Judge Thurman which it will not be easy to forget. His acumen, his logic, his learning, his quickness and intrepidity in debate, have all availed him to stand in the breach and defend the Constitution. He has done yeoman's service in pulling up radical Republicanism upon its desperate course, in bringing it to its senses, and in awakening the whole country to its fatal designs. He has found out how to arrest and put constitutional checks upon the great corporations and monopolies, and has brought the insolence of land-grant railroad companies to swift punishment.

Thurman, Bayard, Stockton, Casserly, Davis, Vickers, Hamilton, Trumbull, and Schurz, by the power and force of their oratory, and the awakened attention of the country to it, wrought a great change in the manner of transacting business in the Senate. Debate was resumed in the Forty-first Congress, after sleeping in paralysis through the Thirty-eighth, the Thirty-ninth, and the Fortieth Congresses. In those former years, under the force of a two thirds majority, it was the practice to concoct and shape measures in caucus, propose them in Congress, allow the Democrats a limited time to speak against them, the Republicans making no replies, and voting down all amendments. Then, after a brief speech by the "manager" of the bill, the Houses passed to the order of the day, the bill was put through under the party lash, and sent at once to the President. But a new order of things, or rather, a return to the old order, began with the Forty-first Congress. The caucus cowhide was less often applied; Republicans, who became individually responsible for measures, found that the combined assaults of the Democratic leaders put them and their bills upon the defensive. The party no longer dared to go to the people upon bills in regard to which public opinion was untried. Thus debate began again, and the opportunity was afforded to the Democratic senators to show the fallacies and the quicksands upon which their opponents were trying to build their fabric of government. This gave a new impulse to the Democratic cause, and enabled the devoted leaders in the Senate and House to seize upon and foster the reaction already beginning in 1869, in consequence of the flagrant incapacity of the carpet-baggers, the prostrate and miserable state of the helpless South, and the uncompromising assaults of Republicans upon the very essence of the Constitution. Extravagant expenditures, disordered finances, and the enormous burdens of the tariff and internal revenue system, all combined to promote this reaction, and the Democrats in House and Senate were prompt to show that the blame for all these disorders belonged to the Republican majority.

There were many able men in the House of Representatives at the time when Mr. Bayard entered the Senate. James G. Blaine, the Speaker, Dawes, Allison, Beck, Voorhees, Sergent, Barnum, are, or have been, senators since then. Garfield, B. F. Butler, Poland, Hale, Morell, Schenck, Lawrence, Bingham, Maynard, Orth, Tyner, Burchard, Hawley, McCrary were all strong men and good debaters on the Republican side. The Democrats were led by Michael C. Kerr, of Indiana, afterward Speaker, and who was ably seconded by James Brooks, Fernando Wood, S. S. Cox, Williams, Beck, and Marshall, in the tariff discussions, and by Clarkson N. Potter, Woodward, Knott, and Voorhees, on matters appertaining to the Constitution and the laws. William S. Holman, the "watch-dog of the Treasury," was probably a better critic of appropriation bills than any opposition party ever had before or since.

In the final analysis, it may be said that the issues in 1869–'70 were quite as important as those of 1865–'7. The civil war was fought out upon the general question of the supremacy of the Union. This having been once and forever finally determined, parties divided naturally and inevitably upon the terms upon which the Union should be reconstituted. Upon this issue, while the Democrats favored *restoration*, with the Constitution as nearly unimpaired as might be, the Republican party almost universally held for *reconstruction*—in other words, for a Union based upon their particular interpretation of the Federal compact, an interpretation which they thought they were entitled to enforce, not because it was logical, or probable, or according to the language of the instrument to be construed, but because they had the power, and because it seemed to insure the empire for which they had spent so much blood and treasure. This, then, was the line upon which parties were drawn when Mr. Bayard first came into the Senate of the United States.

CHAPTER IV.

OUTLINE OF MR. BAYARD'S POLITICAL SERVICES.

Mr. Bayard took his seat in the Senate March 4, 1869. The oath of office was that well-known "ironclad" oath, framed expressly and ingeniously to be a standing obstacle in the way of every respectable person elected to Congress from any State south of Mason and Dixon's line. It was the oath which his father had first taken, and then, in stern resentment that such an indignity should be put upon one who had served the State so long, resigned. Mr. Bayard took this oath, and he has kept it in a religious sort of way not pleasing to his political opponents, who do not agree at all with him in his understanding of the obligations which he assumed in declaring "And I do further swear that, to the best of my knowledge and ability, I will support and defend the Constitution of the United States against all enemies, foreign and domestic; that I will bear true faith and allegiance to the same; that I take this obligation freely, without any mental reservation or purpose of evasion; and that I will well and faithfully discharge the duties of the office on which I am about to enter. So help me God!" From 1869 up to 1880 Mr. Bayard's course in the Senate has made him conspicuously a supporter and defender of the Constitution against its domestic enemies, the only enemies that have seriously tried to overturn it. He has never missed dealing a blow in that cause, nor has he ever had time to take off his armor and rest. For eleven years the battle has raged incessantly, and he has been ever in its front.

No Senator has better or more faithfully discharged the onerous duties of this office, complicated and multifarious as they are. A Senator's duties are to his country, to his State, to his constituents as individuals, to the legislative body itself of which he is a member, to the party whose political doctrines he upholds. The proper discharge of all these particular and constantly recurring obligations, many of which rest upon the man more than upon the statesman, is very fatiguing work. A great many Senators are disposed to break the weight of the burden by doing some of these duties either vicariously or in a very perfunctory way.

Some give but little time, attention, or labor to committee work; some take no part nor lot in debate; some conduct their correspondence, get up their statistics, and prepare their speeches by the hands of " private secretaries"; while others again, restricting themselves to senatorial work, are never to be found upon the hustings, nor showing any interest in public or party affairs. But this has not been Mr. Bayard's way of taking his duties. One of the most accessible of senators, he is one of the most laborious also, plodding away at routine committee work, like a department clerk, even in the moment of preparation of his most elaborate speeches. He is always at his committee table when needed there, always in his seat in the Senate when needed there. It is rarely that he misses a vote on any material question. It used to be said of a distinguished Senator, now deceased, that he always chose a desk near the door, in order to get away quickly when he wished to " dodge an issue." Mr. Bayard has not acquired nor desired to become expert in the art of dodging issues. His votes are as frank as his character, and represent the steadfast consciousness of his mind that he does not hold any opinions which he fears to express, or thinks it expedient to conceal or politic to cloak or veil. He takes a liberal part in all leading debates and discussions, while not so often making set and elaborate speeches. He is a thoroughly business Senator, yet no man in the Chamber has introduced fewer bills for the sake of appearing to originate measures.

Soon after entering upon the duties of his office Mr. Bayard began to serve as one of the Committee of Finance, his name being at the foot of the list, as it now is at the head. His colleagues in this committee were Sherman, the chairman who succeeded Fessenden, Williams, Cattell, Morrill of Vermont, Warner, and Fenton. The lowest place was also given him on the Committee on Private Land Claims, a hard-worked committee, of which Williams was chairman, and on the committee likewise on the Revision of the Laws, when his colleagues were Conkling, Sumner, Carpenter, and Pool. When the first Ku-Klux Investigating Committee was appointed in 1871, and North Carolina was the theatre of inquisition, Mr. Bayard represented the minority. He also served in the searching inquests made in South Carolina, Florida, and Georgia, and he resolutely fought the first "Force Bill" (which grew out of that investigation) at the head of the gallant band of Senators who deserve so well of their country for their struggles in that emergency. When the second Force Bill was attempted to be put through in 1875, with its dire accompaniments of the suspension of the habeas corpus, Mr. Bayard was assigned to the same part in the Senate as that given to Mr. Samuel J. Randall in the House, and the final victory in that grim struggle of the party of law against the party of force is due in a very great measure to Mr. Bayard's tact, endurance, and dexterous qualities of leadership.

One of the best pieces of work ever done by Mr. Bayard was his service to the commerce and the revenue system of the country as a member of the Senate Committee on Investigation and Retrenchment, which looked into the affairs of the New York Custom-House, and exposed the abuses of the general-order system. This committee, which was appointed December 18, 1871, had Senator Buckingham, of Connecticut, for its chairman. There were but two Democrats upon it—Messrs. Bayard and Casserly—and their efforts to get at the facts were continually thwarted by White-House influences; by the adroit, unscrupulous tactics of Senator Conkling, who constituted himself counsel for the abuses and their perpetrators; and by the whole secret power of the New York Custom-House and the detective service of the Treasury, all of which Conkling wielded in his efforts to screen his "henchmen." So complete were the exposures made by Mr. Bayard and Mr. Casserly, however, even in the face of all these odds, that not only were Leet and Stocking, the general-order monopolists, appointed by Grant, removed, and the general-order system abandoned, but the whole atrocious "moiety" system fell with it, the Custom-House was purified by the expulsion of Murphy, and the New York merchants were afforded an almost inexpressible relief in the pursuit of their business.* The trenchant

---

* An elaborate report by Mr. Bayard testifies the ability and vigor of his and Mr. Casserly's efforts to emancipate the merchants of New York from a reign of terror by special agents.

blows dealt by Mr. Bayard at the corruptions and abuses he was thus mainly instrumental in exposing went a great way toward fostering the Liberal Republican revolt against Grantism which culminated in the Cincinnati Convention of 1872.

Another admirable party performance of Mr. Bayard's, with national ends in view, was his service upon the committee appointed to investigate the affairs of Mississippi, previous to the election of 1876. This committee, of which the self-sufficient ex-Secretary Boutwell, the Senator from Massachusetts, was chairman, and James Redpath, the ·peripatetic showman, reformer, and newspaper correspondent, was clerk, proposed to do a great piece of work for the Republican party. The "managers" of that party knew that the election of 1876 would be very close—close enough to make the exclusion of the eight electoral votes of Mississippi very important to them. Senator Morton accordingly moved for a committee of investigation into the conduct of the election of 1875 in that State. The resolution, after amendments by Mr. Christiancy had been accepted, was adopted in March, 1876, and the committee began work in April, the Republicans being represented by Messrs. Boutwell, Cameron, of Wisconsin, and McMillan, while Messrs. Bayard and McDonald were the Democrats. The minority report of this committee, made in August, 1876, was so conclusive that the Republicans were forced to abandon their nefarious design and permit the vote of Mississippi to be taken. This report is one of the best state papers which has ever emanated from the Senate, and the results of the inexpugnable stand taken by Messrs. Bayard and McDonald on this issue were momentous. The Republicans, finding they could not elect their candidate by fair means, determined to secure his being seated by foul means. Senator Morton went to the Pacific and, in connection with Gorham, "secured" the electoral vote of California and Oregon. When even these, it was found, would not be sufficient to serve them, the Returning Board contrivance and the Visiting Statesmen comedy in the Southern States were brought into play, a manufactured majority of one was made ready against the meeting of Congress, and the country was notified that, unless it gulped this witches' broth without a grimace, it must prepare for revolution.

The Electoral Commission naturally and regularly ensued, and of Mr. Bayard's service upon this, as well as upon the other committees which have been named, fuller particulars and illustrations will be found further on in the present volume, the object of this chapter being to show, in briefest outline, the work which the Senate and his party intrusted to one of the youngest members.

All this work was well done, thoroughly done, done cleanly, and done intelligently. The consistency of Mr. Bayard's political and senatorial career is not simply the result of early associations and inherited principle. It is a consistency such as comes from ripe reflection and matured patience in thought, an educated, logical consistency which defies antagonism, because it is fully conscious that it fights in armor of proof and with tempered weapons. He votes, speaks, and acts in every contingency as an honest, loyal Democrat should, but he is a Democrat quite as much by force of the intellect as by persuasion of the heart. He holds his principles and directs his actions under the guidance of right reason, and he is the one man in the country bound to be right in his own mind, whether his party be right or wrong. Unlike Mr. Boutwell, who proclaimed that political economy varied according to degrees of longitude, Mr. Bayard is a man whose principles are cosmopolitan and universal. He is not a better Democrat in Delaware than he would be in Vermont, nor a better revenue reformer in Delaware than he would be in Pennsylvania, nor a better bullionist in Delaware than he would be in Indiana or Iowa, in Maine or in Kansas.

Hence the superior consideration which Mr. Bayard receives in thoughtful, non-partisan quarters, over and above the great majority of his associates in the Senate. These may be his equals and co-mates in appositeness and force of argument, but, when they speak, people are prone to ask, "What is the motive, or the inducement?" while, if Bayard speaks, they ask, "What is it that has convinced him?" It was this which always made Mr. Bayard more than a match for the late Mr. Morton, in spite of the acumen and logical force of the latter's arguments, and the terse vigor with which he put them.

Mr. Bayard's speeches are not ornate; they are not elaborated with great care, but they contain broad views upon large subjects, presented plainly and honestly, and they always carry conviction with them in every quarter, if not of the speaker's correctness, at least of his sincerity. These speeches deal with momentous subjects in a competent and statesmanlike manner. They review pretty much all the history which the United States have been making during the past ten years, and the principles embodied in them will outlast the events in connection with which they were enunciated. More will be said of these speeches, and some quotations be made from them, further on in this memoir, but a word or two in this place in regard to their range and scope, and the influence they have exerted, will not be amiss.

Mr. Bayard, when he first came into the Senate, took ground against the public credit bill (the earliest measure of President Grant's administration), because it did not go far enough, and assure the country also of a speedy return to specie payments. From his position Mr. Bayard has never swerved. Others have trimmed, shuffled, dodged, contented themselves with the half loaf as being better than no bread, but always Mr. Bayard has shown himself to be the Abdiel of currency reform. No matter whether we see him opposing Schenck's Public Credit act of 1869 because it did not go far enough, or Sherman's Funding bill of 1870 and the Resumption bill of 1875, for the same reasons; or combating Senator Merrimon's inflation plan; or writing to Southern newspapers, and visiting Southern assemblages, to awaken those constituencies to their duties; or objecting to the ambiguous clauses of the St. Louis platform; or making war upon the proposition to pay the debt in silver; or proposing, in the face of a timid Senate, to make resumption permanent by making it actual—in every case, not as a party man, not as a believer in expediency, not for his own personal advancement or glorification, but because he recognizes it to be right and necessary, and the duty of the republic—Mr. Bayard has spoken, voted, and acted for the restoration of the currency and the finances of the country to a hard-money basis. He has been as brave on this point as the greater part of his Democratic fellows have been vacillating and timid. He has been as straightforward and consistent on the whole currency issue throughout as Morton and Sherman were throughout insincere, inconsistent, and changeable. His speeches on currency and banking have been valuable and substantial contributions to the literature of the subject, while his votes have been those of a genuine statesman incapable of yielding to any suggestion of temporary expediency.

Next in importance to what Mr. Bayard has said and done in matters of finance are his speeches upon the grave constitutional questions growing out of the post-bellum amendments, the Reconstruction policy, and the Enforcement acts and new election laws established and attempted to be established during the malign ascendancy of the Republican party. In the elaborate discussion of these great questions during the last ten years, Mr. Bayard has labored under the disadvantage of reopening themes already thoroughly treated by the master minds of the republic, and in the immediate controversy upon which he was equally embarrassed by towering associates and astute and skillful antagonists. What chance had one of the youngest senators in the lot in a question of the limitation of powers of the Federal Executive, or of the powers of the States under the Constitution, when he knew that this or that point had already been treated in the "Federalist" by Hamilton or Madison, had already been argued in the Senate by Webster, or Calhoun, or Benton, and, when it came up anew, would be seized upon by Thurman, Stockton, Casserly, on his side, and assailed, on the other, by all the force of Trumbull, Edmunds, Morton, Conkling, and Carpenter? Yet Mr. Bayard's standing as a constitutional lawyer is unsurpassed in the Senate, and his arguments in the Mississippi case, his half dozen speeches about Louisiana, his speeches on the Force bills and the Congressional Election laws, are recognized as among the best expositions which we have. As supplementary to these, in exactly defining the limits of the Constitution, his minor speeches on the question of colored children in the schools, on the Centennial Exposition, on rivers and harbors, and the liquor traffic commission, are especially noteworthy.

CHAPTER V.

LEADING QUESTIONS.—MR. BAYARD'S VIEWS.

THOMAS FRANCIS BAYARD is a party man because, in his view, parties mean something. He does not belong to that "Shifty Dick" school of politicians who have grown up so rapidly since the war, and who hold that party is merely an agglomeration of individuals having a concerted purpose to put some other people out of office and put themselves in. On the contrary, the Senator believes that the doctrine of "principles, not men," means that principles are to be preferred to popularity, and that a man's fealty to party is due to the principles actuating it, and not to the leaders who direct it or the mass who are directed. There is no factious spirit of rude independence in this, but only a deep conscientiousness. "If my party departs from its principles," said Mr. Bayard, in a recent conversation, "it is no longer my party, but something else. It has gone away from me, not I from it. I may follow it, if I choose. I may join the opposite ranks, if I choose, or, if I can approve neither, I am still not bound to make any sacrifices of conscience, for *I can take my hat and go home.*"

The expression is highly characteristic of the man. He will not be tied to any course of action of which his intellect and conscience do not approve, out of complaisance to the terrible "consequences." The consequences have no great weight with him, since, unlike the greater part of the politicians around him, he always has the alternative of taking his hat and going home. Such a man can not be coerced nor "bulldozed," as Mr. Bayard easily proved when the attempt was made to do so at the last extra session of Congress. He proved it when, at the Baltimore Democratic Convention in 1872, he refused, and led the Delaware delegates to refuse, to endorse the nomination of Horace Greeley, already the Liberal Republican nominee at Cincinnati. Mr. Bayard supported Mr. Greeley in the end, and spoke in favor of his election; but he would not recognize him as being the Democratic candidate, and he did perfectly right not to do so. In his speech in that campaign, delivered at Institute Hall, Wilmington, Del., October 4, 1872, Mr. Bayard said, emphatically: "I went to Baltimore, as you know, to represent in part the people of this State. I went there opposed to Mr. Greeley's nomination. No matter what was my cause for it; you may call it my prejudices, or my judgment. I went there believing it was our duty and our right to have a Democrat nominated who should represent us, and we should vote for him upon our own platform worded in our own way. I reached Baltimore to find myself one of the smallest minority that ever assembled in a convention. I have nothing now to say of the scenes there, only that I did my duty as I believed I ought to do it, and as I believed you desired it should be done."

He proved this same sort of independence in his manly speech on the bill for counting the electoral vote, delivered January 24, 1877, in which he said: "Mr. President, in the course of my duty here as a representative of the rights of others, as a chosen and sworn public servant, I feel that I have no right to give my individual wishes, prejudices, interests, undue influence over my public action. To do so would be to commit a breach of trust in the powers confided to me. It is true I was chosen a senator by a majority only, but not *for* a majority only. I was chosen *by* a party, but not *for* a party. I represent *all* the good people of the State which has sent me here. In my office as a senator I recognize no claim upon my action in the name and for the sake of party. The oath I have taken is to support the Constitution of my country's government, not the *fiat* of any political organization even could its will be ascertained. In sessions preceding the present I have adverted to the difficulty attending the settlement of this great question, and have urgently besought action in advance at a time when the measure adopted could not serve to predicate its results to either party. My failure then gave me great uneasiness, and filled me with anxiety; and yet I can now comprehend the wisdom concealed in my disappointment, for in the very emergency of this hour, in the shadow of the danger that has drawn so nigh to us, has been begotten in the hearts of American senators and representatives and the American people a spirit worthy of the occasion—born to meet these difficulties, to cope with them, and, God willing, *to conquer them.*"

But the most signal instances which we have of Mr. Bayard's non-partisan character, and of his determination not to be governed by any rules of expediency, nor to admit that there can be any rules of conduct, even for senators, higher or more supreme than the dictates of a man's own conscience, are to be found in two of his most recent speeches, that upon the bill to repeal test oaths for jurors, made June 5, 1879, at the extra session of Congress, and that upon the resolution withdrawing from United States notes their legal-tender power, made January 27, 1880. This latter resolution, which the Senate Finance Committee finally declined to report, was Mr. Bayard's pet measure, converting, as it would have converted, Mr. Sherman's fiction of resumption into a fact, and an abiding and perpetual one. Mr. Bayard said that he was not a believer in " Congressional alchemy," and he wanted to see any further attempts in that direction abandoned. " Whether the Senate will concur in my views I know not," he said, " for a subject like this has never been and never will be made by me a subject of party caucus, or personal canvass for votes." In the course of this speech, referring to the position of Democratic senators, and the contrast between their immediate action and the ancient traditions of the party, Mr. Bayard said that he could safely take the declarations of party faith and principles—of every national, of every State, of every county convention of the Democratic party from the foundation of the Government down to the present year, and find nothing in them but the denunciation of paper money, and " the steady declaration from generation to generation, in war and in peace, that gold and silver coins are the only true and constitutional money of the United States—*according to the doctrines of true democracy.*" Mr. Bayard added, with his usual frankness, making sure of the vote of Mr. George H. Pendleton in antagonism to this resolution which, if it were to pass the Senate at the present session of Congress, would give Mr. Bayard the position of the leading advocate of hard money in the United States : " In considering so grave and all-important a principle as lies at the root of this discussion, I shall not turn aside to impale individuals upon their inconsistencies ; such occupation would be trivial and unworthy—but when this legal-tender power eighteen years ago was sought for the first time in our history to be exercised by Congress, there was not to be found a Democrat in either House who did not deny it. Look to the record, see how they voted—how they spoke. I am half tempted to recite here the fervent and true eloquence with which some, even now members of this Senate, denounced the assertion of so disastrous a power. But their action has passed into history, and can be revised by those who desire it. I can only say that, if I sought for texts peculiarly condemnatory of such a power as I now seek to withdraw from the paper issues of the Government, I could find them abundantly in the speeches and writings of the most distinguished, trusted, and authoritative leaders of the Democratic party. I am content to follow in their footsteps, and here to-day to plant myself more firmly in their principles, which time has proven to be founded upon truth and justice. And intending no impeachment of others, I must say that I am unable to comprehend the logic and reasoning which, admitting such a law to be in violation of the Constitution, yet justifies a vote to perpetuate its presence on the statute-book. I confess I am unable so to construe the obligation I have taken to support and defend that Constitution, and bear true faith and allegiance to the same." No partisan, no mere politician, none but a firm lover of the truth, and possessed of the highest moral courage, ever spoke thus.

It was said at the time, and has been repeated since, that, when Mr. Bayard opposed the defeat of the appropriation bills at the extra session of Congress last summer, he sacrificed his prospects of a nomination by the Democratic party as their candidate for the Presidency. Those who think well of the Democratic party, and have faith in its destinies and the ultimate success of its principles, do not believe any such thing. But even if it had been the naked, literal fact, Mr. Bayard would have spoken and voted as he did all the same. He is a statesman, who, like Henry Clay, would rather be right than be President; nor does he think it necessary to pose and assume a look of resignation in announcing the fact. In truth, he does not announce it at all, but simply does his duty as he feels himself bound, leaving the action to speak for itself.

In this case it must have been very distasteful to Mr. Bayard, an extremely disagreeable duty, to prefer another course of conduct in regard to this bill to that adopted by the majority of his political associates in both houses. Not only had the caucus sentiment been openly manifested, but Mr. Bayard's sympathies were strongly exercised in favor of the measures in question. In his own words, he held "that the whole course of reformation which these measures illustrate is the sober second thought of the American people." He held then, as he holds now, that the repeal of these obnoxious and partisan statutes, these invidious test oaths, this system of federal supervision of elections, this compulsory attendance of the military at the polls, was a proper issue upon which to go before the people at the presidential election, an issue which would command the support of a large majority of the voters. He believed that the repeals sought to be obtained were measures of the greatest importance. As he said in this speech of June 5, 1879, on the juror's test-oath question: "They touch the question of personal liberty of the citizen; they touch questions of constitutional rights, the dearest and the closest to liberty-loving men." Nor did he approve of the course of the President in vetoing these bills upon the mere technicality of form, and without taking any notice of their subject-matter. He was, as he said, opposed to the policy of "ingrafting matters of general legislation upon appropriation bills," had frequently protested against it, and had often but vainly endeavored "to procure from the Republican majority that overwhelmed us here a recognition of the fact that such methods of legislation were irregular and vicious." But it was too late to object to such things in Congress, and especially too late for Republicans to object. "I may say," said Mr. Bayard, "that there are no more important measures of general legislation now standing on the statute-book of this country than those which have been placed there by the vehicles of general appropriation bills, and that no such thing ever occurred until now in American history that the *method* of parliamentary proceeding was made a cause for presidential criticism and rejection." The "misjoinder" of general legislation and appropriations was not objectionable on constitutional grounds, but, because leading to confusion, uncertainty, and embarrassment. As to this particular measure of repeal, Mr. Bayard expressed his opinion of the need for it in a strain of earnest and fervent eloquence. It was called for in justice and in equity, by the nature of our institutions, by the validity of our faith in our common manhood, by our belief in the principle of trial by jury and our respect for the letter and the spirit of the Constitution. Yet, being such, the President had vetoed the bill, and there were not two thirds of the members of Congress willing to pass the bill in the face of his objection. What then? The veto power of the President was his own. He was an independent branch of the government, and it did not become Democrats to attempt to coerce President Hayes as the Republicans had done by President Johnson. The President was responsible for the exercise of the veto power not to Congress, but to the people of the country. In Mr. Bayard's words: "He is responsible to the House of Representatives for any malfeasance in his office; and to them is given the power to impeach him, and the Senate, upon trial, to remove him, should they consider that his acts have brought him within the constitutional prohibition; but I am very clear that the checks and balances created by our Constitution do prohibit, and are meant to prohibit, any invasion of his just prerogatives; and no exigency, no sense of the abstract injustice or unwisdom of his action, should control me in approving or urging any course of irregularity in order to overcome what I believe to be the errors or the faults of his administration. Equally unworthy and unwarranted would be any attempt at coercion of the Executive by Congress; and such suggestions are only weak and idle."

After denying that the President had any right or justification in assuming that he was the object of coercion, and in impeaching the motives and conduct of Congress, Mr. Bayard added: "Sir, the only coercion I would apply is that of a quickened conscience, based upon a comprehension of the real duties of the great office he holds, the coercion of public opinion demanding great motives from men in high places. It is the coercion of his oath to obey the Constitution, and not the behests of party or the commands of those who have never heretofore treated him with even ordinary respect."

Mr. Bayard then went on to say that he held the invasion of one department of the government by another to be utterly unwarranted, dangerous, and to be strictly guarded against. Differences must be met in a spirit of comity and mutual accommodation, not in a spirit of obstruction. "I hold," said he, "that no spirit but that of high public duty should actuate any man possessed of public power; that personal exasperation, official bickering, partisan revenges and manœuvres have no just place in the execution of the trust of public power, wherever it may be placed." Mr. Hayes, it was quite apparently Mr. Bayard's opinion, could not criticise Congress with a good grace. The fact that there was such a wide difference in political sentiment between him and Congress gave him no right to speak, but rather would admonish any modest man in his position to hold his tongue. "We know," said Mr. Bayard, "at least those who compose the majority of the Senate and of the House do know, and we do believe, that the sentiment which caused the election of a Democratic majority of the present Senate and House of Representatives also elected a Democratic President. Right down in the heart of every man composing the majority in either branch of Congress lies the solemn belief that would induce him to walk readily to that desk, and with uplifted hand, or his hand upon the Holy Book, swear that he believes that the individual who now holds the executive office was not elected to it by the votes of the American people, but that he holds an office justly belonging to another.

"I have nothing to say in referring to the history of the events of 1877, when, having a single eye to the welfare of the American people, believing in the necessity for the existence and support of a government of laws, believing that it was better, rather than that strife and confusion should throw this government into the hands of the body of men who stood only too ready to clutch it by the throat and put it under the mailed hand of armed power—we proposed and preferred that the forms of law should be created, should be followed, even though the gravest disappointment arose; and we believe that the result was the overthrow of the will of the American people expressed at the polls.

"Those are the facts, and I believe history will record them as beyond dispute. Such was the honor of those who did maintain this ground in a period of profound excitement, in a period when they were convinced of the grossest injustice, who did believe that the public opinion of the American people would in the end be a safer refuge than the rush to arms for the purpose of vindicating a clear right. Upon that faith we have rested, 'that truth was omnipotent, and that public justice was certain.' On that we stood then and on that we stand now; and upon that great issue the American people will be called upon at a day not long distant to decide.

"But these facts only conduce to what? They render our situation even more difficult and trying. The Congress of the United States have their duties. They are endeavoring to execute them faithfully and well. They are endeavoring to shape legislation in accordance with public sentiment, so that this country shall be free, and safe, and prosperous, and happy, that the Union shall be perfectly and really restored, that the public credit shall be guarded and maintained, that all the functions of this great government shall be duly exercised, and proceed properly in their execution. That is our great wish; but if there is in our propositions of themselves anything wrong, if they are unwise instead of being wise, if they are unpatriotic instead of being patriotic, we have the opinion and conscience of the American people to appeal to. All that I would ask is that they may clearly comprehend the issues which lie before them. It is upon their intelligence, their sense of virtue, it is upon their capacity to comprehend aright, and distinguish between the just and the unjust, that we form our chief hopes.

"But, sir, suppose in these efforts we meet obstruction, suppose in these efforts we meet the interposition of the constitutional powers of the Executive, and he stands in the way and says, with or without reason, 'I execute this power; I will taunt you, I will harass you, I will endeavor to inflame you and place you in a false position before your countrymen,' what is your answer? That that may be his measure of duty; but, thank God, he can not impose the measure of ours. Our responsibility and our sense of duty are measured only by ourselves, only by our own conscience.

"This government is placed, so far as the legislative power is concerned, in the hands of the majorities composed of the Democratic members, and we propose so to conduct it that the people of the country shall feel that honesty in the first place has marked every law, that the lobby that so long here infested the corridors of the Capitol and controlled the legislation has been routed and put an end to, that the treasury shall be protected, that every branch of the government shall be amply supplied and maintained with vigor, economy, and justice. This is our proposition.

"Our first duty is to continue this government. Our first duty is to supply everything needful for the honor and welfare and protection of this government and all of its people. Is our measure of that duty to be taught us by a hostile, a harassing, and an obstructive executive? Sir, our measure of patriotic duty is not to be dictated by him. It is to be measured by the oath that we took to support this government. It is to be measured by our own discretion as to what the safety and the welfare of the government require at our hands.

"Mr. President, I sometimes fear that this great complicated machinery of the civilized government of a rich and populous country is not fully comprehended. It seems to me, when I consider all the forms of property, they lie only in the shape of accumulated credits, where once what we called wealth meant nothing but cattle or arms or jewels, or the precious metals. The property of a civilized country is the creation of its laws, and is dependent for its existence on those laws. The great body of its property is its credit in all its forms, which only by the close observance of law and maintenance of order can retain their force and vitality and value. This country is no longer a mere collection of Indian villages, in which peace and war was a matter of every day's chance occurrence. Confusion in a government like ours is pregnant with the deepest danger and with the greatest disaster and suffering. You can not throw out of gear for one moment such complicated machinery without producing almost irremediable injury and wide-spread distress. Therefore, the man who idly talks about stopping supplies to the government, or who disingenuously or dishonestly charges others with endeavoring to stop the supplies of the government, either suggests a great public crime, or he makes false accusation of one against his neighbor. I hold it to be the great mission of the organization called the Democratic party to maintain this government in all its parts, and, under the limitation of its written charter of powers, to protect it against all enemies, domestic as well as foreign, to prevent confusion from rushing in upon it and disturbing its orderly progress. I do not hold it to be in the power of any executive, unfriendly and unjust as he may be to the principles and the objects, and to the *personnel* of that organization, to lessen or alter its measure of duty, or place it in a false position before the American people.

"If I did not believe that party was to be trusted I would not belong to it. If I did not believe that the credit, the safety, the welfare, and honor of the American people were safe in its hands I would abandon it. But shall it be that an officer accidentally vested, and vested, as I have said, against our belief of right, with the enormous powers which have accumulated and grown around the executive office, shall succeed in placing this great party, with all its patriotic objects and intents, in a position of suspicion and doubt before their fellow countrymen? Ah, sir, it will require two to make up that issue. It is a false, dishonest, untruthful, disingenuous attempt to slander his neighbors. No, sir, this government shall move on. It shall be supplied regularly and fully. We will put an end to political jobbery wherever it appears; we will reform all the wrong and injustice that are caused by bad laws that we may; we will supply everything needful for the strong, vigorous, just exercise of every constitutional power in every branch of the public service, and we do not mean that any obstructive executive, any unfair political opponent, occupying power against our belief of right, but to which we submit under the forms of law, shall pervert the truth or raise false issues between us and our countrymen.

"Therefore it is that I have said this much, and it may save me the trouble of repeating it again. I have said it in connection with a measure to which the Executive has returned no objection. I can not imagine that there will be objection to it. I do not mean to say that there can be none manufactured—for when there is a will, a way will always be found for anything—I will not say that men's minds may not be so constituted, or so controlled by their prejudices and passions, that they may not find good reasons exactly in the opposite direction from those I have endeavored to state. But what I ask, and all that I ask, is that the issues now forming between the two houses of Congress, as represented by their dominant majorities, and the executive branch of the government, may be plainly, and clearly, and fairly understood by our fellow countrymen, because, when they are so understood by them, I am satisfied they will find reason only for renewed confidence and increased respect for the party whose motives have been so unjustly called in question, in regard to the grant of supplies for the support of our government, and who are *honestly* seeking to reform abuses, and redress the actual grievances of the American people."

These are instances of what Mr. Bayard meant when he said: "If my party departs from its principles, I can take my hat and go home."

No man knows better than Thomas F. Bayard what Democratic principles are. No man has studied them more closely. No man has more constantly waited for conviction before he gave adhesion to these principles, and consequently none can hold to them with a firmer faith. No man has defined these principles and doctrines more accurately and logically, and none has conformed to them more rigidly. There is to-day no better expounder of the Constitution and of the teachings of the fathers in relation to it than Mr. Bayard. Plain, practical, straightforward, he goes to the heart of a matter, and gives always the solid, substantial reason for his votes. These reasons rest upon the foundations of common sense, upon axioms of law and equity, upon the reasonable sense of the Constitution. Stated, they become the form and substance of Democratic doctrine, and his speeches might be taken for a text-book of pure and unadulterated Democracy, not "Jeffersonian," nor "Jacksonian," but constitutional.

Thus, in his late speech * on the bill for the restoration of General Fitz-John Porter to the army, as in a great many other speeches, Mr. Bayard uttered his warning against the danger of the growing tendency to centralization of power.

"There is," he said "a spirit of centralization; there are centripetal forces at work that in my judgment the people of this country would be most wise to check, and it is well that the centrifugal forces should be set in motion, in order that the orderly distribution of power intended by those who founded this government should once more prevail, because they did intend that liberty should be protected by preventing the undue concentration of powers in any one hand, or in any one department of the government."

In the same speech he called attention to the danger of even talking of the equality in dignity of military courts and military commissions with the judicial courts of the United States. This was a danger which our forefathers realized, and provided against in the Constitution. "They made," said Mr. Bayard, "even before the formation of our present government, their immortal protest against the British king, and among their reasons for

* March 8, 1880.

claiming independence of his rule was that he had affected to render the military independent of or superior to the civil power." "Sir," he added, "there have been many suggestions in this debate, many things that have occurred in the course of this debate, there is too much in the air nowadays throughout this country, that does tend to aggrandize the military power to the danger of civil and constitutional liberty. We have heard here in effect proclaimed that military courts and courts-martial are in substance part of the judicial power of the United States, that they have equal dignity, that they are as wholly irreversible in their decisions as those of the judicial branch of the government. I dissent *in toto* from such a proposition. I say, on the contrary, that military rule is obnoxious to the American people, and it is justly so to all people who would remain free." Then he goes on to show how, while the military is a part of the executive arm, the judiciary is a separate, independent branch of the government.

This power of *definition*, as a means of setting forth the limitations of the Constitution, is a very distinctly marked characteristic of Mr. Bayard. In consequence of it all his speeches bristle with pregnant sentences, which shed a glow of electric light upon the subject. His illustrations are arguments in themselves; his very tropes are syllogisms compressed. When Senator Morton, in opposing the admission of Mississippi in 1870, asserted that "definitions progress," and that, in consequence of the thirteenth and fourteenth amendments, the constitutional guaranties in 1880 were different from what they were in 1787, Mr. Bayard said that the expression was the most alarming proposition—"the largest stride toward legislative omnipotence" that had yet been heard of.

"Why," said he, "its result would be to resolve this Congress into a committee of public safety. It would be to pass that senatorial decree of ancient Rome, that it behooved the Senate to look to the safety of the republic; and after that what remains of civil or constitutional liberty?"

Speaking of "reconstruction," Mr. Bayard said: "After all, sir, what bald humbugs and wretched shams are your reconstructed governments, and your 'resuscitated States,' as they have been termed in the course of this debate! What honest man but must laugh in scorn at these specimens of radical manufacture set up here as republican States! The machinery of our own constitution of government, designed only for operation through the exercise of the will of a free people, has been distorted and perverted to purposes of tyranny and usurpation. Hence the failure of all these schemes of reconstruction; hence they will always fail, for *you can not ingraft the principles of despotic power on the tree of liberty!* You may mutilate that tree, and insert your unnatural scions, but they will never grow!"

"Loyalty," Mr. Bayard calls "that mysterious word, that many-colored garment of political favoritism." It was in 1870 that Mr. Bayard, with a prescience which the holders of Virginia and Tennessee and Louisiana and Carolina bonds must sigh to think they did not recognize, declared the newly constituted negro voters to be "*natural-born repudiators.*" The Republican party to-day affects to despise the alliance which Senator-elect Mahone, of Virginia, offers them. They can not deny, however, that Mahone and the "readjusters" owe their supremacy in the Old Dominion to this race into whose hands they recklessly thrust the suffrage, giving practically the control of property to a class not only ignorant of the laws and semi-barbarous, but creators of inevitable insolvency by the mere bent of their "lavish, simple-minded, thriftless, easy-going natures." Mr. Bayard's moral texture was never shown in all its strength and purity better than in the unconscious enunciation of his creed in the little speech on equal rights in public schools in the District of Columbia. Said he, "Minorities may have terrors to some men, but I have been in one too long, and *I have found too much of comfort in being there*, to let such propositions have any terror for me. A man who makes the performance of duty his object, I am satisfied, will be happy, whether he be successful or not."

Mr. Bayard's intellect is, like his moral nature, pure and clear as a bell. He thinks largely and broadly as becomes a man upon the high plane on which he moves. Speaking of the changes of party and individual opinion in regard to currency matters, he said, "What was truth then is truth to-day. The laws of health do not change because men become sick—indeed, it is then they must be most carefully consulted and obeyed." The credit system which finally exploded in 1873, he called "the system that had stimulated men to believe that the great primeval decree that men should eat bread by the sweat of their face was in some way repealed, and that people could grow rich without labor, and Congress could ordain that people should be prosperous and happy without following natural laws." "Heaven help us," he said, in his harvest-home speech at Newport, Delaware, "if the time shall come when the value of every man's farm and every contract he makes is to be determined by some accidental majority in Congress that may change every two years." "At the bottom of all human dealings," he said, "lie certain simple principles implanted there by the Author of our being. One of these is truth—nothing that is not based upon truth can long subsist, and honesty is but one form of truth. The reason why gold and silver are accepted among men as a standard of value is not merely because of their attributes, their indestructibility, their durability, but because these metals truthfully represent so much human labor expended in obtaining them, and are worth so much as commodities, because it costs so much to procure them. If gold and silver are adulterated they are no longer true, but false." "We live in sad and troublous times," is Mr. Bayard's opinion, "and we must live through them like honest men. On shipboard, when the storm is raging, and hope seems almost dead, the cry is often heard, 'Break open the spirit-room!' but the true captain will have a firm guard at the door to keep the men back, to save his ship and save the lives of the wild and foolish creatures who invoke their own destruction."

Thomas F. Bayard has shown himself to be this "good captain," whenever the hour of peril forced him to take the lead. He showed it in the case of the Electoral Commission; in the case of the debates and votes on the appropriation bills in the extra session of 1879; in all the financial issues since 1879, in which period so many of his fellow Democrats have gone astray, their heads lost in the fogs and bewilderment, and their feet mixed in the quicksands, of the "Ohio idea"; and he showed it in every contest between the majority and minority of Congress on the issue of federal usurpations and violations of the Constitution.

It would be easy to draw up the chart by which this "good captain" does his plain sailing—the platform of this true, loyal, pure Democrat, which, indeed, is the only platform upon which true, loyal, honest Democracy can find room to plant itself. Integrity, honesty, economy, these three words sum it all up.

First. Mr. Bayard clings with religious deference to the Constitution as it was understood by the founders, and has been construed by their successors, and to a strict and rigorous limitation of the delegated powers of the government, to the end that one branch may not suffocate the other, and the States disappear under the wheels of the Juggernaut of centralization. It is Mr. Bayard's doctrine that "The framers of our government sought to limit power, and accomplished their end by the distribution of power. The very distribution of power was to work its limitation."

Second. He does not approve of class legislation, which always follows from the consolidation of power. Power, he holds, is always stealing from the many to the few, and class legislation promotes this. Whether it takes the shape of tariffs for protection, the creation of national banks, the subsidizing of roads and steamship lines with grants of lands or money, he is hostile to it, because it tends to break down the safeguards of freedom, to increase the expenses of government, make the rich richer and the poor poorer.

Third. Honest money he demands, because Congress had no right to give us any other. "The Good Book tells us," he says, in one of his open-air speeches, 'Remove not the ancient landmarks which thy fathers have set,' and, in the name of our fathers, of Washington, of Hamilton, of Jefferson, of Madison, of Webster, of Jackson, and of Calhoun, I ask that the ancient landmark of an honest money be not removed." He demands it also for the sake of the poor man, robbed of his earnings by fraudulent money, and in order to enable our productive classes to compete with Europe. "Our competition with other nations," he says, "is close, and growing closer; we must buckle down to our work, and neglect nothing. We have honest weights and measures fixed by law; let us insist upon the restoration of THE GREAT MEASURE OF MEASURES, AN HONEST MONEY."

Fourth. An honest and frugal administration and civil service. "We are in debt," Mr. Bayard says, "and have got to pay it or be disgraced; and I will not admit there is any alternative to the American people on that subject. Now, we must study rules of economy to do this." Dishonest money and a government devoid of respect for the limitations of the Constitution have led to extravagance in government which must be reformed. "A habit of dealing with large sums in a reckless way" (so Mr. Bayard puts it), "in other words, an utter loss of the sense of values has resulted, and the man who loses the sense of relative values is a most unsafe guardian of the public treasury. There has grown up a vast body of civil officials, appointed under a system which can not bear examination—a civil service which, of itself, threatens almost the permanence and success of republican institutions. The idea that the public offices of the country were established for the benefit of the persons who fill them is wholly wrong. The office is instituted for the public service; it is not for the benefit of the man who holds it; it is for the benefit of the people whose laws created it and whose service is to be performed. The good and faithful servant of the public is entitled to be secured and maintained on the same principles precisely as the good and faithful servant of a private employer. The man who does his duty in public office owes nothing to the public. He has rendered them back *quid pro quo.* He has given them that which they were entitled to, and they have paid him no more than justly was his right. But when office has been, as we see and know, dependent, not upon the excellence of the manner in which its duties were performed, but is made a reward for mere partisan exertions, sometimes services which would not bear close examination ; and when the holder of the office depends upon the pleasure of the appointing power or the whim and caprice of the party to which he must look for maintenance in his place, you may be assured that his duties will not be the first and chief point of his consideration. But rather that his time will be spent in contriving how little he may do for the post, and how he may best continue in the enjoyment of his official emoluments.

"An intelligent Englishman, holding a high station in his country's government, in discussing this question not long ago, told me he would be perfectly willing to undertake the conduct of our departmental business, conducting what may be called the entire clerical business of the great departments of our government with one third the number of our present officials, provided he could procure the same class that were employed by his government at home, men who had been trained for the work, and who knew if they did their duty they need not fear being displaced, but would find a long life of public service met at the end with pension, reward, diminished labor, and public thanks.

"I have been one of your representatives at Washington for some years past. I can well attest the great pressure there is for official appointment, and the evil, it strikes me, is not in the fact of the salaries being too high. On the contrary, I think, for the character of the service demanded, they are, in many instances, less than they ought to be. It is to the superfluous number of persons employed, and their precarious tenure, that we owe our imperfect system which has led to such enormous expense."

Fifth. No subsidies; no waste; sound laws, honestly administered; the civil power supreme in the state; the fostering of that spirit of amity and conciliation, of mutual deference and concession which the peculiarities of our political situation render indispensable, and without which the Union can not be restored—these things comprise Mr. Bayard's platform, as declared in his speeches and emphasized in his actions. In both word and act he is frank and sincere to such a degree that all he says and all he does count at their full value. Mr. Bayard never seeks to accomplish his objects by indirection. He has a noble scorn of the art of "looking one way and rowing another" in which politicians are supposed to excel. Still more does he despise the tribe of Pecksniff and all others who make pretense for pelf. "I do not spell humanity with a large H," said he, when voting for an appropriation to relieve the starving freedmen gathered at Washington, "nor freedom with a capital F; but I am, nevertheless, willing to do what I can to relieve distress and suffering where I find them."

CHAPTER VI.

THE UNION AND THE CONSTITUTION.

In the excited times that preceded the outbreak of the war of 1861 there were two—parties we can not call them, for they were not held together by party ties, nor can we call them sections, for they were not separated by geographical boundaries—two aggregates of men opposing each other, and actuated by diametrically antagonistic principles and purposes. These were the peace men and the war men on both sides of the line.

The war men of the two sections, led by such men as he who said at the South, "Give me the sword, or I will take it myself," and he who declared at the North that "the Union was not worth a rush without blood-letting," bitterly hostile as they were in other respects, agreed in this, that they wanted war rather than peace, and so played into each others hands with the skill and concert of two partners in a game. Each angry expression, each taunt or threat, each lawless act of the one scored a point for the other, and was adroitly used to inflame the popular mind and draw recruits to their ranks.

The peace men of both the Republican and Democratic parties were those who believed that war was no remedy for the evils they felt or feared, and who held the only remedy to be in constitutional legislation and the good sense and patriotism of the whole people, if the madness of the hour could be cured. But to cure this madness was what the others least desired. All their efforts were directed to exasperate it; and to compass this they used every instrument—the public forum, the press, the stump, the pencil, and the pulpit. With the fire-eaters of the South we have nothing here to do; but the radicals of the North gained the masses to their side and established themselves in power by persuading them that the war was only to save the Constitution and the Union—the Constitution which they had repeatedly broken, and the Union of which they had openly declared their abhorrence. No wonder that the calmer patriots, who saw the spirit that ruled the hour, dreaded the result, and feared that, however the war might end, constitutional liberty would be lost, never to be regained. For this in chief was the object of their devotion, and the Union so far as it was a means to this, for which end, as the Constitution recites, the Union was established. Liberty without union would be weakness and discord, union without liberty would be even a worse evil—organized despotism. The duty, then, of all true patriots, throughout the war and after the war, was to resist all encroachments upon constitutional liberty, and to shield as far as might be the whole people from a worse fate than the sword had brought upon the defeated States.

The war ended. The conquered South accepted the decision of the sword. There were then two courses open to the party in power: the one, to heal, as far as they could be healed, the festering wounds, to quench the embers of hate, to restore constitutional liberty, and bring back peace to all hearts and prosperity to all homes. But this course was not chosen by the radical leaders. Preferring party success to the country's welfare, and knowing that a return of good feeling would terminate their tenure of power, all their efforts were exerted to keep up the war in other forms, and to prevent that restored union which had been their professed object. No means were left untried to keep alive the passions of the war, and so to fasten their own grip upon power while these passions lasted that it should afterward be impossible to wrest it from them. Under these two heads may be summed up the whole monstrous mass of radical legislation and administration from 1865 to 1876. Never once, though often challenged, has the radical party announced the principles by which it proposes to lead this union of States in the paths of peace and prosperity. Measures to serve a temporary purpose they have in plenty, but, when asked for a platform, they rant about "saving the Union," which they did not save, and "wave the bloody shirt." To denounce all Democrats as secret or open traitors, to fix upon whole States the stigma of "brigands," to rekindle hate and suspicion, to stifle the voice of the people, to subordinate the civil to the military power, to make the federal legislature a council of war, the judiciary a military court, and the executive a provost-marshal-general —this has been the radical policy. To these ends have been directed the reconstruction acts, the force bills, the Ku-klux legislation, the packing of courts with partisan juries in the box and pliant judges on the bench, the expulsion of honest officers, and the enrichment and exaltation of knaves. From this policy, as its natural consequence, came that saturnalia of lawlessness, violence, fraud, and robbery that disgraced the eight years of Grant's administration.

Against all these things, and each as it arose, Mr. Bayard has always steadily and fearlessly uplifted his voice, not as a partisan opposing party measures, but as a citizen and legislator of the whole country, resisting measures that tended to its ruin. Whenever the choice lay between hatred and enmity, between law and breach of law, between good faith and bad faith, between the Constitution and violations of it, between liberty and the encroachments of power, between honesty and fraud, men could always predict with unerring certainty where Bayard was to be found. His attachment to the union of the States was not reiterated so vociferously in cheap and empty rhetoric as was the fashion among some, with whom, perhaps, there was greater necessity. He was never a dealer in fine sentimentalities, and, instead of bragging of his patriotism, preferred to show it by a steady devotion to the Constitution and the principles on which the Union was founded. He preferred patriotic legislation to patriotic flourishes, nor desired to boast in words of that which he could best illustrate by his actions.

Yet, with all his loftiness of principle, there has been no impracticable quixotism, no aiming at things palpably impossible, or refusing a lesser good because a greater was not to be had. He has always known that the duty of a legislator is to do the best that he can, not the best that he would.

The only course open to the upright conservative statesmen in those days, when such formed but a feeble minority in Congress, was steadily to offer an exemplary, if ineffective, opposition to all unsound legislation; to repeat, though to unwilling ears, the true principles on which the government had been founded; and to warn his countrymen, on every fit occasion, how far they were drifting from their true course, and the rocks toward which they were driving. All legislation for party purposes, everything that savored of chicanery or sharp practice, everything that tended to lower the standard of public honor, he boldly denounced. Thus, when it was urged that, owing to the loose wording of the law imposing a tax on tobacco, the treasury was likely to lose heavily, to avoid which a modification was proposed, which, under certain circumstances, might entail the payment of a double tax, he said: "I can see how this government may afford to lose money, but I can not see how it can afford to lose character, and fail to keep good faith with the citizen .... I trust that the United States government, in dealing with the people, will always set the great example of the uttermost good faith with those who have striven to keep their obligations with it; and, if under existing laws there be imperfections in ascertaining the proper amount of tax to be levied, I think that the government should suffer that, and not the people who have striven to do their duty toward it." *

Measures of temporary expediency he was equally averse to, knowing that the permanence and fixedness of the laws were next in importance to their justice. Thus, when, in 1872, a bill had been introduced taking the duty off tea and coffee, Mr. Bayard opposed it on the ground that it was "a piece of the demagogy of politics"; that those who introduced it knew well that, while it might serve a temporary purpose, it would certainly be rescinded before long; and that, above all things, the business men of the country "had a right to ask that stability should be an element of the laws." The whole commerce of the country, he said, had suffered more by the "wavering and staggering" of Congress on the subject

---

* Remarks on the tobacco tax, April 8, 1869.

of these very duties than from any imposition, however heavy.

At the same time that he opposed this piece of demagogy, he reiterated his adhesion to the sound Democratic doctrine of a revenue tariff. "I consider," he goes on to say,* "that, as a matter of justice to the business of the whole country, we should not proceed to deal by piecemeal with the revenues of the country. . . . My own hope is that the tariff will be reduced to a revenue standard. I believe that for that purpose, and that purpose only, is it justified."

In the same way, and on the same ground that openness, fairness, and good faith, expected of all, were above all to be expected of statesmen legislating for the common good, has he shown himself the unwavering foe of caucus legislation. The caucus, in some form or other, is probably an unavoidable feature of party government. It is necessary, with regard to grave measures, that the party shall act in concert; and, so far as a caucus does no more than provide for this, and equal privileges are allowed to the opposing party, it can not be objected to. But the caucus was abused by the majority so as to form a secret legislature, where, with closed doors, measures were concocted, every man's part assigned him, and they were then sprung upon the legislative body without warning, and rushed through without time allowed for consideration or debate.

Speaking of this strategy, he says: "I can not regard with respect or approval, and I must consider it as destructive of the spirit of our constitutional form of government, that it has pleased the majority in this, as in other

---

* Remarks, April 30, 1872.

cases, to consider grave public questions in the secret councils of party alone, and then suddenly to promulgate them by party orders, and call upon their associates in this chamber instantly to act upon them before they can be known, before they can be fully comprehended, or that proper preparation made for their deliberate consideration which every man in this chamber owes to a question before he casts his representative vote upon it. . . . The preparation of public measures in party caucus, and their enactment into law without public explanation or debate, is a defeat of the spirit, if not the letter, of our government."

It may be seen from these illustrations, and will more fully appear in other pages of this sketch, how far Mr. Bayard stands above the ordinary partisan leader. To meet innovation by counter-innovation, to defeat a measure by shifty finesse, to win a party triumph by adroit jugglery—such was never his idea of statesmanship, nor his mode of opposition. He has never forgotten that he was a legislator for the whole country; and, if he has desired the success of one party rather than another, it is because he believes the fundamental policy of that party to be the best for the people of all parties and of all sections. His hope and aim have been to bring back the whole people to the ancient regard for constitutional liberty, in which alone there is safety; to their ancient respect for law, which can never be recovered unless the law-makers show themselves worthy of confidence and respect; to their former wise dread of the usurpation by one branch of the government of the functions or powers of another, or of the enlargement of powers which the Constitution has most wisely and cautiously limited.

By such ways has he endeavored to check the headlong course of the party in power, and to pave the way for a restoration of sounder government and better footing. Amid all the turmoil of party warfare he has kept in view the true issues of the great struggle, on the solution of which our political destinies depend. These issues are so clearly put in his speech of October 4, 1872, at Wilmington, that we quote at some length:

"The issue which I tell you has been formed in this country, in one shape or another always asserting itself since the formation of the government, is the issue between the tendencies of power, wherever it be placed, to increase and centralize itself, and the corresponding effort under our Constitution to prevent that centralization and insist upon a distribution of power. Let me endeavor to place this idea clearly before you.

"The men who formed this government had, as you know, suffered from arbitrary power. They had been coerced by an arbitrary government. They took up arms to relieve themselves, and, under God's providence, were successful. Their sufferings you know; they are part of the history of your country, and I am sure it ought to be a most important lesson for us in all time. Having suffered from arbitrary power, the men who laid the foundations of this government determined that they would put limitations upon power, no matter where that power was deposited. They knew the weakness of the human heart; they knew that if you give a man power he will exercise it for the most advantage to himself and in ways not intended; and they therefore determined that in the Constitution of the government of the United States there should be no grant of power that was not limited, no such thing as absolute power, no power that was to be without limitation both as to its extent and duration.

How did they accomplish that? By distributing powers, by dividing our government into different departments, all of which should be coördinate and equal, none of which should be absolute or superior.

"The national legislature was created with ample power to make laws, but not absolutely, for the President had his right to veto. There was also the check of a written Constitution that those laws should not pass the subjects or the extent of power conferred by its provisions; but, in case they did, there was the other great check upon them, the judicial department. Even if the Congress and the President assented to the law, it was to be subjected to the test whether, in the minds of the judiciary of the country, it was, or was not, an infringement of the limitations imposed by the written charter.

"They further distributed power over this country so that the national executive, the national legislature, and the national judiciary, all checking each other, should not even when combined be omnipotent, because they left to our system of States the whole mass of powers not delegated and enumerated in the grant of powers to the general government. The general government had none but certain delegated powers; all the rest were expressly reserved to the States; they were diffused broadly throughout the land, and they were intended by that distribution to be a check upon each other and a check upon the federal government, and the federal government was intended to be a check upon them. Our fathers arranged this system with perfect harmony, so that in the mind of any honest man, determined to obey both the laws of the United States passed in pursuance of the Constitution and the laws of the States which are subjected to the State constitutions and to the federal Constitution also, there can not be a question of conflict which can not be relieved by a fair and candid examination of these different instruments.

"Do you understand me ? The framers of our government sought *to limit power, and accomplished their end by the distribution of power. The very distribution of power was to work its limitation.*

"Now, gentlemen, what is the result ? If you destroy the distribution, then you destroy the limitation, and the power becomes consolidated and absolute. It is this issue coming up in our history at different times, but never before looming up in the dreadful proportions which it has now assumed, which has been the issue upon one side of which the party called the Democratic party has ever without fail been found. I claim for that party, not that it contained better men than others, not that they were less fallible than their fellow citizens, not that they were more learned or more wise; nay, I will not say they were more patriotic, but that the reason why it has had vitality and existence from the foundation of our government until to-day, yea, why it will exist so long as the very forms of freedom are left in this country, is because it is based on the principle of freedom, of opposition to centralized power, and an insistence on the distribution and limitation of powers for the public safety.

"I care not what may be the issue that arises, the true test is, does the measure proposed tend to destroy the limitations upon power that keep us a free people, or does it tend to centralize power in any hands ? If it tends to centralization, it is anti-Democratic in the best meaning of the word ; if it tends to the diffusion of power throughout the land, then it is in accordance with their sentiment.

"If I read the history and the meaning of the Democratic party of the United States aright, it has always been the organization which has advocated the distribution of power, and never its consolidation.

"Nowhere in the history of this government under a Democratic administration will an attempt be found to gain or retain control by the consolidation of powers. Never under Democratic rule was an attempt made to usurp the just powers of any State, nor to invade the prerogative of one branch of the government by another.

"Thus, there was no class legislation, no creation of vast federal corporations, no imperial grants of lands, no chartering of a whole system of banks; but, on the contrary, an examination of its record will disclose the truth that the doctrine of the distribution of power and the prevention of its consolidation has been from first to last the steady principle which the Democratic party has followed in or out of power. The preservation of the rights of the States, of the rights of the people of the States to fully exercise all the powers of self-government in relation to their internal and domestic affairs, has never in the most heated party times been attempted to be interfered with by the Democratic party.

"In one word, the course of that party has always favored the doctrine of limitations upon power wherever that power was deposited. If the axiom be true (and who can doubt it?) that power is ever stealing from the many to the few, then in a country like our own, whose institutions were intended to be as free as was compatible with the preservation of good order and safety, the party that most jealously opposes the consolidation of powers is not only essential for the welfare of the country, but will be likely to prove its greatest safeguard. A party with such a principle underlying it will always exist while a shadow of freedom remains, and it matters not under what name.

"I believe it was for this reason, thus broadly stated, that prosperity, good feeling, and good order existed throughout our land. Simply because no power of the government was urged out of its proper sphere, and the harmony between federal and State governments was suffered to remain undisturbed, in accordance with the wise system arranged by our forefathers. Nothing but the truth, the actual vitality of this principle that governmental powers, always seeking to aggrandize themselves in one form or another, are steadily to be kept in check by the will of the people over whom they are sought to be exercised, has ever enabled the Democratic party to maintain its existence amid all political fluctuations, changes of events and conditions in this country during the whole of the present century.

"It has contained good men and bad men, and both classes at times have had power under its organization, but both were alike compelled to administer the government in subordination to the principle I have referred to. Hence, we of the Democratic faith have always inscribed 'principles, not men,' on our banners.

"Let us look a little further at the wisdom of the men who framed this government. They knew the inevitable tendency of power. You give a man a little power, and he uses it to obtain more. He gets the more, and then the easier is it for him to increase it. It is like the snowball that is begun by the school-boy, beginning a little pack in his hands, it presently rolls itself into a mass that can not be moved. That is the onward increase of power if left to its own laws, unchecked by human contrivance, virtue, or efforts.

"The men who formed this government had other ends in view. Not only did they mean the people of their generation to be free, but they meant their posterity to be free; that the government was to be preserved by the constant exercise of the principles upon which it was founded; and, therefore, when they distributed power so that centralization should be checked and absolute power made, as far as, humanly, it could be made, impossible, they by that very act gave the people throughout the country the *right and opportunity of local self-government*. What does that mean? It means the school of government; it means the opportunity to learn how to be a citizen of the United States by learning what the functions and duties of a citizen are; and how can you learn unless you practice and try? Take a man among the many whom I see here to-night, whose hands and whose arms are hardened by honest and steady toil, and I ask you how long could those arms and hands, stalwart as they are, perform their task unless they had been taught to do it by exercise and practice? If you tie up a man's arms and he does not use them, will not the muscles wither and grow weak? Will he not lose all power of control over them? Undoubtedly. And is it different with your faculties of mind and heart? Certainly not. Take away from a people the opportunity to exercise their power to think on public subjects, take away from them the right of local self-government, and their mental faculties will weaken just as their muscles would if not used.

"Therefore, I beg you to understand the wisdom of the men who founded this government. They accomplished a double object by distributing powers, insisting upon the State systems and the great rule and principles of local self-government in opposition to centralization. They did that for the purpose of educating the people to become a self-governing nation. The wisdom of all this plan is this: unless the people are practiced in self-government, they will not be fit to govern themselves, and, unless they do govern themselves locally according to their local interests, central power will seize upon them and their liberties and control them. So that, in order to be free, in this broad land, two things are required: that power shall be diffused throughout the country and not centralized at Washington, and that the people shall exercise their powers in order to fit them to carry on the government.

"The rights of the States were just as fixed and positive, and are to-day as essential for the good government of this country, as the rights of the general government. They were part of the same system, and you can not take away the rights of the States without weakening our whole system, without destroying the power of the people by exercise to make themselves fit for self-government; and you can not take away the rights of the general government without making it ineffectual to carry out the wishes of the people and make fit laws for them. The harmony of the system must be preserved, and there is no more reason to suppose that the great object for which this government was created will be defeated by the act of the States than by the act of the central government. There is no reason to presume suicide from one cause more than the other, and, to use the language of the Supreme Court of the United States, in a case lately there decided, 'Such being the separate and independent condition of the States in our complex system, as recognized by the Constitution, and the existence of which is so indispensable that without them the general government itself would disappear from the family of nations.'

"The exercise of local self-government, I have said to you, was essential for the education of the people. Where, in the history of the rule of this country under the Democratic party, was there an attempt on the part of the general government to invade a State? When, under the rule of the Democratic party, was there ever a disposition on the part of the general government to allow a State wantonly to invade its just authority? When there seemed to be an attempt, in 1833, on the part of South Carolina to destroy the harmony between her and the federal government, whose administration was it whose wise, firm rule brought that State to her proper bearings, and caused her to resume her proper place within the national family without the shedding of one drop of human blood? Was it not Andrew Jackson, backed by the Democratic sentiment of the country, who, simply by the beneficent, regular operations of power under the federal Constitution, compelled the disorderly spirits of that State to render obedience to the United States Constitution and laws? Therefore, you will observe that not only does the record of that party show you that peace and good order were maintained by leaving to the States their just powers, but whenever there was any attempt on their part to assume powers not belonging to them, or refuse their due allegiance to the general government, it was met and checked promptly. In my belief, my fellow citizens, it has been the adherence to that principle that has enabled the Democratic party to maintain its organization so long; and, so long as it is animated by that spirit of true freedom, that just regard for the spirit of our institutions and our laws, so long it will exist, until even the forms of election and popular expression are destroyed in this land."

Again and again he warns the party in power against the narrow-minded and short-sighted policy of distrust.

"Do not," he says, in his remarks on the Mississippi election, "do not base all your legislation here upon the presumption that the States of this country do not propose to do their duty by all their citizens. Do not suppose that the best refuge and the best sanctuary for the rights of an American freeman are only in the federal courts of this country. It is the same spirit through all. All are American courts. Do not for the sake of this temporary power which is yours to-day, and may leave you to-morrow, invoke an authority which some day may be used to interfere with that right of free local self-government which is the very foundation and the very soul of our system of government. . . . I beg of you, with all the feeling of one American toward another, to trust the American people. Trust the people of the American States. Do not let it go forth that the men of this country, white or black, have no protection except in federal liberality. It is unjust to the States; it is unjust to the people; it is creating a certain collision of feeling and of sympathy between the States and the federal government, which ought to move along, each in its own orbit, undisturbing and undisturbed."

We might fill many pages with quotations from Mr. Bayard's speeches in which similar warnings and appeals are made. It has been the ever-recurring burden of his discourse, because it touched the very heart and root of the evil. With restored confidence and with a spirit of equal justice to all, once more filling the hearts of the people, north and south, the men whose whole political capital consists in stirring the embers of discord would soon find themselves plucked from their high places, and their seats filled by statesmen who, however they might differ on points of policy, would have all the same aim, the good of the whole country. A manly appeal like this from his speech of February 4, 1879, is worth all the "spread-eagle" rhetoric and phrase-mongering that have tickled foolish ears for a generation:

"I believe that I can see in these resolutions and in others of a similar tenor a desire to renew doubt, suspicion, and distrust in one party and one section of our country against the other. Sir, we have had too much of that already. I believe that all the difficulties that have arisen in our land, that have darkened our homes with mourning, and spread their baleful shadow over the face of our country, have chiefly come from the fact that our countrymen were ignorant of each other; it was the want of proper mutual understanding, it was the want of proper confidence that bred strife and confusion. If this spirit of renewed confusion is to be invoked, if the exigencies of party shall still call upon men to raise the standard of strife and distrust among their countrymen, whatever may be the result, I shall be found on the other side invoking the methods of peace and good will, and not those of war, invoking generous confidence and kind feeling, and not suspicion and hostility; asking our countrymen to dwell not upon their mutual faults, but upon their mutual virtues, of which every day and every hour we can witness happy illustrations if we do but seek to realize and comprehend them.

"This country to-day needs peace and rest, recuperation from the losses of war, and from the unwisdom of angry legislation. The man serves his country best who seeks to avoid confusion and strife, who seeks to disarm suspicion and to re-create confidence: and if this is to be the issue that this hateful, dangerous geographical line of sentiment and action is sought to be established, I, for one, will not accept it; I will be of no party, I will aid in no legislation that shall not recognize the right of each man in all parts of this country, and their duty to do that which no legislation can enforce—I mean the great duty of the creation of a spirit of nationality among the inhabitants of this broad land. How can that be created if men are to be permitted to stand on this floor and elsewhere, and denounce, with railing accusations and unmeasured assaults, whole sections and States of our Union, and hold them up to scorn, to opprobrium, to detestation? Mr. President, there must be, and, please Heaven, there shall be yet, the unwritten law that will visit with popular execration and denunciation the man who seeks to establish the domination of a party at the cost of the peace and security and welfare of the entire American people."

Nothing more strongly marks the extent to which men's minds have been warped by the principles and practice of the party in power, than the way in which they have learned to look upon the government as something above them to control them and dictate to them, instead of a body of public servants of their own creation, with strictly limited powers and responsible for their use. On this point Mr. Bayard touched in his speech of May 4, 1872, on the bill "to secure equal rights in the schools of Washington and Georgetown."

"This bill," he remarks, "would not be complete at the present time if it did not contain some portion of that coercive disposition which seems to mark so unhappily the legislation of this country for the last twelve years. The idea that this is a voluntary government sustained by the people because they love it, the laws executed because they represent the will of the people, seems to be nearly passed out of sight. There seems to be now no law that shall speak to the people by its own voice and by its own majesty, relying upon their ready assent to it because it is the law. No, sir, there must be a penalty; there must be something to drive them to obey; and such seems to me to be the unhappy feature in almost every public law that is now proposed. There is no longer trust in the desire of the people to execute the laws of their own free will; but you seem to rely only upon the fact that they are to be scourged with fines and penalties, and driven to the work which can never be so well performed as when the heart shall dictate the act which the hand performs. Congress has been so in the habit of driving and coercing the people of this country, that it seems to me now that they have taken up that as the ruling principle of mere despotism in regard to every act of Congress, no longer trusting upon the hearty loyal wish of the people themselves to carry into effect voluntarily the laws which their representatives have made, and which, if wise, would commend themselves without recourse to penal threats. . . . I have seen too often the Congress of the United States relying much more upon the force they could bring to execute a law, than upon the moral sentiment of the community that they would obey it because it was the law. I long for the day when this coercive tone shall be silenced. I long for the day when the real wishes and the happiness of the people of this country—'the consent of the governed'—shall be the underlying principle of every act of legislation."

In the same spirit when he was denouncing the interference of Congress to frustrate the popular will in Mississippi, and one of the advocates of that measure suggested that there might be a reversal of parties in Delaware, he flung back with scorn the covert implication. "It may occur," he said, "but God forbid that, when my people shall express their opinion against me and my party at the ballot-box, I should come here and ask Congress to revolutionize any State government for the sake of giving me party advantage!"

This is the ground-tone that runs through all Mr. Bayard's speeches. Open them where you will, you will find the faithful watchman's cry announcing danger, even though it should fall upon heedless ears. The usurpations of power, and, what was still worse, the growing public indifference to those usurpations; cynical disregard of the most solemn obligations and plighted faith; the systematic adoption of a policy of chronic mistrust diversified by paroxysms of active hatred—these were the poisons that were tainting the blood of the whole country. His reiterated appeals for a return of good feeling were not a sentimental *eirenicon*, an entreaty to forgive and forget. They rested upon far deeper grounds; upon the knowledge that what harmed one part of the country was harmful to all; that a blow that pierced South Carolina wounded Massachusetts; that the South could not be deadly sick and the North long remain sound. Yet these views were sneered at as old-fashioned, the exploded doctrines of a by-gone age, by men who were incapable of looking beyond party advantage or seeing that he was in truth defending the real interests of their constituents far better than they were themselves. They were old-fashioned doctrines, no doubt; they were as old-fashioned as the Constitution and the fathers that framed it; nay, they were of an older fashion still, of the old fashion of truth, honesty, and kindness, before hatred struck the first blow and insolently asked, "Am I my brother's keeper?"

Of a truth, in no other way can the country be saved from ever-recurring perils, and the general prosperity planted upon a firm foundation, but by going back to fundamental principles. The war has changed much, and we all accept its changes; but it has not changed these. We can, if we please, stand where our fathers stood in 1787, differing in opinion, but all striving for the good of the whole. The cry "Let us have peace," though uttered by one who brought not peace but a sword, finds now as then an echo in every honest heart. Let us have men in power who will once more look to the good of the whole country, instead of bounding their low ambitions by a party triumph; let us have men who regard obligations, who will keep and enforce good faith, and once more bring back integrity where it has been so long a stranger, and set in themselves an example of the doctrines they preach; men who see no difference in morality between a public and a private obligation; whose hands are uncontaminated with bribes, whether of the grosser sort, or that subtler kind which appears on no check-book or ledger; whose principles have not varied to suit the exigencies of the hour, but have been always the same from first to last.

These are the principles that have guided Thomas F. Bayard through all his public career, not only when in a feeble minority, but when the tide of public opinion had turned. Through all the storms, the confusions, the uncertainties, the ever-shifting changes of the last eleven years, the eyes of both friends and foes have turned to him, knowing that he would be found erect as a tower

"That stands four-square to all the winds that blow."

CHAPTER VII.

FINANCE AND THE CURRENCY.

At the outbreak of the war, when many thought, and the Administration professed to think, that it would be of but short duration, it was believed that the necessary expenses might be met by an issue of convertible treasury notes and a loan for their redemption, without the necessity of resorting to extraordinary means. When, however, events showed that the war was about to assume gigantic proportions, and might be of indefinite duration, it was plainly necessary to make provision for enormous expense. There were two ways of doing this: one by increasing taxation so as to pay for the war as it went on; the other, to carry on the war on long credit, and lay the burden of the debt on future generations.* The former would have been the fairer way; and men well versed in finance and acquainted with the country's resources believed that it could be done. But the administration was afraid to risk the heavy taxation that such a course would have required; they knew how much more terrible seems a near than a distant evil, and they believed that the people would rather mortgage their future prosperity than pinch and economize to pay heavy taxes. So one make-

---

* "The extension of the debt over future generations" was actually urged as one of the soundest features of the policy adopted, by one of the senators from Massachusetts.

shift was tried, and then another, until in February, 1862, the legal-tender bill was signed, and the country was flooded with "greenbacks," made by law a tender for all dues except duties on imports and interest on the public debt.

That this law was unconstitutional was maintained by the conservatives, and afterward decided by a majority of as able judges as ever sat upon the Supreme bench, with Chief Justice Salmon P. Chase at their head. That it was impotent for good and very powerful for evil, any tyro in finance could see. It is perfectly plain that no act of Congress, no royal edict or imperial rescript can ever give *value* to anything whatever, though it may compel men to accept it as value. The sole value of the greenback consisted in its being a promise to pay, as its face expressed. If, instead of the words, "the United States will pay," it had read, "the United States will *not* pay," no power upon earth could have forced it into circulation. Had it been redeemable on demand in specie, of course it would always have been at par; but, as it was, three elements of uncertainty entered into the estimate of its value: would it ever be redeemed? how would it be redeemed? when would it be redeemed?—and as the possibilities or probabilities in these respects varied from day to day, so did the purchasing power of the greenback, compared with the steady value of gold. By a fallacy like that which makes us say the sun rises and sets, whereas it is the earth that moves, men talked of the rise of gold while it was really the paper currency that was falling. Had gold really risen ten per cent. compared with other values, all the precious metals of the world would have flowed into America; as it was, long before gold had "risen," as it was called, to 200, every ounce of specie had either fled from the country or disappeared from circulation. A certain portion, diverted from its legitimate purposes, ran round and round in a charmed circle, from the treasury to the bondholder, from him to the importer, and from the latter to the treasury again, and it was made the basis of colossal gambling on the stock exchange; but as a circulating medium it no longer existed.

Of course, all who made contracts under the new order of things regulated their prices by the existing value of the currency, and the probabilities of its rise or fall; and in this way the whole business of the country was dragged, perforce, into the vortex of speculation. The United States treasury—that is, the money of the whole people entrusted to certain public servants for special purposes—had to pay the constantly rising market rates for its enormous expenditure, and this increasing drain was met by new issues and new expedients, still further increasing the volume of the public indebtedness, and, as a natural consequence, lowering the value of the public promises.

It was for a while the fashion to talk about the greenback having "saved the country"; but no greater folly could be uttered. What brought the war to a successful close was the unshakable faith of the great majority of the people in their final success, and in the ultimate good faith of the government. In fact, the legal-tender act was a blow to the public credit, at home and abroad, as it amounted to an official declaration that the people had not faith in the ability or the purpose of the government to meet its obligations; and as such it was answered by the immediate stoppage of the sales of bonds abroad. And "yet the financial interests of a great nation for an indefinite future were staked upon a desperate resource, to tide over a temporary exigency. When the lessons of history were quoted, they were answered by the flag and eagle. When caution was urged, in view of possible future exigencies, it was answered by prophecies of military success and denunciations of rebels. When the need of deliberation was urged, it was answered by clamor in regard to the necessities of the government. When it was said that irredeemable paper had always wrought ruin, it was answered that our resources were unlimited, and that these precedents did not make a rule for us. When it was prophesied that the paper would depreciate, and that we should not be able to retrace our steps, the prophets of evil were indignantly pointed to the 'pledged faith' of the United States, and asked if they thought that would be violated. The inference that the notes must be made legal-tender because the government needed money was never analysed, and its fallacy never shown. The question whether it is necessary to issue legal-tender notes is a question not of law, but of political economy; and political economy emphatically declares that it never can be necessary. The proposition involves an absurdity. Whatever strength a nation has is weakened by issuing legal-tender notes."*

A provision, however, was made for the redemption of these notes by the funding system; that is, the holders could buy United States bonds, bearing interest, and redeemable within a certain time. It was the conversion of one form of debt into another form; more burdensome on the country, since it bore interest, but of a sounder character, since a time for redemption was fixed. Into the various issues of these and the way they were "floated"

* "A History of American Currency." By Prof. Sumner, of Yale College, pp. 201–2.

by selling at par in a depreciated currency, so that the country was pledged to pay from a dollar and a half to two dollars for every dollar received, besides interest in gold, and all the ingenious devices by which the market was "rigged," and the overburdened public dragged deeper and deeper into debt, it is needless to enter here. Take one example, a sale under the nine hundred million loan act:

"Gold being at 140–150, that is, the paper dollar worth 65 or 70 cents, 75,000,000 ten-forties [loan redeemable after ten years, interest to cease after forty years] were taken at about par at six per cent. The Secretary was now led to try the ten-forties at five per cent., but the currency was not sufficiently depreciated to float them at or near par, and they were not taken. He then used his alternatives, issuing 175 millions one and two years treasury notes. Gold rose to 200–220, or above, making the paper worth 45 or 50 cents, at which point the five per cent. ten-forties floated."*

That is, the Secretary of the Treasury, the guardian of the public money and the public credit, purposely depreciated the value of the currency by lowering the general trust in the public faith, in order that he might entail upon the people of the United States a debt of two dollars and interest thereon for every dollar received. Nor is this said by way of reflecting upon the character of Secretary Chase; but to show to what desperate expedients even honorable men were driven by the false and ruinous policy that had been so recklessly adopted.

The disease, bad enough in itself, was rendered much worse by extravagant inflation, or an increase of the volume of the currency beyond the needs of legitimate trade.

* Sumner, p. 207.

Of course when two dollars had only the purchasing power of one, it took twice the amount of currency to carry on the business of the country. The larger figures looked like larger values, the scarcity of gold increased the foreign exports, the lavish expenditures of the war stimulated nearly all branches of trade, the rapid fluctuations in prices fostered wild speculation, and the people, deceived by a fallacious show of prosperity, demanded more money.

Thus the disease produced the morbid craving, and the indulgence of the craving aggravated the disease. To complicate the situation further, the national bank system, then an untried experiment, was established, and the old State banks taxed, for the most part, out of existence.

At the end of the war, in October, 1865, the total debt of the country was $2,808,000,000; the total currency, $704,000,000. Under the management of Secretary McCulloch the process of contraction—that is, of liquidating that part of the public debt that was represented by the greenbacks—was begun, but it was in part neutralized by the increased issues of national bank notes. This retirement of the notes was kept up until January, 1868, by which time $44,000,000 had been retired, and the amount in circulation reduced to $356,000,000, the national bank circulation being then about $295,000,000. At this point Congress stepped in and stopped their further retirement.

The resolution of Congress had called for the "retirement and cancellation" of these notes; but, though retired, they were not canceled, for in the fall of 1872 Secretary Boutwell re-issued $5,000,000 of them, which Congress afterward called in again. In the next year

Secretary Richardson again re-issued $26,000,000 of these "retired and canceled" notes, and Congress legalized the proceeding. The volume of legal-tender currency was now within $8,000,000 of what it had been ten years before. The resumption act of January, 1875, redeeming 80 per cent. of United States notes for every $100 issued to the banks, brought down the legal-tenders to $347,000,000; but the act of May, 1878, stopped further contraction by requiring the *re-issue of the redeemed notes*. Such is a brief outline of the action of the government in regard to the legal-tenders.

On March 15, 1869, a House bill, called "a bill to strengthen public credit," was introduced into the Senate. It began with the preamble: "That, in order to remove doubt as to the purpose of the government to discharge all just obligations to the public creditors, and to settle conflicting questions and interpretations of the laws by virtue of which such obligations have been contracted, *It is hereby provided and declared* that the faith of the United States is solemnly pledged to the payment in coin, or its equivalent, of all the obligations of the United States," etc.

On this bill Mr. Bayard made his first speech of any kind in the Senate, and we cite his remarks at some length, as they give the keynote to his constant financial policy: "The title of this bill [which had been amended] now reads, 'A bill to strengthen the public credit.' Its title so far is a challenge to American respect. But do the object and effect of the bill upon examination bear out the high-sounding phrases of its title? I apprehend not. Is this bill to have the effect 'to strengthen the public credit' in reality? What is our public credit? The confidence of the public that the government of the

United States will thoroughly fulfill all its obligations in their letter and their spirit. That is our credit.

"Now, sir, to obtain and justify this confidence, I know of no royal road. I never have been able to understand the difference between the principle that should be applied to the honest extinguishment of a private debt and a public debt. I take it they both rest upon the same sound principle, and they must both be treated, if treated honorably, in the same manner and to the same effect. The payment, in my opinion, of any debt, public or private, is a mere combined question of ability and integrity. Every law, therefore, that we may pass which shall have a tendency to increase our ability to pay our public obligations will strengthen, in fact, our public credit. Therefore, every act of economy, every act of retrenchment, is an act of this character, and I will most cheerfully vote for it upon all occasions when I have the opportunity. More than that, sir, every act which tends to create popular confidence in the permanence of our government is an act of this character. Every act which tends to restore order and regularity to our proceedings, and to distribute governmental powers in accordance with the intent of the character of our government, is of this character. . . .

"But, sir, this act professes to be a declaratory act. The language of it is that it is intended to 'settle conflicting questions, and interpretations of the law,' in virtue of which certain obligations of the United States were incurred. Now, I invite the attention of honorable senators to this fact: something is due to our own character, and the character of our body. Each bill should do in substance that which upon its face it professes. If anything would be derogatory to, and tend to weaken the character and credit of, the United States, it would be that under the guise of one measure you seek indirectly to accomplish something that you dare not place fully on its face. If this act, however, called merely a declaratory act, be intended in any degree to add any new stipulations of an obligatory character upon the government of the United States; if it be intended, either expressly or by any implication of the present law, to give any new right of action in claims of the public creditors under the law under which these obligations were issued, then I protest against its passage as being fraudulent upon its face, and untrue; and I claim that if such an intent is to be urged hereafter, directly or indirectly, let our action appear, that men may clearly know what it is they vote for."

The speaker then proceeded to show the nature and origin of declaratory acts, which had their rise under the English system of government, and were intended to preserve the traditions of an unwritten law, but were not germane to the government and laws of the United States. After briefly touching upon some of the possible results of the passage of this bill, he continued: "I do not, however, propose at this time to make any extended remarks upon that which lies in the future. 'Sufficient for the day is the evil thereof'—sufficient for me it is in considering this bill to find it in a shape that I can not give my approval to, because it transgresses that which was always with me, and I trust ever will be, the rule of my action in treating upon governmental matters. It is an attempt by Congress to invade the prerogatives of another branch of the federal government, and I believe that I can strengthen my government no better than by keeping the proper departments each within its proper sphere.

Our danger at this time is that men lose sight, it seems to me, of the dividing lines of power; that there are departments in public justice, and that if those departments are over-ridden, if those barriers are broken down, confusion will come, the first name of which confusion will be, perhaps, an elective despotism, and the word 'anarchy' will come in soon after. . . .

"While I am perfectly willing to support the amendment of the honorable Senator from Kentucky" [that the just and equitable measure of the obligation of the United States upon their outstanding bonds . . . is the value at the time in gold and silver of the paper currency paid to the government on those bonds], I can not vote for the bill in its present shape, for I think it can not have any effect to strengthen the public credit; but I think it may have this effect, in regard to which I either feel indifferent or hostile—it may temporarily inflate the bonds of the United States government, but for what good end? Is the legislation of this country to become a matter for the use of speculators? Already the creation of your so-called lawful money of paper has given rise to an elasticity of business which has destroyed credit, which is making everything in the country purely speculative; and I am not disposed to dignify such a mere stock-jobbing result as the temporary puffing of these bonds into an increased price as worthy of an act of Congress, or of anything that we should give our assent to.

"Then, if it is supposed that by raising these bonds in their value temporarily you may induce a larger portion to be held by foreign holders, to that I say, as at present advised, I can not give my assent or approval. As this debt is to be paid, and as it is to be paid with such enormous interest upon it in this other lawful money so superior in value to the paper which bore that name; if the people of the country are to pay the interest, I wish that it should be paid to our own fellow citizens, and not to persons who reside abroad. The strange paradox seems to have pervaded men's minds at the present time that the greater a man's debt, the richer he is; and that the more the bonds of the government could be held abroad, so much greater the proof that we were a prosperous, a rich, and a great nation. I can not so consider it. Look at the great debt of England, not, proportionate to the amount of accumulated capital, or to the amount of interest paid, one half as great as our own; those who are fond of citing that as an illustration of our consolidated ability to meet it, should remember that there ran always with it the proposition that it was mainly held within the British empire; in other words, that, if the people of England were taxed to pay this heavy debt, the people of England received the benefit. So, if our country is to be taxed to pay this debt, and to be taxed to pay the interest upon it, let us, at least, if it can be so arranged, see to it that our own people shall get the benefit of the great sacrifices which will be necessary to be undergone by the American people in order to meet this debt in any proper and reputable shape. Therefore, sir, while I am not, and never propose to be, interested in puffing the price of United States bonds for the purpose of creating a foreign demand, and creating a still greater outflow of gold into foreign countries from the hard-wrung toil and labor of my countrymen, for that reason, if for no other, should I withhold my assent to this bill."

The bill passed the same day, Senators Bayard, Carpenter, Casserly, Cole, Davis, Morton, Osborn, Rice, Reve,

Spencer, Stockton, Thurman, and Vickers voting in the negative.

Very wisely did Mr. Bayard suspect this act with its specious title. And how was its promise fulfilled? The Secretary of the Treasury, instead of redeeming the greenbacks, and so restoring public credit and specie payments at once, employed the gold at his command by selling it and buying up with the proceeds bonds not due at a high premium, and leaving the currency as it was, thus giving a splendid profit to the bondholders, while the masses were suffering all the evils of an inflated currency. And this masterly policy was pursued until 1874. No legislation could strengthen public credit while it rested upon such foundations. To quote Mr. Bayard's words, "it was not only a house built upon sand, but it was a house of straw built upon sand; there was neither substance above nor below, and no human ingenuity could give it permanent stability or safety."

No doubt the great masses of the Republican party were as sincerely anxious for the prosperity of the country as were the Democrats. But they had suffered themselves to be deluded by unwise or selfish leaders, and had committed the fatal error of disregarding and loosely interpreting the Constitution. Had they held fast to that and rigidly adhered to its limitations, they would never have fallen into these errors; but, in that case, they would not have been the Republican party. The Constitution gave no power to Congress to make paper a legal tender; but that was over-ridden on the plea of military necessity. The Constitution straitly limited and defined the powers of every branch of the federal government; but, under a Republican administration, the legislative usurped the powers of the judiciary, or the executive of either, upon any plea that was convenient for the moment. The Constitution carefully specified the powers of the federal government, declaring all others reserved to the States respectively, or the people; but now the rights of the States and of the people of the States were invaded by legislative enactment, by executive action, by military force, without any plea whatever.

The party in power had so overwhelming a majority in both Houses that they were at no pains to conceal the cardinal principles of their legislation, and occasionally avowed them with an effrontery almost cynical. In March, 1869, Senator Sprague introduced a "bill for loaning the public money," and providing for a "United States council of finance," with a commissioner, deputy commissioner, auditor, and twenty-four councillors, all salaried, to do a grand bill-discounting business with the public money, all the while that the people were groaning under the interest on the public debt. That the United States should turn money-lender and note-shaver was bad enough; but that it should do this on a capital of its own unpaid promissory notes was something stupendous. But the cream of the whole business lay in the brief remarks with which the Senator introduced it. He said, "I desire to call the attention of the Senate to this bill. In my judgment it will perpetuate the power and the existence of the Republican party for twenty years. Then it will put out of existence great bankers, great traders, great shipmasters, great manufacturers, great telegraph, railroad, and other corporations." That is, it would ruin the great productive industries of the country. That was one thing. And it would keep the Republican party in power for twenty years. That was another thing. And these two considerations, he thought, ought to recommend it to the majority in the Senate.

The brain grows dizzy in attempting to follow all the schemes and devices proposed in Congress in regard to currency and finance. To change one form of debt into another form of debt, with a provision for its possible conversion into a third form; to make one kind of bond acceptable because it was long, and another because it was short; to devise some super-dexterous juggling by means of which capitalists could be inveigled into lending their money at less than the market value; to propose, with a grand flourish about honest payment, the redemption of one kind of currency, with the condition that it should be replaced by an equal or greater amount of another kind of currency just as irredeemable—these were some of the expedients proposed, instead of the simple, straightforward plan of paying off the debt as fast as it could be paid, and in that way bringing the notes to par, which was all that was needed. No words can describe the chaotic character of the debates on this subject. Everybody had his grand nostrum for doing by not doing, and for attaining something by striving for just the opposite; and speaker after speaker arose, with his sheets of carefully arranged figures, and, after a flourish about the public credit, proceeded, according to the measure of his abilities, to stretch out the line of confusion in theory, and lay the stones of emptiness in practice.

Conspicuous among these darkeners of counsel was Mr. Sherman, in whose dexterous hands facts and figures were like cards in those of Robert Houdin, multiplying or diminishing at his will, coming no one knew whence, and vanishing no one knew whither. In March, 1870, he introduced his grand funding bill, "to authorize the funding and consolidation of the national debt, to extend banking facilities, and to establish specie payments." Of course, it provided for an issue—they all provided for an issue of something or other, either of more paper, or another sort of paper into which the old sorts were convertible (and the bankers and brokers made a pretty penny by all this converting and reconverting; but this by the way). It provided for an issue, of course, and this it was: the government (to establish specie payments) was to issue not more than $400,000,000 in 5 per cent. bonds, fifteen-forties, and not more than $400,000,000 in 4 per cent. bonds, twenty-forties, these last to be sold to national banks, formed or to be formed, as a basis for further extension of their circulation. Here was a way indeed "to establish specie payments"!

Mr. Bayard opposed the scheme in his speech of March 7th. He showed the evils under which the country was laboring, and the real cause—"It was chiefly because, departing from all our traditions, from the principles of finance stamped indelibly upon our written Constitution, in spite of the warnings of every generation of our statesmen from the formation of our government until the present time, the Republican majority of Congress in 1862 resorted to issues of paper money to sustain public credit. They created a money of credit which had no intrinsic value. It was a blunder in finance, which, as the witty Frenchman said, was 'worse than a crime.' It did more to place the laboring masses of this country in the hands of capitalists than all your other measures combined. It unsettled values by destroying the only standard of value. You might as well have repealed all laws for the regulation of weights and measures. It placed a strip of india-rubber in lieu of the yard-stick, and jugglers' bottles in place of fixed measures or quantities.

"This was not done without debate, or heedlessly. The evils of this system had all been foretold. But party power was dearer to the majority of that Congress than public faith. The founders of our government had suffered bitterly from the use of paper money. The system had proved its falsehood and its perfect worthlessness in our war of independence. If any man doubts this, let him read the debates of the convention which formed the Federal Constitution, and his doubts must be all removed; and the lessons so taught us by the sages of 1787 had been repeated by our wisest and best men in every generation since.

"It has been owing to the disregard of the lessons and warnings, and by direct, flagrant violation by the Republican party of the provisions of the Federal Constitution, that our people groan to-day under at least $900,000,000 of the present debt; and this is a moderate estimate of the cost to us of the paper-money issue. The most reasonable and reliable calculation I have yet seen places sixty-six and two-thirds cents on the dollar as the average sum received for our present federal securities."

He disdains to enter upon the idle and endless task of untangling the maze of figure and calculations which had been prepared and propounded to prove that not doing a thing was the same thing as doing it, and that increasing a debt was the way to pay it, and strikes at once at the root of the matter.

"My proposition respecting the funding of this national debt, desirable as I think it for the purpose of diminishing the large rate of interest we now pay, is this: that we must postpone any such measure until we shall have reached a real basis of value for our currency, when we shall have a *constitutional currency of coined money of value* to rest our debt upon before we talk of funding it. So long as our basis of currency is one of credit only, without intrinsic value, just so long uncertainties and fluctuations will distress the land and disturb all legitimate business. Let us resume specie payments before we offer new loans."

And he concludes that the only honest and feasible plan is "to go back until our feet rest once more upon the solid rock of the Federal Constitution. The currency of the country is a matter of enormous importance, and that currency can not, in my belief, be lawfully or safely anything else than a currency of value—the gold and silver coin directed by the Constitution."

It would be wearisome and unprofitable to follow up all the devious courses and analyse the patent nostrums of the Republican financiers of those days. Against all these tricks and devices Mr. Bayard steadily set his face and recorded his vote. When, in December, 1873, Mr. Sherman was pressing a bill providing for national banks without circulation, Mr. Bayard opposed it, asking where Congress got the power to multiply indefinitely banks of deposit. "It was far better," he said, "to go back to the great principles of finance, as in all other questions of government, of letting the people of the locality, through the exercise of local self-government, remedy the evils under which they suffer by the light of their own experience." "I am strongly in favor of disconnecting the banking system of the country from the treasury of the United States. I do not believe that one helps the other."

In the minority resolution offered by him on December 15, 1873, he gives his view of the one duty of Congress, in the matter of the public finance, in few words:

"*Whereas*, a just regard for the interests of every class of the community demands that the national basis of finance shall consist of a uniform standard and intrinsic value; therefore—

Resolved, That the Committee on Finance be, and they are hereby, instructed to report to the Senate measures which will secure, at the earliest practicable day, a return to specie payments."

"A uniform standard," not two weights and two measures, nor the "strip of india-rubber"; "intrinsic value," not "fiat-money" and promises not to pay, not even promises to pay, as a basis; and a return to specie payments as soon as practicable. This was his and the minority's answer to Mr. Sherman's proposition to establish a currency "adjusted to meet the changing wants of trade and commerce." His views on the subject and his suggestions for a practicable way of gaining the end desired will be given elsewhere; but this, in brief, was Mr. Bayard's position first, last, and all the time. When some of the Democratic leaders, forgetting the true principles of their party, became greenbackers and inflationists, they left him standing where he had always stood, on the firm foundation of honest payment of debts in honest money, and as soon as it could be done.

When we remember that the bonds of the United States had been bought at far less than their gold value, and that Mr. Bayard himself never owned a single bond or a single share of bank-stock, one might have supposed that his sympathies with the bondholders and the banks would not be strong. But his sympathies with justice and honesty are more than a principle—they are part of his very being; and, on the question of making the debased silver dollar a lawful tender for all amounts, he pleads the cause of the banks and the bondholders as if he were one of them, for there it is the cause of right, of good faith, and of the whole people. He, never himself a capitalist, becomes the earnest defender of capital when it is proposed to wrong capital, or to defame it as if it were the enemy, instead of the ally, of industry. In his speech of February 4, 1878, he says: "Let it not be forgotten that the banking capital of the United States to-day almost wholly, with the rare exception of State banks of discount and deposit here and there, is based upon the bonds and credit of the United States government. The stock of the banks of course depends upon the security of the bonds. It does not stop there. The business of the country, the accommodation to the borrowers, all the circulation, has this ultimate dependence upon the credit of the bonds which lie at the foundation of security for every bank in the country. You can not strike down that interest without striking men who never saw a bond, who never owned a bond, of the United States government.

"If a bank is crippled, can it continue accommodations? And, if it can not, who shall suffer? If stringency and distrust shall mark at once our business, who shall suffer? The men engaged in business, and not simply the banks, which are the instruments and the instrumentalities for distribution and discount and of currency. Oh, no, sir. A blow so blindly leveled will reach objects it never was intended to strike; it will prostrate interests of which we now can have but slight comprehension. For better or for worse, the fate of the banking capital of the country is rooted in the prosperity of the communities in which the banks are organized."

And a little further on: "What is capital? It is but the accumulation of labor. The very highest instincts of humanity are exercised in procuring and amassing it. It is the glory of our institutions, and nowhere have I ever heard that more resoundingly pronounced than on the floor of the Senate that the institutions of this country offer no impediment to the poor man, or the poor man's son, rising to place and power and property; that all the avenues are thrown open to him; and does not this senate chamber itself proclaim the fact? How many men who hold their seats here to-day, how many of those men who have held seats here in times gone by, have known youths of poverty struggling against adverse fortune, and who have triumphed and gained place and gained fortune and power by the liberal, generous, equitable institutions of American government! Sir, the people of this country are not downtrodden. The history of this country proves by the men who have been your presidents, your rulers, yes, your millionaires to-day are men who started at the lowest round of fortune's ladder, and have had their upward path impeded by no obstacle whatever.

"Why, sir, there is not an apprentice in the land who does not hope to become a journeyman; there is not a journeyman in the land who has not his visions of becoming an employer of men; there is not an employer of men who is not struggling daily to better his condition, and to place himself in a position of independence pecuniarily. What becomes of the virtue of thrift which we so commend—the virtues of self-denial, of self-control, and of industry? They are all meant for one purpose, to lift men beyond the risk of temptation and place them where every good man would wish to be, in a condition of being able to help others less able or fortunate than himself. The man who overvalues money is simply unwise, but the man who undervalues it can not be said to be wiser."

When the possibility of resumption had at length almost been reached, we find him, in May, 1878, resisting, with all his energies, the act to forbid the further retirement of the legal-tender notes, and thus turn the ship's course away from the land that was just in sight. In his speech on that occasion he reviewed the whole subject, and offered an amendment that the notes should be deprived of their legal-tender feature, but should be receivable for all dues to the government except duties on imports. Those duties being the source from which the treasury received gold to pay the interest on the public debt, cutting off that source would compel the treasury to purchase gold in the market, whatever the premium, and we had had sad experience of the effects of that kind of finance. With the notes at par in gold, there was no conceivable reason why they should not be retired, or, if desired as a convenient circulating medium, be continued without the compulsory clause, and standing on their own merits alone.

His latest utterance on the subject is found in his speech of January 27, 1880. The Senate, having under consideration the joint resolution in relation to United States treasury notes, the minority of the Committee on Finance submitted the following recommendation and resolution:

"The undersigned, believing that the industrial, commercial, and financial prosperity of a country, in order to be enduring and secure, must be based upon a money of actual and intrinsic value, and that our government has no power and is incompetent to endow its paper obligations with such value, and the United States Treasury notes in existence and in circulation being now redeemable in gold and silver coin at the option of the holder, do therefore recommend the withdrawal of the present compulsory legal-tender power from such treasury notes by the passage of the subjoined joint resolution.

"T. F. BAYARD.
"FRANCIS KERNAN.

"Admitting the principle of the resolution as to the power of the government to make paper legal-tender, I reserve my action upon the resolution as to the time of the withdrawal of the power given heretofore.

"WILLIAM A. WALLACE.

"Reserving the right of amendment.

"JUSTIN MORRILL.

[Joint resolution in relation to United States notes.]

"*Resolved by the Senate and House of Representatives of the United States of America in Congress assembled.* That from and after the passage of this resolution all United States notes shall be receivable for all dues to the United States excepting duties on imports, and shall not be otherwise a legal tender; and any of said notes hereafter reissued shall bear this superscription."

Mr. BAYARD: "Mr. President, my object in urging the adoption of the present resolution is to bring about an *actual* resumption of specie payments. Whatever else may be effected by this resolution is secondary, and merely incidental to this one cardinal object.

"I ardently desire the prosperity of my country; I wish it to endure, and I know that to be permanent it must rest upon a sound basis, and I know that a sound currency is essential, and that real money is the only basis of a sound currency.

"I have said that I desire to effect a *real* resumption of specie payments, for I do not believe what is at present called resumption is real or reliable, because, although since January 1, 1879, United States notes are redeemable in coin at the office of the assistant treasurer of the

United States in New York city; yet, by the act of May 31, 1878,

"'when any of said notes may be redeemed or be received into the Treasury of the United States, they shall not be retired, cancelled or destroyed, but they shall be reissued and paid out again and kept in circulation;'

"so that while there is a resumption of payment in specie, it is neutralized in all its resumptive effects by the immediate reissue of the notes just redeemed. To 'resume' by such a delusive process is as idle as to bail water with a sieve.

"I am for actual resumption and a restoration of real money in place of any substitute therefor, unless such substitute is voluntarily agreed upon by the parties to any contract. Plainly, then, this resolution is intended to secure the resumption of a standard of value—based upon value, and not upon mere credit.

"It is not intended to destroy the convenience and assistance of the present paper currency; but, as that paper rests upon the credit that it *is* convertible into specie and *will be paid*, so do I feel assured that, by letting men feel a confidence that a stable standard is ultimately to measure all their contracts, they will naturally feel safer to enter into contracts. This will give them assurance that the lapse of time will not bring with it alterations in the basis upon which their agreements were formed. This will encourage capital to embark upon enterprises which will give employment to the laboring classes, and will insure to labor an honest equivalent for every hour of toil. Such, I believe, will be a part and a part only of the benefits to flow from the adoption of this resolution.

"Mr. President, I would pause here, and ask the consideration of the Senate to a confusion of terms, which I am sure has led to a great confusion in thought, in dealing with this subject. It is unfortunate that notes should be called 'money,' as it tends to produce confusion and injustice; at best, notes are a promise, and, until that promise is paid in *money*, it is unperformed.

"When power was given to Congress 'to borrow *money* on the *credit* of the United States,' the words had a definite meaning: not to borrow evidences of debt, but to give their evidences of debt for money. The issue of the notes was a proof that the government had no money; that they thought it unadvisable to tax the people to obtain it; and, therefore, the United States notes were merely instruments of the government to obtain supplies to carry on the war without paying for them.

"The very issue of these notes was a confession that the government had no money. To make them circulate in the place of money, and enable the holders to get rid of them, they made them at first convertible into the interest-bearing obligations of the government, and created them a legal tender for all debts, public and private. And let it here be noted that making notes legal tender does not oblige any man to sell his property for such notes; it only compels him to receive them for a debt *then due*. In other words, legal tender is a debt-*paying* power, but can never be made a debt-*contracting* power; and no amount of tyrannical force in the history of the world has ever been able to accomplish this last. To define the difference between money and its substitute, I will accept the definition of Lord Liverpool, in his famous report upon the coins of the realm of Great Britain:

"'The money or coin of a country is the standard measure by which the value of all things, bought and sold, is regulated and ascertained; and it is itself, at the same time, the value or equivalent for which goods are exchanged, and in which contracts are generally made payable.'

"Paper currency, in all its forms, bills of exchange, promissory notes, bank bills, all are useful auxiliaries of money, but are evidences of debt, and not of wealth, and possess no inherent value.

. . . .

"In no civilized country can all the exchanges of property be carried on by the agency of *coin alone.*

"Paper notes are an essential auxiliary to coin, but never let it be forgotten, they are *not coin*—are not *money*—but are *substitutes* for it. They are not *actual* payments, but promises to pay—*evidences of debt* which the law will enforce—and do not give *value for value;* and their acceptance must be based on their credit, on their convenience, and be *always voluntary in order to be safe.*

"When a paper note, an evidence of debt, is made a *compulsory tender* in payment of a debt—the great law of honesty—the great *law of money—that value is to be given for value,* is broken and disregarded.

"Mr. President, we have heard in this chamber allusions somewhat vague, but none the less alarming, to an unseen, undefined, but terrible, 'money power.'

"What is meant by these ominous warnings against this invisible, intangible, immeasurable power?

"What is meant is, I suppose, the power of capital.

"How shall the law deal with it?

"Capital is the result of labor and frugality; it is by the virtues of thrift, economy, and self-denial, working under the instruction of intelligence and enlightened self-interest, that capital is first created, and then accumulated.

"Wealth and property of all descriptions are but forms of capital. Encouragement is given by the institutions of property, by the creation of government, by the enactment of laws, to induce men to exercise their faculties to gain wealth. Is all this founded upon fallacy and wrong? Is there to be discrimination, suspicion, and assault visited upon those individuals of society who have been more successful than others in the accumulation of property? Is it not 'money power' that enables a poor laborer to become the owner of the pick-ax or shovel with which he prosecutes his daily task? Is it not 'money power' that enables him to procure a wheelbarrow? Is it not 'money power' that enables his savings of a year's labor, temperance, and frugality to give him the means to purchase a horse and cart? Is it not 'money power' that enables him to educate his children and fit them for an improved condition in life? Is it not the same 'money power' that crowns his life of honesty, sobriety, and industry with an old age of comfort and respectability?

"Such, sir, are the humble, but honorable and useful, careers that America offers to the poor of all lands; and, of all institutions to secure such results, a money having real value is the chief, because it is the true and only road by which the laborer honestly becomes the capitalist. . . .

"The issue of these United States notes was, until these later days of 'greenback' finance, always stated to be 'a war measure,' growing out of the exigencies of the times, and to be ended just so soon as peace was restored.

"In his annual report of 1862, Secretary Chase said:

"'The recommendations now submitted of the limited issue of United States notes as a wise *expedient for the present time* . . . are prompted by no favor to excessive issues of any description of *credit moneys*; . . . *for, just so soon as victory shall restore peace,* the ample revenue already secured by wise legislation will enable the government *through advantageous purchases of specie to replace at once large amounts, and at no distant day the whole of this circulation by coin,* without detriment to any interest, but, on the contrary, with great and manifest benefit to all interests. The Secretary recommends therefore no mere paper-money scheme, but, on the contrary, *a series of measures looking to a safe and gradual return to gold and silver as the only permanent basis, standard, and measure of values recognized by the Constitution.*'

"The language of Secretary McCulloch, in 1865, I have read already to the same effect, and the 'cordial concurrence' of Congress. To this I could add abundant proofs from the debates, and from the valuable 'Financial History of the War,' by Mr. Spaulding, to show that the issue of treasury notes was at no time intended as a permanent measure with or without legal-tender power.

"The peace looked forward to by Secretary Chase came three years after he wrote the words I have read, and fifteen years have passed since the war ended, and yet we find this measure of confessed temporary expediency still in force, and by many urged to be continued *in perpetuum.* And senators say 'these notes are now at par— are redeemable by the government at the will of the holder in gold and silver coin.' 'Therefore let well alone,' and 'it is inexpedient' to *do anything now* to make resumption permanent and fix gold and silver as the only basis, standard, and measure of values recognized by the Constitution. The proposition to restore our constitutional and safe basis of value for all money is called 'tinkering with the finances.' To this complexion have we come—that a proposition to adopt measures of admitted safety and wisdom to secure a permanent prosperity is called 'tinkering with the finances.'

"Mr. President, such a condition of sentiment alarms me, and only causes me to be more vigorous in my efforts to secure my countrymen against such manifest dangers.

"When I see error so supported, my efforts will be redoubled to defend the country against it—to warn my associates here, and my countrymen everywhere, against the seductions of false measures of finance and the necessity of securing a sound basis for their business prosperity.

"This assumed legal-tender power is like the germ of a deadly fever, that needs only the heat of excitement, of speculation, of war, or of distress to develop its deadly powers; and it is while it is dormant that I would put an end to its existence. . . .

"The stock of gold and silver in this country was never so large as it is to-day.

"The report of the director of the mint informs us the amount of coin and bullion in the country, on October 31, 1879, was, of gold, $355,681,532, and of silver, $126,009,537; making a total of $481,691,069. And he says: 'Should the unprecedented flow of gold continue from foreign countries unchecked by its reaction upon prices here and abroad, the metallic circulation of the country at the end of the fiscal year (June 30, 1880) will have swollen to *over* $600,000,000.

"Wisely appreciating this high tide of opportunity, the banks are converting their reserves into coin; and a table furnished me by the Comptroller of the Currency will show that by far the greater portion of the reserves of the banks (which are largely in excess of legal requirement) consist to-day of coin.

"Mr. President, centralization of power in any government is to be dreaded. Under it 'the individual withers,' and local self government, in which are grown the seeds of hardy, self-reliant virtues and capacities, is destroyed. If this be true of other governments and peoples, how especially true of our own, where a territory so vast, embracing populations so heterogeneous in race, pursuits, and traditions, are brought into a union under a single Constitution, which is the supreme law of the land. The gradual absorption of jurisdiction by the general government in so many ways during the past fifteen years, its invasion of the domain of the States, its interference with subjects and matters so essentially proper for local cognizance and control, have justly alarmed those who have at heart the preservation of the Union under our federal theory and constitutional government.

"I believe this recognition is widespread, and the necessity admitted of a re-diffusion and re-distribution of powers which, in the emergencies and heat of civil war, have been unduly absorbed by the national government. Let us call to mind the legend upon our national seal, '*E pluribus unum*'—that the States form a *union* 'out of many'—not a *unit*. But let me ask, what act of centralization is so potent or in any degree equals that which assumes to create values by the fiat of Congress, and compels such values to be accepted as an equivalent for any indebtedness? In my view, all other steps to centralization are as nothing compared to this.

"Ten years ago I endeavored in vain to impress this Senate with the manifest and paramount duty of restoring and establishing a sound currency, a *real* money of daily measure of all contracts.

"In a speech made by me March 7, 1870, on the funding bill, I endeavored to show how much more pressing and important was the need of a sound foundation for all contracts than a prepayment and refunding of our bonds not due.

"But my efforts were in vain, and the deplorable policy inaugurated by Mr. Boutwell in his administration of the treasury was continued. From 1869 to 1875 the sale of nearly $500,000,000 of gold coin received from customs duties and its investment in United States bonds at high premiums was continued, and all that time the currency was suffered to stand unredeemed, and no step taken to resume specie payment. Such a policy precluded resumption, and to it I attribute in a large degree the sufferings which followed the crash of 1873.

"What I have said to-day is little more than repetition of what I have been moved to say more than once before, in regard to which I have been vindicated by events.

"I wish to say a few words to explain why the resolution before the Senate does not allow the United States notes to be received 'for duties on imports or interest on the public debt.'

"By the act of February 25, 1862, under which the first issue of these notes was authorized, it was, in section 1, expressly provided that—

"'Notes herein authorized shall be receivable in payment of all taxes, internal duties, excises, debts, and demands of every kind due to the United States *except duties on imports*, and of all claims and demands against the United States of every kind whatsoever *except for interest upon bonds and notes, which shall be paid in coin*, etc.'

"And by section 5 of the same act it was provided:

"'SEC. 5. *And be it further enacted*, That all duties on imported goods shall be paid in coin, or in notes payable on demand heretofore authorized to be issued and by law receivable in payment of public dues, and the coin so paid shall be set apart as a special fund, and shall be applied as follows:

'First. To the payment in coin of the interest on the bonds and notes of the United States.

'Second. To the purchase or payment of 1 per cent. of the entire debt of the United States, to be made within each fiscal year after the first day of July, 1862, which is to be set apart as a sinking fund, and the interest of which shall in like manner be applied to the purchase or payment of the public debt as the Secretary of the Treasury shall from time to time direct.

'Third. The residue thereof to be paid into the treasury of the United States.'

"I am unable to construe this law otherwise than as a distinct restriction of the notes—that they should never be receivable for duties on imports—and coupled with it the distinct pledge that these duties shall be paid *in coin*, and be 'set apart as a special fund' for the security of the interest on the public debt. It was, in my judgment, unwise and derogatory to a government like our own thus to 'put in pledge' any one of its sources of revenue specially—it savored too much of pawnbrokerage—but it was nevertheless done, and the contract made by the authorized agents of the American people. It may seem useless, now that credit is established and the bonds above par, when they have been called in and exchanged, that this law should be enforced; but the law of 1862 has never been repealed, but stood in full force as the utterance of the government when the new bonds went out in place of old ones, and the inscription on the notes is the same as it originally was. I propose to be strict in the performance of public obligations, because we can not infuse the spirit of honor and good faith, nay, *uberrima fides*, too much into our public acts. It was for the security of the holders of our public obligations that these pledges were made, and they alone can release us from them.

"It may seem now a useless formality to pay at the custom-house to the government the gold and silver coin we have drawn from its treasury on its own notes, but it is a formality carried out in a spirit of exact performance of a contract, and that alone makes it dignified and proper.

"Mr. President, at much greater length than I desired I have expressed my reasons for urging the adoption of this resolution, and, in concluding, I can only say how incompetently I feel I have dealt with a great subject, profoundly affecting the happiness, the morals, the welfare of our country. But I have, at least, tried to treat the question in a worthy spirit, and do my best in the service of truth and justice. Whether the Senate will concur in my views I know not, for a subject like this has never been and will never be made by me a subject of party caucus or personal canvass for votes; but I believe that good sense and right feeling are permanent and enduring forces in American politics, and in that faith I shall rely upon these qualities vindicating themselves in the minds of my countrymen as time shall pass on.

"The issue is nothing less than whether there shall be security to labor for its savings, to thrift and industry of their just results. The painful earnings of daily toil and the accumulated wealth of generations are alike involved, the creation of property by labor and its transmission to posterity are all alike affected by what I have proposed, and, not being a believer in *congressional alchemy*, I ask that we now abandon any further attempts to make it successful."

CHAPTER VIII.

TARIFF AND REVENUE REFORM.

WHEN Senator Bayard first came into Congress the revenue and fiscal service of the country was one of the most extortionate and oppressive ever recorded in history. It rested upon favoritism and class legislation, yet, a few years before he took his seat in the Senate, there had been extorted from the country some $650,000,000 in a single year by those questionable modes of taxation. The internal revenue system was obstructive and inquisitorial. The tariff laid duties upon some four thousand articles, for the benefits mainly of manufacturers in a few localities and few in number. Mr. Bayard, in coming to Congress, could truly say that he had had nothing to do with the enactment and the perpetuation of this disastrous system; and the section of the State of Delaware from which he was mainly elected was much more interested in manufactures than in agriculture. Wilmington is in many respects an offshoot from Philadelphia, and few men enter Congress from Philadelphia, no matter what may be their views in regard to federal politics, who are not avowed and active and *serviceable* protectionists in regard to revenue matters. In this respect Democrats and Republicans have equally agreed, and the policy of *quieta non movere* was long since very generally accepted.

Mr. Bayard, however, was a Democrat after an older

and better order. He knew how the country was suffering in consequence of these oppressive tax laws, and, while he heartily sympathized with the desire of his fellow citizens in Wilmington and other parts of the country to build up, extend, and diversify their industries, he did not believe they should be permitted to do this at the expense of the whole country. He saw, moreover, that, under the system of federal taxation for purposes of internal and customs revenue, the burden of the general taxes paid was much more costly even to the manufacturers of Wilmington than the specific measure of protection derived by them from the tariff. The system gave them the chance of taking in two cents extra in the shape of illicit profits, but compelled them to pay four cents in extra expenses. It was a lottery, in which, for every $100,000 worth of prizes awarded, the subscribers paid in $200,000.

Mr. Bayard was, besides, a strict constructionist of the Constitution, and he did not believe that the grant of power to raise revenue conveyed with it the power likewise to extend "protection." He did not believe that the power of Congress to derive income for the government upon the imports of iron from Cardiff could be stretched into a power to prevent these imports for the benefit of forges in Pennsylvania, so that every buyer of iron, in any shape, in the whole country through, had to pay these high duties to the home manufacturer, while the government derived no funds at all from the duties imposed by it to bring revenue in. If duties could be laid at all by government, they could only be laid for revenue; and, if they did not result in revenue, but, instead of that, in taxation of all classes for the benefit of one class, or a few classes, they were unconstitutional, and should be repealed.

There can be no mistake in regard to Mr. Bayard's

views upon such matters. He believes that there is no power under the Constitution to frame tariffs upon this principle, and that if the power did exist it would be inexpedient to exercise it. "I need scarcely say here," he remarked in connection with the bill providing for the Centennial Exhibition,* "to those who have taken the trouble to note my course on legislation, that I am a strict constructionist of powers under the Constitution. I believe that ours is a government only of special and enumerated powers, and not of general and unlimited powers; but I am unwilling to say that language which has been placed so carefully, not simply in the preamble of the Constitution, but carried affirmatively a second time into the very enumeration of the powers delegated to Congress, was placed there so that it should have no effect, and to be mere idle words which can be left out of consideration at will. . . . That is the most familiar, and, in my opinion, the safest principle of construction of the Constitution—*expressum facit cessare tacitum*—that, in construing a grant of express power in the Constitution, you can not ingraft upon that an implied power. . . . One of the troubles of our times," Mr. Bayard said in another speech,† "is that so many well-meaning and respectable persons consider that everything that is right in itself should necessarily be performed by the Congress of the United States, forgetting that *this is a government of limited, enumerated, and delegated powers*, and that the desirability of a measure is no test whatever of the right of Congress to enact it into a law. I believe, sir, it is an indifference to this truth, and it is a disregard of this truth, that has led this country into most of the difficul-

---

* February 26, 1874.
† Liquor Traffic Commission, February 26, 1874.

ties from which we have suffered and which still surround us."

So, in regard to subsidies, Mr. Bayard stands upon the general idea, and demands * "upon what principle, except that of using the associated powers of the government to interfere with competitors and certain individual enterprises, can you *bestow bounties upon selected individuals* and confine those bounties to favored cases?" That sentence embodies in a nutshell the whole proposition in favor of protection, and, even in stating, refutes it, not only upon the issue of constitutionality, but upon that of good policy also. For, as Mr. Bayard says in another part of this same speech, "There are other reasons why in our form of government such propositions are especially dangerous and difficult. In the past, one of the great difficulties in the history of our government has been the prevention of local jealousies and discontents proceeding from supposed inequitable and unjust administration of government favor. The expenditures of money in one part of this country or the other, the passage of laws that were supposed to work favorably to one section of the country at the expense of the other, have all given rise to great difficulties in the past; and no wise and considerate legislator but will appreciate the great danger of exercising the power of granting government aid in local enterprises—and that one great element of public safety is the restriction of this function of federal power to the minimum consistent with the execution of the essential powers of government. What is this principle of subsidy? *It is the assistance from the public treasury to individual enterprise; it is a gratuity from the public treasury in aid of a private undertaking* Communism,

* June 25, 1878, Roach Subsidy Bill.

as I understand it, is the principle of acting through the association of government as opposed to individual competition. Under governments where such doctrine does not prevail, individual competition is left to stand or fall, according to its own merit, energy, or force; but where you shall array the associated powers of the government, and make them the controlling element of every enterprise, you have what is termed communism."

It must be understood, however, that in this matter of subsidy, of tariff, as likewise in the kindred subjects of the banks and the entire fiscal system of the government, Mr. Bayard is a reformer, not a revolutionist. There are many things, the result of Republican misrule and of the riot of unchecked power since 1861, which he wants to see reconstructed and reformed. But it is part of this Senator's well-balanced and conservative instinct that he is not a destructive nor an obstructive in anything. He does not wish for himself, nor does he encourage or countenance his party, to pull down anything until the time is ripe to substitute something better in its place. "I do not favor sudden changes," said he, in his first speech on the financial question.* "*Festina lente* is a wise maxim for governments as well as individuals, and reforms to be wholesome must be gradual. This is one of the sources of the strength of the English government, from whom it is wise that we should borrow lessons of experience. Their reforms have been gradual and not sudden, so that the people of that country have had timely warning and opportunity to accommodate their affairs to meet the proposed alterations in the governmental system."

He knows how the present revenue system was set in motion in 1861, how unjustly and invidiously, with what

---

* March 7, 1870.

midnight haste and utter disregard of all propriety, advantage was taken of the secession of some Southern States and the consequent defection of Southern senators,* to hurry through a bill substituting an entirely new tariff system for that which had been maintained by so many Democratic administrations to the material benefit of the country. He knew how this first tariff effort of Mr. Morrill and his friends had been retouched and expanded until it culminated in the Morrill tariffs of 1865 and 1866, the most monstrous revenue system ever contrived for hampering the industries of an enlightened people. Mr. Bayard knew how the people were oppressed and stifled under the burdens and inequalities of this system, but he knew also that under it industries had sprung into existence, capital had been largely invested and labor diverted into new channels, and that any sudden and violent changes would visit complete, irremediable, and unmerited disaster upon these. He knew, finally, that the government must have revenue, and that, to obtain this, it must, in part at least, in pursuance of old established precedent, continue to depend upon that form of indirect taxation known as tariff duties—not abstractly the best mode of impost, but that which people tolerate with the least complaint, so long as it is prudently and fairly levied. Hence, Mr. Bayard entered the Senate, not as a free-trader, but as a revenue reformer, an advocate of tariffs so far as needed to yield necessary revenue, but no further. Taxation, he held, was a necessary evil, but an evil still. Therefore, expenses should be reduced to their minimum, and simplicity and economy should rule in every department of the government, in order to keep the evil of taxation down to its mini-

* In March, 1861.

mum likewise. Revenue reform, in Mr. Bayard's view, meant three very essential things: It meant the defense of the people from an oppressive volume of tariff taxes; it meant their further protection from the still heavier burden of a class legislation which, while it produced one dollar to the government, taxed the people six dollars, by compelling them to purchase necessary goods and articles from favored manufacturers, whose industries had become monopolies, defended by act of Congress; and it meant, finally, by curtailing revenue and expenditures, to put a period to the disgraces of official corruption and profligacy.

Mr. Bayard was never doctrinaire, but always practical and matter-of-fact in treating these important questions. He asked himself in regard to every part of the revenue system: "Does the Constitution allow it? Is it expedient to be done? Will it advance the public interests if done?" These simple rules of conduct have enabled the Senator to initiate and carry through some substantial and valuable reforms, which have given material and valuable relief to the mercantile and commercial communities. How practical he is, how humane, how little wedded to abstract ideas in the face of solid reforms, let a word of his in discussing the tariff bill of 1870 bear witness to. The question was on the taxation of official salaries, which Mr. Sherman upheld, but Mr. Bayard said: "I think that every reason which existed for the repeal of the income tax exists for the repeal of this tax upon salaries. Salaries are the remuneration for labor— a fixed compensation; and I regret that this discrimination, or this tax that we have refused to continue on all other sources of income, should continue on a very hard-worked and poorly paid class of people, and a class of people who have no means of getting rid of their tax in the way that one class had who have been relieved, to wit, the landlords and property-owners of the country. There is no means by which this class can escape from the burden hereby imposed. I should be very sorry, while any private income I might have derived from any other source than my salary here should be exempted, to still continue a tax upon the salaries of officers, clerks, and others, poorly paid, as I have said, in the main, for the labor they have done. I trust the Senate will not agree to it."

This tariff act of 1870 very sensibly reduced the burden of general taxation, though it intensified the injustice of "protection" in a great many individual instances, and the sugar schedule, in particular, was a monstrous abortion, which has destroyed the importing interest, prevents the consumption of raw sugars, has eaten up the capital of honest refiners and driven them out of the trade, delivering over to their successors the entire control, manipulation, and distribution of the sugar supplies of 45,000,000 people, consuming 1,800,000,000 pounds of sugar every year. Mr. Bayard argued as strenuously for the good features of this tariff bill as he combated its unjust ones. In his speech of June 23, 1870,* he took strong ground against the income tax, especially in regard to its discriminative features. This discrimination against property *per se*, Mr. Bayard argued, was most unjust, and most unjustifiable. "It was discrimination against the *measure* of property. It was defensible on no grounds on which laws should ever rest. It was in effect a punishment for the possession of wealth, and tending to deter men from

* Appendix to "Congressional Globe," Forty-first Congress, 2d session, p. 522.

following successfully all those pursuits which a wise public policy is disposed to encourage."

In the end of his speech Mr. Bayard summed up the reasons which compelled him to vote against this bill, and which have made him the opponent of every bill of the same sort that has been introduced in Congress since he came there—"Mr. President," he said, "believing that this tax is under our written Constitution forbidden by the clauses which I have read; believing it to be an unjust tax in its results; believing its discriminations to be utterly unjust; believing its exemptions to be utterly delusive, failing to affect favorably those classes who appeal most to our sympathies and our sense of protection—I mean persons of a decent condition of life with fixed incomes, drawn from the stock of incorporated companies, who are deprived of all benefit by this so-called exemption under the present form of our law; believing this, and further, that the demoralization arising from the pressure upon men either to conceal the proper amount of their incomes to escape tax, or upon those who are struggling under financial troubles to exaggerate their income in order to gain credit, and delude those to whom they are indebted; believing it to be accompanied by inquisitorial features which tend to create discontent in the hearts of the citizens against the government under which they live—all these things justify me in expressing the hope, and I certainly shall indicate it by my vote, that this income tax may cease to exist as a feature of American legislation."

But there were other reasons why Mr. Bayard opposed the perpetuation of the income tax. He believed that the revenue to be derived from this source could be obtained from the taxation of United States bonds, and this he strongly favored, both because it was equitable and because public opinion generally consented to it, and demanded it as strongly as it repudiated the policy of perpetual income taxes. Mr. Bayard's views upon this subject are valuable as illustrating his force and character as a *practical* legislator, a profound believer in the "unwritten law" of public opinion and that "common consent" which we weaken by confounding with the very ordinary and, as commonly used, unmeaning phrase, "common sense." Said Mr. Bayard:

"The policy adopted by the treasury officials of the United States has forced these securities to something above their value in gold; and yet the cry is that a guarantee, the advantage of which they have fully enjoyed and more, a guarantee that was upon its face temporary only, shall now be continued in their behalf for ever. Sir, I think as there has been no lack of favor to them, no short-handed allowance of good faith toward them, they should be satisfied now to take their rank with other classes of the citizens of the United States, and to be dealt with according to the same measure of even-handed justice. I would deal with them with perfect good faith; but I would not exempt them from paying their fair share of the public burdens, nor discriminate in their favor against other classes of my countrymen. Then, sir, the object of this income tax having ceased, other means for procuring the same amount of public revenue being, as I have stated, directly at hand, the retention of this five per cent. upon the interest of the public debt, the same rate which it has been paying heretofore, a tax imposed directly upon accumulated property, will, I think, amply supply the deficiency which may be caused to the public revenue from the destruction of this income tax upon other property.

"Sir, it has been said that there is an opinion in the community more acute, more able, and more wise than that of even the wisest individual in it; and that is the great result called public opinion. Many men in the mass come to conclusions perfectly just and irresistibly true, for which, perhaps, they could give you but lame reasons if they were pressed individually. It is what may be called the sum and essence of popular intelligence that forms to my mind one of the safest guides for legislation. I do not believe that this income tax would have reached the unpopularity that it has, that it would be felt to be so injurious to the public as it is felt to be, if its evils were not real instead of imaginary. I do not think it would be difficult to trace the reasons why these evils should be felt, and be felt by the poorest man as well as by the most wealthy, simply for the causes that I have given here, of the easy method by which these burdens that are paid by the landlord and the capitalist in gross may be transferred to his dependents in detail. The consumer will pay it at last; the poor tenant will pay it at last; and you may take from the lands of the rich landlord what you please, he simply has an immediate remedy by tacking that amount to those from whom his revenues are derived. Such is the case; such it has been; such it always will be; and, when the people of this country complain of the payment of a tax of that kind, they know precisely where the shoe pinches, and they best can judge of their own sufferings under it."

The vexed question of reform in the "sugar schedule" agitates Congress and the country to-day, perhaps because the frauds under it are more glaring and conspicuous than they are in respect of some other provisions of the tariff. This schedule was put in very nearly its present shape at this session of 1870, from which we have already quoted, and Mr. Bayard easily saw through and sharply denounced the new complications in the methods of taxing imported sugars which had been put forward by Mr. Schenck, of the House Committee of Ways and Means, and by Mr. Sherman, of the Senate Finance Committee, as tariff reforms. Mr. Bayard would accept no such palpable and transparent sophistries. He made a short speech on the subject, and on the general matter of hurried tariff legislation,* which is representative of his ideas on such subjects, and full of wisdom and soundness. It affords another instance of the thesis which has been maintained throughout this entire sketch, that Mr. Bayard is as signally conservative as he is confessedly statesmanlike in all his views.

"There is one proposition that I think will be assented to by all who hear me, and that is, that, in dealing with a question so broad as the rate of duties upon imports, a comprehensive view of the situation is demanded for anything like justice, or anything like a statesmanlike result. How are we asked at this time to consider this question of duties upon imports? Why, sir, not as a whole, not as a general system, not in a comprehensive glance at the interests of our entire country, with all our demands and with all our productions; but we are called upon to consider it in a mere fragmentary state, as a mere patchwork upon this bill, in which necessarily you will be prevented from doing justice, because you will exclude from your consideration nineteen twentieths of the interests which you ought to consider at the time you attempt to tax the rest.

"I am not only strongly in favor of a reduction of

* June 27, 1870.

taxes, but I am an equally positive believer that in the amount of taxes now raised there can be far more comfort and justice to the country by having them readjusted in different forms, and to fall with different weights than they now do. But can this be done now? Is this a proper time, or is the Senate a proper body, to take up this question and consider it, as I say, only in this patched and fragmentary condition? Why, sir, what was the result? . . . I will simply say this: that of all exhibitions of human selfishness, of all shortsighted human selfishness that I have ever known in my life, that which I have witnessed in the past four weeks has exceeded all. What has it been? A mere scramble for different interests rushing down here in the closing weeks of a session, each man anxious and willing to thrust his portion of public burden from his own shoulders, and pointing out the convenient back of some neighbor on whom it might rest.

"It was not the dictate of justice; it was not dictated in the broad light of necessity for the public welfare and a systematic reformation of public burdens. It was nothing in the world but what I have described, some means by which individuals might profit, and that profit should be gained at the expense of some other member of society. I do not say this struggle of human interests will not always occur; but I do say that over and above all that there must suspend the judgment of those who are unable to comprehend the entire field. In order that men should undertake to settle a tariff for a great nation like this, with all the variety of its demands, with all the intertwining of interests among a people so vast in number, so varied in pursuits, with all the demands of so varied a climate and soil as our own, there should be at least a full, large-minded grasp of the whole subject before you attempt to deal with any part in the fragmentary way that is now proposed. . . . If this list of tariff duties is to be discussed, long time must be occupied in it; each individual interest will wish to be represented; and there is none more interesting or more important to the people at large than probably the very subject now under discussion. There are admitted defects in the present system of assessing and obtaining your duties upon sugar; there are opportunities for fraud, opportunities for error, which result in injustice under our present system; and yet, great as are these opportunities growing out of the complications of the law, and the difficulty of establishing this standard of color, which is the one resorted to as a test of duty, the propositions of the finance committee in this respect rather increase than diminish them. I do not say they do not place the matter on a fairer basis in the abstract, but I say that, practically speaking, they increase all the difficulties of the present law.

"Sir, there is one other matter in this affecting questions of commerce; and that is, that although a law is perhaps unjust in itself, yet if it has been suffered to solidify by time, and the interests of commercial men have been suffered to accommodate themselves to its existence, it is better to keep it, though it is defective, than by sudden changes to disarrange the arrangements of men in commerce. What contracts may have been made by merchants upon the basis of existing duties I do not know; but no doubt they have been large and important. There can be no doubt that while some men may be benefited, the great mass of those engaged in a particular trade are injured, by a sudden dislocation of the rates of duties, and a change in either the mode of collecting them or in the amount to be collected. . . . Let the tariff stand as it is until the next session of Congress, when it may be examined, not in parts, not in this fragmentary way, but as a comprehensive whole. It should be certainly a system and not a simple statutory remedy, picking out here and there some article which is to be favored by what is termed protection, or else to be put upon the free list in order to benefit in some other way equally selfish some manufacturer. I trust that in these cases and in all others the present rate of duties upon imports will be retained, without regard so much to the merits of the individual proposition taken by itself in part as this, that when a change of the tariff is made it shall be made in obedience to a comprehensive system of alteration."

The tariff attorneys in and out of Congress had so arranged matters as to bring the House bill into the Senate just at the tail-end of the session. They now further proposed (June 28, 1870), on a resolution offered by Mr. John Sherman, then chairman of the Senate Finance Committee, as he is now Secretary of the Treasury, "that the debate on House bill No. 2,045, to reduce taxation, shall after to-day be confined to debate of not exceeding five minutes by each senator on the amendment pending, when such debate arises." This resolution, though without any precedent in the history of the Senate, was adopted by *quasi* unanimous consent, but not before Mr. Bayard had emphasized his objections to any gag-law of the sort. "I take leave to say," he said, "that there are in this bill features that can not reasonably and justly be discussed in the time stated. There are propositions in this bill to which I, in advance, avow my utmost opposition; there are propositions in this bill to make the people of this country pay tribute to a limited number of individuals, the patentees of certain processes of manufacture, that can not have all said that ought to be said against them, and that would be said, but for the interference of this rule, within the short space of five minutes."

In another speech in the debate on this same tariff, Mr. Bayard adverted to *ad valorem* duties. Such a tariff he regarded as a misfortune. "It requires in the first place a system of oaths from the importers. *The system is to set the oaths of men, their sense of truth, against their pecuniary interests;* and I am sorry to say that the history of mankind shows that those two matters can seldom come into collision without injury to the former." These views are in pointed illustration of Mr. Bayard's principles, that "it is vain to sing pæans to public credit and to national honor, and do those things that make it impossible to preserve either."

Let us now glance at Mr. Bayard as a practical revenue reformer. We have already briefly alluded to his position, with Senator Casserly, in the minority of the Senate Committee on Investigation and Retrenchment. That committee reported in June, 1872, and, in spite of the fact that the Senate took no action, and the White House would not desert its favorites "under fire," and all the corrupt influences of the New York Custom-House were brought into line to keep things in *statu quo*, the general-order system of warehousing was abandoned, Leet and Stocking forced out of business, Collector Murphy removed, and the moieties to informers broken up. All this was in consequence of the facts brought out by Mr. Bayard and Mr. Casserly, and the strong public feeling which they called into action.

These matters are worth discussing just now, for the

system which Mr. Bayard condemned and exposed was not only tolerated and encouraged, it was in great measure *established*, by General Grant and his understrappers in and out of Congress. General Grant is again before the people soliciting a third term in the presidency, and his pretensions are eagerly sustained and urged by the old Custom-house ring of New York.

The Committee on Investigation and Retrenchment was charged to investigate alleged abuses and extortions in connection with the general-order warehouse business, the monopoly of which, with enormous profits, was practically in the hands of George K. Leet, said to have had "some connection" with the White House; to find out what was the "mysterious power" sustaining this scandalous system of robbery against the voice of the merchants of New York and the judgment and voice of the Secretary of the Treasury himself; to discover if unlawful charges were made for cartage and storage; if customs officers took bribes ("presents," they were called); if they connived at "irregular practices" (another name for smuggling); if merchandise was stolen *in transitu;* if compromises with merchants under the moiety system led to losses of revenue, and finally, "whether the patronage, officers, or employees of said custom-house were used to influence or control either or both of the last two State conventions of the Republican party in New York, and whether assessments of money have been made, or contributions of money exacted, to be used to control primaries, secure delegates to State conventions or for other political purposes, and whether any of the said officers in said custom-house have been or are used as instruments of political or party patronage."

When only a part of the testimony had been taken,

the investigation threatened to be so damaging to those involved that it was cut short, and the majority of the committee, without intimating the fact or consulting with the minority about it, prepared and adopted a "white-washing" report. This report, in manuscript, was submitted in the last hours of the session, when there was no possible chance to examine and consider it promptly, and when Mr. Bayard was absent as one of a committee of conference on the tariff bill. The minority report, therefore, of Senators Bayard and Casserly was necessarily a hurried and incomplete document, yet it was able to accomplish all that we have said. After premising that, in consequence of New York city being the great gateway of our commerce, the chief officer of customs there occupies a position and becomes an officer scarcely second to a cabinet officer in national importance, the report proceeds to consider the abuses which have grown up in this office in consequence of partisan mismanagement. The history of the general-order stores and bonded warehouse system is given, and it is shown that there was no maladministration until "the young man Leet" was forced upon Collector Grinnell by a note of recommendation which he bore from President Grant, which practically was a mandate to appoint him. In Leet's behalf Grinnell withdrew the general-order privilege from the steamship warehouses in Jersey City, causing great injury and loss to New York commerce. Under Leet's system, it cost fourteen per cent. more to store goods for forty-eight hours in a New York bonded warehouse than it did to transport them across the Atlantic. When Grinnell declined to give to Leet and his partner, Stocking, the entire monopoly of this general-order business, he was removed by the President, and Thomas Murphy became collector. Murphy proved more pliant, and, as the minority report shows, "from September, 1870, onward and until after the committee had left New York in February, 1872, the general-order business was a monopoly in the hands of Leet and Stocking, who concentrated it in the two localities above stated. Backed by the official sanction of the custom-house, this monopoly became grossly exacting and oppressive to the merchants of New York. Their charges for storage, cartage, and labor were enormously increased, and delay, inconvenience, and loss followed to the community."

The testimony of leading merchants, such as A. T. Stewart, H. B. Claflin, B. H. Hutten, C. W. Schultz, and others, mainly elicited upon cross-examination by Mr. Bayard, went to prove that Leet's charges were double those formerly made, double what was needed, and that goods handled by him were not well guarded. It was proved that his profits were enormous, variously estimated at from $60,000 to $200,000 a year, and it was partly proved that somebody in Washington, and near the White House—some of "the mess" to which Leet had belonged—probably shared these profits with him. Leet's clerks testified that the books of the firm were never balanced, nor could the committee get these books before them. The entire capital put by these adventurers in their business was $1,000 in cash, advanced by a third party, and Leet's "certificate" from Grant, stating that he had been the General's headquarters clerk at Vicksburg, and enjoyed his confidence.

The minority showed also that customs officers took bribes in defiance of the statutes making such action a criminal offense. These violations of law were habitual in every department of the service. Gross frauds were also shown to be probable and likely in the weighing and appraising of merchandise. It was proved that merchants were held at the mercy of spies and informers under the "general-warrant" system, by which a promiscuous seizure of books and papers and a general obstruction of business was allowed. It was proved that these seizures were often made, and that merchants were forced to pay heavy sums in "compromise," in order to save themselves from ruin. The system encouraged gross corruption in the detective officers, and encouraged merchants also to commit crimes against the revenue. As the minority report aptly said: "What would be thought of the administration of law which permitted a forger to go free upon repaying the amount he had gained by the commission of his crime? How would counterfeiting be stopped if the false money could be redeemed by good and the offense wiped out? or if the robber, who was caught coming from your premises with his plunder, should relinquish his basket of plate and go unwhipped of justice? Yet such is precisely the present system of disposing of highly penal offenses against the revenue. Such is the result and consequence of settlement and compromise for offenses for violations of the revenue laws, as systematically conducted by United States treasury agents, district attorneys, informers, and seizure-bureau officials. Who can doubt that one resolute prosecution to conviction, the presence of one dishonest importing merchant in the prisoner's dock, the consignment of one such criminal to the penitentiary of the State, would do more to reform abuses and discourage frauds upon the revenue than a thousand compromises and settlements? Who can estimate," the report adds, "the amount of undiscovered frauds and their cost to the government? The object of the informer being gain alone, a bribe of superior dimensions to the informer's share would at any time secure his silence, and perhaps connivance. When a government relies upon nothing higher than the love of money in its public service, it may well doubt the security of its revenues."

It was proved that officials made extravagant gains from forfeitures and amercements. The naval officer's share from these sources, above his handsome salary, was $114,704.27, and that of the surveyor $101,206.12, all in four years, besides a divisible interest, to a much larger amount, in undetermined seizure cases. It was proved that Jayne, Howe, Brush, Chalker, and other special treasury agents, in their search after moieties, stooped to bribe the clerks and confidential employees of merchants to betray their most private affairs. "Can such abominations as these," said Messrs. Bayard and Casserly, "be justified by the pretense that they are meant to prevent or punish frauds upon the revenue? Who will not say that the remedy is not ten times worse than the disease? What security is there that the bookkeeper or clerk so suborned by the informer shall not make such entries in the books of the merchant, unknown to him, as would be proof almost conclusive of criminality? Such a system would honeycomb society with fraud and dissimulation, and banish all confidence between men."

The minority report finally exposed the New York Custom-House as a political engine in such an effectual way as to compel the men who came after Grant to pretend at least to prohibit government employees from levying assessments, and "managing" primary elections. All the reforms either made, or mapped in this direction, started from the disclosures embodied in this report of

Messrs. Bayard and Casserly. The Liberal Republican revolt in 1872 and the very liberal Republican platform (not acted up to) of 1876 are among the other fruits of what the report revealed. On these subjects is said, among other things:

"Of the utter demoralization and wide-spread injury to the public service caused by this perversion of official power and abuse of the patronage inherent in the bestowing of public office, we have abundant and conclusive testimony. Indeed, the frauds, the misdemeanors, defalcations, and abuses to which we have referred in the foregoing pages, have their well-spring in the necessary corruptions that flow from the prostitution of appointments in the civil service to mere party ends. It would be a Utopian idea that so vast a machine as the New York Custom-House could be operated without the incidental results of human frailty and sin. But when the governing ideas of such an institution are based upon the very lowest views of political morality and partisan expediency, the result must necessarily be such as is disclosed by the present testimony."

It proved that the Custom-House ring was in sympathy with and friendly to the "Tammany ring," had intimate relations with and did underhand work for Tweed, Sweeney, Connelly, Smith, and Hall. In those palmy days, Mr. Alonzo B. Cornell, Conkling's present governor of New York, was naval officer at the port, and then, as now, a strenuous adherent of General Grant's. The conclusions to which Messrs. Bayard and Casserly came have peculiar value. They cover the whole subject of civil service reform, and how to effect it, and they express Mr. Bayard's views in regard to this most important matter.

"We believe," the report says, "that the extracts made of the testimony taken in this case, in relation to Mr. Murphy and his method of conducting the affairs of the collectorship, will render it obvious that he was a very unfit man for the position, totally without a proper comprehension of its duties, and almost totally without the capacities to fulfill them. The tenure of the political office under his administration was made solely dependent upon bald partisan service, generally of the basest character. Merit in office was overlooked or disregarded, if it did not accompany the most facile and slavish obedience to party demands. Personal unworthiness and profligacy were totally disregarded if unhesitating political adherence was given. The result was necessarily fatal to the public service. To be a good and reliable public officer means to be a reliable man and good citizen. The qualities that form our security in private life are our best safeguards in public life. A public official who will sacrifice his personal convictions of right and independence of thought to gain or keep an office will be unworthy of trust when in office. If such an example be set by those high in authority, nothing can be expected but that it will be followed by their subordinates. Like master, like man. If the collector of the port be nothing better than a ward politician, with the habits, instincts, and tone of his class, his subordinates will, very shortly, be found to follow and imitate him. If Mr. Murphy totally overlooked what was due to the public service in making his appointments, if he bargained and sold the places of inspector, weigher, gauger, and the like, how could it be expected that his appointees would be faithful to the government, or that bribery and corruption, delinquency and abuse, should not mark nearly every department and feature of his administration?"

As to the principles regulating tenure of office, it says: "It seems to us that those principles of compensation and employment which are found useful, and lead to success in the business affairs of private individuals, are not less true when applied to the public service. To make tenure of office dependent upon the mere will of the superior or upon the shifting tides of political party ascendancy, is a system which would soon lead to the bankruptcy of the private merchant who adopted it. By a course of reasoning equally applicable to public affairs, the government that adopts it must suffer. It can not well be denied that good behavior in office should be the only condition imposed upon permanent tenure; that the public service should be the only thing to be regarded; and the individual who performed that might feel assured that he would be allowed to enjoy his individual opinions upon political and other subjects in perfect self-respect and without fear of the frowns of his official superiors. Certain it is that this rule could safely be applied to all offices simply ministerial. In others of a grade that necessarily reflected the political policy of an administration, such as cabinet officers, it may be necessary, and probably is so, that concurrence of sentiment with the executive should be an additional condition of official tenure."

And upon the general subject we find these very wise conclusions: "The principles of good government are, after all, although profound in their operation, very simple in their nature. At the very base, strict and rigid pecuniary honesty must lie. If this be wanting, if pecuniary delinquencies shall be condoned because the public treasury, and not an individual, is the sufferer, then from such an admission proceeds a whole catalogue of evils and corruption. If a man in official position bestows an office of trust and emolument upon another because he is a personal or political friend, and without regard to the fact whether he is competent and willing to render a just equivalent of service for the salary he receives, then the public treasury is defrauded, is robbed to the precise amount of that friend's defalcation in duty; and in dishonesty the crime is not proportioned to the amount that is taken, but to the departure from moral principle which is involved. Public men have no right to receive personal favors at public cost. They have no right to enrich themselves, their families, or their friends, at public cost. It is a breach of trust when such things are permitted; and no public service where they are tolerated can fail to become corrupt and worthless.

"We have pointed out the evils that resulted from an unwise, impolitic law, such as that permitting the seizure of books and papers of merchants. But the great mass of the abuses to which we have referred are those of maladministration; and, until men shall be placed in power who realize the requirements and are competent to understand and execute the duties of civil administration, without personal favor, and with a single eye to public interests alone, the evils we have pointed out can not be expected to diminish, but, on the contrary, to grow worse and worse.

"The evils which have been proven to exist have their source, as we have said and now here repeat, much less in the existence of imperfect or mischievous laws than in the want of capacity and fitness on the part of those who fill the offices. The fundamental cause of this great abuse and the real responsibility for it are to be found in an improper administration of the appointing power in the government.

"By the Constitution and laws of the United States the President has plenary power over the civil service of the country. Nearly all appointments to office proceed directly or indirectly from him. By the Constitution he is commanded 'to take care that the laws be faithfully executed,' and by his oath of office he binds himself 'faithfully to execute the office of President of the United States.' He is to put fit men in office, and to see that the laws do not fail of execution by their misconduct.

"His power over the subject is exclusive. So is his responsibility. His duty is equally plain and paramount.

"Having all the power necessary, if he has the capacity and will to give to the country an honest, efficient civil service, he will do it. If he fails to bestow this great blessing on the people, it is not for want of power in himself. It can only be for want of either the will or the capacity; it may be, of both. Whatever the cause, the evils of his failure are manifold and serious. His abuses of the appointing power are reproduced with mischievous fidelity through the body of the subordinates in the civil service, to the scandal and oppression of the people, and the gradual general lowering of their moral tone.

"The cure for the evil must be sought in the same high quarter where the evil had its rise. It is there that the power, the duty, and the responsibility lie. There the cure is to be applied. Anything short of this is trifling with the evil. It is dealing with the effect instead of with the cause."

CHAPTER IX.

"THIS IS A GOVERNMENT OF LAWS."

AMONG the calamities which war brings in its train, there is none more pernicious or more lasting in its baleful effects than this: that it familiarizes a people with the substitution of the rule of force for the rule of law. The jealous vigilance with which any approach to illegality should be watched by a free people becomes relaxed, or superseded by a spirit of acquiescence, if not of submissiveness. During the late war so many violations of civil rights and order were perpetrated under the plea of military necessity that the people grew callous, and, even where such necessity did not exist, looked on, perhaps with regret, but without astonishment, and almost without indignation. The war and its results established the radical leaders firmly in at least temporary power, and lifted one of the victorious commanders to the highest office in the country, and they must have had less than the common share of human frailty if they had not regarded the modes and the instruments of their success with peculiar affection.

By a natural confusion of thought they had first identified the country with the administration, and then with their own party; and as once whoever canvassed the acts of the President was branded as disloyal, so now they could not help feeling that a dissenter from their views or opposer of their policy must be a traitor at heart. To cast a Democratic ballot was an act differing only in degree, but not in kind, from firing a rebel bullet; and a Democratic body elected to replace a Republican body was, in the view of these extremists, merely a hostile force that had surprised a fort, and must be dislodged at any cost.

The President of the United States, a trained and veteran soldier, was naturally partial to those summary modes of procedure with which he was familiar, and which in his hands had proved so triumphantly effective; and he was surrounded by advisers and subordinates who urged—if urging was needed—and eagerly applauded their use. When members of the legislature of a State were thrust from their hall by an officer of the United States army, at the head of a file of soldiers; when a general of cavalry proposed, in time of peace, and with all the courts open, to deal with a community as "banditti," a prompt and hearty approval from "all of us" flashed back with lightning speed. No matter how complete the machinery of civil government, wherever there were "outrages," there the military must interfere; and there were sure to be "outrages" in plenty just before an election, except in districts certain to be carried by the Republicans, and there a halcyon calm prevailed. Of no use was it to expose the preposterous character of the testimony adduced, or to inquire how a handful of Democrats could "terrorize" overwhelming majorities of their political opponents; the spectres of "Ku-Klux" and "White-Leagues" were made to stalk solemnly up and down the halls of Congress until the farce could be played no longer.

But these things were not the worst, for from these

there was sure to be a reaction; worse than these was the growing indifference to law, the feeling that the party in power was entitled to have things their own way, which was the legitimate offspring of a loose construction of the Constitution, and that doctrine of "a higher law" invented to justify, and even to sanctify, profitable perjury.

No wonder that the conservative minority in Congress did their utmost to check this growing demoralization, which was eating like a cancer into the very vitals of the country. Among these Mr. Bayard was constant in his warnings, not to the Senate alone, but to the whole people, that something far more momentous than party failure or triumph was at stake—that nothing less than republican government and free institutions were at stake, if the great truth were forgotten that "this is a government of laws."

"Would to God!" he exclaims, in his speech of February 15, 1870, on the admission of Mississippi to representation in Congress, "would to God the people of this broad land could fully realize how fatal to the cause of civil liberty, how hostile to the very genius of our institutions, is the doctrine of coercive powers, upon which now alone the radical party propose to govern this country.

"When will the leaders of that party recognize the truth that the true strength of our government rests, not in the number of bayonets it can command to overawe and subdue local discontents, not in penal statutes and test-oaths and disfranchisements of the ablest and most intelligent citizens, but in the love and respect which exist in the hearts of our people toward it and their rulers? That its 'cheap defense' will be the ramparts which patriotic sentiments shall construct to guard it, and that the 'consent of the governed' is the only just and firm foundation upon which we can build our hopes for the perpetuation of the free Constitution of our fathers, designed by them to be our shield and safeguard against all tyranny and usurpation, whether from within or from without?"

And elsewhere in the same speech:

"If the doctrines enunciated in the speech of the Senator [Carpenter] yesterday in regard to the limitations upon the centralizing power of the federal government, in regard to the recognition of the wisdom and the necessity of leaving to the state governments the control of their local matters and institutions, matters which so necessarily and so reasonably belong to them, can be followed out, and can be brought in good faith into practice by the party of which the Senator is so distinguished an ornament, I will rejoice in their success. The power and spoils of party which may attend their political success I shall not envy, nor disturb their enjoyment. To me the happiness of seeing my native land once more enjoying that civil and religious feeling which can only exist under a government of laws, under a government of well-defined and limited powers, will more than compensate for the absence of the supposed exultation consequent upon a mere partisan triumph."

So in his speech of May 21, 1872, in opposition to the bill giving the President power to suspend the writ of *habeas corpus* in any State at his pleasure, thus giving really absolute and dictatorial power, and "substituting his irresponsible will for the safeguards of the Constitution"—for so shamelessly reckless had the radical party grown, that they were not only willing but eager to lay the liberties of the whole country under the feet of a military autocrat, rather than risk their own expulsion from power.

"Mr. President, it is to me an appalling and fearful thing to witness how the frail bands of constitutional limitation are snapping and parting in the fire of party spirit and sectional animosity. It seems to me the principles on which our system of government was based are day by day more and more effaced, and their very existence forgotten. Legislation by Congress seems day by day to be assuming the form and shape of mere military orders. Reason, argument, persuasion, moral power, are supplanted by the argument of arms. Our government is fast becoming a government of mere will, and a government of laws is being forgotten or discarded. We have seen lately in this very chamber how the decisions of the judicial branch of our government are met by the majority. When heat and passion have induced the passage of an act by Congress violative of the Constitution, and therefore invalid, and in calm and temperate methods the Supreme Court of the United States, without a single voice of dissent, so declares it to be, loud and disrespectful denunciations of the exercise of just judicial prerogative are heard from the leaders of the majority; denunciations of the decision which thwarted their hostile intent, and something approaching threats against a coördinate and equal branch of the government.

"And let not the people of the Northern States believe that this power so greedily asked for by the President, so shamelessly sought to be awarded him by his party friends in Congress, can be exercised or will be exercised to subjugate the Southern States, and destroy the liberties of that people alone. It is the first step that costs. That

8

which is pretended as a law to-day for but part of the country, a temporary law for part of the country, will shortly become the settled law for the whole country. The emergency of party, the needful party success, will be the only regulation that its authors and its executors will recognize."

Yet monstrous as that bill was, it would have become the law of the land, had not the Liberal Republicans in the House joined the Democrats in defeating it. Here is its history, from Mr. Bayard's address at Wilmington, October 4, 1872:

"I know the history of those events. As one of your representatives in the Senate I witnessed them all. I know how close was the shave by which that wicked and monstrous law was defeated; and I know by whose aid the Democratic party was enabled, standing of course a solid phalanx itself, to thwart that disastrous attempt. Why, look at it. The Senate passed the bill to give this power for one year more to the President. There was full debate upon that in the Senate; but you know how weak in numbers is the minority there. Then were heard, however, the voices of liberal and true men of the Republican party protesting against this act. They acted with the Democrats in endeavoring to prevent its passage, but in vain. It went to the House of Representatives; fresher from the people, with more responsibility for their acts to the people, than many of those in the Senate. There the Liberal Republicans, acting with the Democrats, succeeded in tabling that bill, and laying it under some hundreds of measures that could not be acted upon, and refusing to give it precedence.

"Then what happened? In the Senate of the United States we were considering a bill to appropriate moneys for the expenses of the government. For the purpose of facilitating business, the Senate unanimously adopted a rule that no amendment but such as was germane to the appropriation bill should be received, and that but five minutes should be given to any one to debate any given subject; it being a business measure entirely upon which lengthened discussion was out of place, and which the condition of the session rendered also impossible. The nomination of General Grant had been made. The nomination at Cincinnati had been made. The conclusion was almost foregone at that time that the Democratic party would ratify the action of the Cincinnati Convention. At least there had been then so general an expression that such result was understood throughout the country to be highly probable, although there were many members of the Democratic party, among whom was he who now addresses you, in opposition to such action. In this emergency the Republican leaders, feeling that their position was desperate, that they must give this power to the President in order to re-elect himself, and to have this bayonet bill once more enforced over the entire country, in utterly dishonorable disregard of the intent and meaning of the rule they had adopted, procured a fitting instrument to offer an amendment to a money bill, giving the President the right to suspend the writ of *habeas corpus* at his pleasure in any part of this country for another year.

"The dishonorable proposition was immediately denounced by the Democrats. It was debated; but the temporary Chairman of the Senate, forgetting what was due to himself and to his position, ruled the amendment to be in order. Upon a motion to take an appeal from his decision we were afforded a poor opportunity of debate, because, if the amendment had been received as in order, but five minutes would have been given to discuss such a question, which, of course, would have been fruitless and absurd. In order to bring before the people of this country the monstrous nature of this proposition, the little band of Democrats, throughout the whole of that weary night, discussed that question, so that the people might be aroused to the danger of the attempt that was being made, and that the House of Representatives might also be put upon their guard and understand the true nature of the question. But human endurance has its limits; and those few worn and weary men, the Liberal Republicans and Democrats of the Senate, a scanty handful, were at length compelled by sheer fatigue to abandon the contest, and, as the gray light of dawn entered the Senate Chamber, that amendment was offered, and it was adopted by a vote of the Senate.

"The bill went to the House, and what was its fate? There spoke Democracy; there spoke Liberal Republicanism—both uttering the same voice and saying: 'This dishonest act shall not become a law.' I well remember the anxious, weary hours that I and others in that Chamber passed in watching the fate of a bill that seemed to me to involve the fate of my country. What! give to a candidate for re-election the right to take away the great writ of liberty from all his opponents! Is it not enough to make you shudder? Is it not enough to make men ashamed that such things ever were proposed? Is it not enough, my friends, to make you feel grateful that there were Liberal Republicans to aid the Democrats in such an emergency."

As President Grant was the ready and willing instrument to execute a policy that would have laid the whole

American people prostrate beneath his feet, and made constitutional government, a government of laws, mere things of the past, Mr. Bayard took occasion in the same speech to review his action, that, from what he had already done, the people might judge what he was ready to do.

"What rebuke has the President of the United States ever administered to a dishonest official? What encouragement has he ever held out to a pure and honorable one? Early in the history of his administration there was a gentleman who was his Secretary of the Interior, whom I never heard spoken of by any man who knew him except in terms of respect: I mean Jacob D. Cox, of Ohio. He was a pure-minded, honest administrator. A proposition was made that all the clerks of his department should be assessed upon their salaries for political purposes, and Mr. Cox said nothing of the kind should be done in his department; that those men were there for public service; it was optional with them what they should subscribe, but that he never would make himself a party to a scheme for raising partisan funds by assessing the wages of those overworked and ill-paid men. What was the result? The political managers of the canvass were not satisfied because he would not make himself an instrument for this disreputable business. They went to the President with complaints that he would not do this dirty work of politics. What did the President do? You know that he parted with that honest man; he sustained the corruptionists, and he let Mr. Cox retire from his cabinet, and refused to sustain him in the honest position he had taken.

"While he turned Mr. Cox out of his cabinet because he would not league himself with these disreputable operations for partisan purposes, he kept in his cabinet and close in his counsels Mr. Creswell, the same postmaster general who allowed the claim of one Chorpenning to his law partner, when he himself had previously examined it and disallowed it, when three postmasters general had previously disallowed it after full examination. Mr. Creswell allowed a claim for $454,000 when the man who claimed it never had a just claim for one cent, and had really been paid three times more than he ought ever to have received.

"I take the record, and I show you that Mr. Dawes, the chairman of the Committee of Ways and Means of the House, came into Congress at the opening of the session in December, 1870, and introduced a resolution to repeal a former resolution, which had been obtained by fraud and misrepresentation, allowing the Chorpenning claim on the recommendation of the postmaster general, or authorizing him to make the settlement. Mr. Dawes explained the fraud, and the resolution under which Creswell had acted to pay this claim was unanimously repealed. It came to the Senate, and it was also unanimously repealed there. The payment of the money was stopped; it was saved to the treasury against Mr. Creswell's efforts to get it out; and after that time twice, upon the statute book, stands a proviso to appropriations of money for public purpose that no portion of that money should go toward paying the claim known as the Chorpenning claim. This occurred two and a half years ago. It was one of the most scandalous things that ever occurred in Washington. Yet Creswell is still held close in the councils of the present administration.

"You have heard of Governor Holden, of North Carolina. You know, perhaps, that he was an ultra secessionist; that he did his best to educate his people up to the doctrine of secession that carried North Carolina out of the Union; that he was an ultra Southern man in all his doctrines; that finally, when the war closed, and he found the cause of secession had failed, he whipped around, and became a violent Union man, so called, and took sides with the victors; that by dint of military and negro aid he was made the Governor of the State of North Carolina, and also the head of the Union League of that State, which embraced almost every black man within its limits; that a legislature, elected by the like means, met and voted away bonds of the State to the amount of nearly $15,000,000; that this man assisted in the robbery and the beggary almost of his people; that there is not to-day in North Carolina a hundred miles of good railroad to be seen for the $15,000,000 that were expended for the purpose of creating them. The money was stolen bodily by various people who were Holden's friends, and with his assistance and approval. An election followed. A legislature opposed to him was elected. He was impeached and convicted. His conviction was accomplished by the votes of Republicans as well as Democrats in the legislature. He fled from North Carolina and took refuge in Washington, where a requisition could not reach him. He there became the editor of a Grant newspaper. Now, mark you, this is the case of a man who had connived at robbery, who fled from his own outraged people, and has remained away from them ever since. That man, with that record, a year and a half after these events, was nominated by President Grant to be our minister at Peru. This is another case of General Grant's appreciation of the necessity of honesty.

"What shall I say of Bullock, of Georgia—the fellow who went down there and robbed those people out of some five or six millions, and then fled to Canada? I remember perfectly well when that scoundrel was in Washington endeavoring to procure the aid of Congress, and did procure it, to get soldiers and disperse the legislature that would have impeached and removed him. He had the presidential ear. But they could not withstand the progress of public opinion. A legislature was elected which was honest in its sentiment. Honest men were driven together by their sufferings, independent of former political views; and, when he found that his conduct was to be inquired into, Bullock ran away, and never will go back to Georgia, unless he goes back there to jail.

"What shall I say of Bowen, of South Carolina, who, after the war, became a violent partisan of the Northern government? When the war closed and his party was defeated, he went to the strong side. This man came to Congress. He disgraced the country and his position by selling his cadetships. They turned him out of Congress. He went back to South Carolina and married two wives, having them both living at the same time. He was indicted for bigamy in the District of Columbia. He was convicted by a jury upon which were negroes, who were his particular friends; and he had not been in jail two weeks before General Grant takes him by the hand and pardons him, just as Geary pardons this man Yerkes and the other fellow who was assisting Hartranft in the robbery of the State of Pennsylvania.

"What shall I say in regard to the discoveries made in the city of New York by a committee of which I was a member during the last winter? What shall I say in regard to all the rascality and robberies on the merchants of New York, which were there exposed? Were they not proven? Do not your public documents show you, not by statement of mine, but his own statement under oath, that a young man, formerly one of General Grant's own aids, Leet, an unknown, obscure man, was enabled, by a letter written and signed by General Grant, to go to New York and extort from the collector a perquisite called the general-order business, by which he was enabled to make enormous sums annually by plundering the merchants in overcharging them for the storage and the labor on their goods. Those outrages were all laid before the public; they were all printed at the time. The most efficient aid that that committee had in the discovery of frauds in New York was through Mr. Greeley, who himself came as a witness before that committee, and exposed the dishonesty of the Republican party.

"But, gentlemen, all these things appear on the record. Leet plundered the people of New York. General Grant was told of it. His former friend, Mr. Alexander T. Stewart, informed him of it. There was no ground to presume his ignorance. He knew it all—that a young man, not knowing a soul in New York, going there with nothing but General Grant's personal recommendation, who had been upon his staff, connected with him personally, had abused the confidence he had reposed in him, and that he was there plundering that community. The President knows that fact to-day; he knew it two years ago; and yet he has never lifted his finger to make him disgorge his plunder or to turn him out.

"Take, further, his ideas of politics as developed by his friend, Mr. Thomas Murphy, of New York, the late collector. Mr. Murphy seems to have been on terms of confidential intimacy with General Grant. I have not the time nor the disposition to read you, as I could from the public documents, Mr. Murphy's own statements in regard to his acts, or to read you the conversations which are sworn to in regard to Mr. Murphy's report from the President, of the part that the President wished the government officials to take in the canvass, but they amount to this: that Mr. Murphy was authorized to sell, and did sell and barter, the government offices in the custom-house at New York in exchange for party power and delegates to party conventions; that he made merchandise of the public offices of the government just as much as any marketman sells his produce. He did it openly, notoriously, so that all knew of it. Finally, as you all know, so great was the storm of public feeling on the subject, so powerful was the denunciation of Murphy's dishonesty and improper action, that even General Grant was forced to intimate that he would accept his resignation, and when he left he received a letter of the most effusive nature, praising Mr. Murphy's honesty and good conduct in the public service. Indeed, the only effect which these shocking disclosures seem to have had upon the President is, that he ordered the prosecution of the merchants who had been compelled to pay money to his corrupt subordinates, and who disclosed the truth of these abuses before the committee. What is the President doing to-day in Pennsylvania? Is he not sustaining a man running for governor who is confessedly corrupt, in whose aid the jails of the country are emptied in order that convicts may come out and speak in his favor, the speech in his favor being the price of their escape from justice?

"In all that wild carnival of dishonesty which has had no parallel in human history before, in the robbery of the Southern States by the adventurers, black and white, who have settled there upon those unhappy people, when public treasuries are robbed, when individuals are robbed, when offices are bought and sold, when scandals of the most infamous nature are exposed, constantly, I ask you whether one word has come in a presidential message, in a presidential speech, or in a presidential paper of any kind, to rebuke these things throughout that country? Not one.

"Therefore I say that pecuniary honesty, simple, rigid, and plain, which the humblest comprehension can understand, should be the corner-stone of a government. If it is not so, of course the larger the sphere of action, the more gross must the corruption become. What hope have we with an administration that sees no wrong in these things? While I do not propose to make, but, on the contrary, have purposely abstained from making any charge that would link the President with the personal receipt of any portion of these ill-gotten gains, I do say without fear of contradiction that no rebuke of a dishonest man in or out of office can be found in the official career of Ulysses S. Grant as President of the United States."

When one calls to memory the eight years of President Grant's administration, it seems almost inconceivable that the American people could have borne such things. Violence in one section of the country, fraud and rapacity in another, the laws and the Constitution trampled under foot, and the Murphys, the Durells, the Leets, the Caseys, the Bowens, the Belknaps, and the whole swarm whose names were to become a stench in men's nostrils, not merely unwhipped of justice, but carrying high their brazen foreheads, as the chosen friends of the Chief Magistrate, and the men whom he delighted to honor. It was urged as a noble trait in the President that he never forgot a friend or a service, and it was truly urged. Nay, the coarser the service, the more vulgar the friend, the more certain the gratitude and the more substantial the reward.

Those were the times that tested the courage, the patriotism, and the endurance of the minority in Congress. The majority seemed to think that they were above all responsibility, and superior to law. When the news came that De Trobriand with his soldiers had expelled by force the lawful members of a State legislature, and Sheridan's dispatch followed, asking permission to deal with the Louisianians as banditti, member after member rose, in either House, to justify the acts. When the minority, alarmed at the rapid strides of unlicensed power, proposed to ask of the President what information he had upon the subject, they were tauntingly told that the Senate "had better not try to make a law to guide the acts of the President"; that the President might give the desired information, or he might not, and, if he did not, "what were they going to do about it?" That was the sneering remark of the Senator from Wisconsin. In those times, patience, full debate (when it was allowed), that the public at least might know what was going on, and steady record of their votes against obnoxious measures, were all that the minority could do, and this duty they faithfully performed, none more faithfully than Mr. Bayard. When the admission of Pinchbeck to the Senate was on the verge of accomplishment, he remained in his place for twenty-eight continuous hours, resisting that monstrous disgrace and wrong; resisting, not only then, but at all times, the doctrine that this is something other than a government of laws, a government of defined powers, a government in which, while majorities rule, minorities are protected by the shield of the Constitution.

Yet, what other than that state of things which prevailed during President Grant's administration was to be expected from the teachings of the radical party? The beginnings of illegality are as the letting-out of water; the little breach once made, swiftly becomes a crevasse. Granted that the Constitution might be strained a little for a special need; that a little unwarranted power might be taken in a case of emergency, and the rest followed as a logical consequence. Yet many well-meaning citizens, who viewed with abhorrence the carnival of misrule of which we have spoken, still thought that they might,

"To do a great good, do a little wrong,"

and strain the limited powers to gain a desirable end.

It was to such as these that Mr. Bayard addressed such warnings as those with which he began his speech of February 26, 1874. The abuse of alcoholic drinks is a great and most deplorable evil, as all men admit. But many worthy men, who have given attention to the subject, have grown to think that outside of that there is scarcely any evil at all; and to repress it, or even to experiment in repressing it, they would consent to a far worse abuse—the abuse of unlawful power. And, as another set of gentlemen thought that the chief duty of Congress was to devote all its thought, its care, its solicitude, to making the negro contented and happy, so these would have had the same body undertake the charge of the liquor-trade. It was on this that Mr. Bayard remarked:

"One of the troubles of our times is that so many very well-meaning and respectable persons consider that everything that is right in itself should necessarily be performed by the Congress of the United States, forgetting that this is a government of limited, enumerated, and delegated powers, and that the desirability of a measure is no test whatever of the right of Congress to enact it into law. I believe, sir, that it is an indifference to this truth and it is a disregard of this truth that have led this country into most of the difficulties from which we have suffered and which still surround us."

So in his speech on the appropriation bill (February 26, 1879), when he recalls the noble struggle that the minority made for constitutional liberty in 1870 and 1871:

"When on the floor of this Chamber there stood with me a scanty handful of men, among whom, ever conspicuous, was my honored friend from Ohio [Mr. Thurman], that we steadfastly opposed the enactment of the so-called enforcement laws, and stood here, by day and by night, endeavoring, by strenuous debate, to awaken the American people to a sense of the dangers contained in such legislation, and to make some attempt, vain though it should be, to dissuade the great party majority that enacted these laws, I believed then that those laws were arbitrary; that they violated the spirit of justice which laws must contain in order to be useful and respected; that they were violative of those limitations upon federal power which the Constitution had imposed. I then endeavored to point out their capability for gross abuse and injustice; and all the dangers that I then apprehended, and the injustice and the mischief which such laws would necessarily cause, have been more than fulfilled in what we have witnessed in the last four years.

"For what purpose and in what name and in what cause were these laws enacted? They were professed to be in the interest of peace and purity of elections. Have they been productive of peace? Have they been productive of purity? Have the agencies which the administration have employed to carry out these laws been such as can, with common honesty, be claimed to be in the interest of peace, good order, and purity in elections? Have they not rather been proven to be agencies for corruption and for the grossest intimidation? I ask, plainly, all over this country have these laws been administered in the cause of public justice, or have they been administered in the cause of one political party? In all the millions of money that have been appropriated and spent, has one dollar, one farthing of that money, ever reached any but a partisan's hand? Has any man, but the members of one of the great political parties, ever felt the adverse power of this legislation? Has any man but a member of one political party felt his dishonest or improper action restrained by this legislation? Can the records of any federal court show any indictment found or prosecuted against any but the members of one of the political parties of this Union? Can any senator suggest the record of a single case in which this unjust and partisan discrimination has failed to be made?

"I said I intended to walk in the path of law and the spirit of law, and to find, under law, remedies for all injustice, for, in my belief, one danger of our time is the confusion in the public mind and in the minds of honest men of the spirit and meaning of the laws which should protect our liberty. Sir, there can be nothing more insidiously dangerous than to accomplish injustice under the pretended forms of justice, nothing more dangerous than to overthrow law under pretense of enforcing law. Laws perverted from their meaning, laws in which the letter is followed and the spirit is killed, are the most essential frauds upon a free government. By all the decisions of the courts, by the decision of every parliamentary body in a free country, the presence of armed forces at the polls of popular elections *ipso facto* avoids the result of that election at the demand of the defeated party. To my sorrow as an American be it said, I witnessed the other day the array of the united majority of senators on the other side of this chamber in favor of the doctrine, that in time of profound peace it should be lawful to bring a standing army to the peaceful polls of election—not one voice of all, not one man in that array of intelligence and ability, was found to be willing to raise his voice in favor of a principle so plain and essential that I had not believed there could be a difference about it among those who intended to preserve a government of laws."

And he concludes with words that should sink into the heart of every honest American, whatever his party, who truly loves and cherishes his country and his liberty, nor believes that what our fathers bought so dearly should be lightly flung away: "Mr. President, I believe that all over this country, outside of those heated partisans who make up the rank and the file of the two great parties, there stands an authoritative mass of intelligent, independent, upright, liberty-loving American citizens, who will never consent that the principle of free election, that great safety-valve, that great American substitute for revolution, shall be invaded or overthrown, directly or indirectly. When the American people, having the facts and the issue broadly, fairly, and openly presented to them, shall say that it is lawful for the executive branch of the government to have unlimited power to take possession of all the police powers of any State, to place at the polls an authority paramount to any which the State could place there, officials without number, beyond the power of arrest, officials paramount to any State authority, and so go through the form of an election, or allow the people to go through it, in the grasp of such a mighty power as I have described—I say when the American people shall look on and decide in favor of that, then my hope of republican government in this country will have died within me. I do not believe they will ever so decide. I do not believe that they are prepared to part with their liberties; I do not believe that, when fairly and honestly and straightforwardly this issue is presented to them, there will be a doubtful voice or a doubtful expression of that voice. I do not believe that they are prepared to bid farewell to this grand system of republican government which has so dignified humanity, which has been so fair and so just, so glorious and so noble, which has given the plain poor man in this country the status of his manhood, and recognized the true dignity of humanity; I do not believe they will part with all this at the bidding of any political party for the sake of continuing itself in power. And, sir, I can only say that, whether it be with the great majority, which I think I shall find with me in that issue, or whether it be in the feeblest minority that, mindful of the Constitution of our fathers, mindful of the liberty for which they struggled, mindful of the principle of laws under which they endeavored to establish this government, I shall ever be found steadfast; for I know that it involves the vital spirit of republicanism, without which our system would become a despotism, or sink into anarchy."

From such principles and such practice as have been referred to, there followed, as a natural consequence, a habit of considering all restrictions to a proposed line of action as vexatious and offensive hindrances, to be cleared away as expeditiously as possible. True, the time was not ripe yet for quite as summary measures everywhere as had been used in some of the States. They could not put a Bond or a Durell on the Supreme bench of the United States, or send a De Trobriand to purge the House of Representatives at the bayonet's point; but what they could do they did. The Supreme Court of the United States had long been consecrated in men's minds as the inner line of defense against wrong, as that which in our whole fabric of government was most upright, most stable, most august. But the Supreme Court stood in the way of invasions of the Constitution, and was therefore at once the object of attack. They spoke of it with scarce concealed scorn, talked openly of "repudiating" its decisions, if these threatened their plans, and found a still more effective mode of undermining its influence and lessening its title to respect. A decision against the constitutionality of the legal-tender act stood in their way, and must be reversed. How was the reversal accomplished? Not by changing the opinion, but by changing the *personnel* of the court. The number of judges was increased, and a gentleman added to the bench who was known to be in favor of the act. This, and the opportunity given by the resignation of another judge, enabled them to construct such a court as they wanted. To say that this only differed in enormity from the offense of packing a jury would be to use harsh language; but we are unable to frame any form of words to express a distinction so refined. But there was still a minority in the Supreme Court, as there was a minority in Congress, and the legislation that would have confounded all the departments of the government and swept away every safeguard of the Constitution was not permitted to go on unchecked.

Next in importance to the supremacy of law is the

stability of law, and on this point, too often overlooked, Mr. Bayard has insisted with great force. A great evil in this country has been the habit of temporary legislation. A law may be just in itself, it may excellently answer a temporary purpose, and yet it may be a very unwise law, because, that purpose once accomplished, it becomes obsolete, and is either a hindrance to justice, thus defeating the end of all law, or its breach is connived at, thus bringing law into contempt. Of course, the imperfections and the changing conditions of human society necessitate changes in legislation; but what Mr. Bayard has urged has been that legislation should be made as stable as possible, and that permanence should always be an end kept in view. Some of his remarks on this subject have already been cited, and he adverts to it in his speech on the bill "to strengthen public credit":

"I think that it will destroy, in a great measure, that certainty which it should be the object of all legislators as well as judges to reach. . . . *Peace and certainty* ought to be the ends of litigation as well as legislation."

So in his speech of December 19, 1873, the proposed repeal of the bankrupt law being under consideration:

"The trouble of our legislation is its want of stability. It is this continual yielding to an ignorant and popular demand for change when the necessity for change does not exist. Our people do not let their laws stand long enough to understand their general result, their ultimate effect. A law can not be judged by single cases of its influence and operation; it must be judged as to its general policy after years of experience."

But Mr. Bayard is not one of those who imagine that in legislation alone is a panacea for all human evils, and think that men are to be made good and happy by a statute framed to meet every case where they are bad or unhappy. He has always insisted upon the great principle of the "unwritten law"—not "a higher law" which releases men from legal obligation when it becomes inconvenient; but rather a lower law, a law which is the foundation of all legislation that is at once both just and wise. Of this he has given his views so forcibly in his address at Cambridge, June 26, 1877, that we can not do better than to transcribe a part of his remarks:

"It is the most difficult of all problems in the science of government to determine when and where and how it is wise to interfere by the authority of law with the motives which are usually called the natural motives of men —as it is evident that the force of laws and their value depend almost entirely upon the assent or the consent with which those to whom they are addressed shall meet them.

"The law can not prescribe the performance of the virtues; but it is addressed to the reason, and seeks to influence human action by and through the will, by presenting an alternative to each prohibited act. More than thus appealing to the reason and presenting an alternative the law can not do!

"It is this consciousness of the limited power of the law which should instruct us that it must be addressed to reason, and command the assent of all reasonable minds; otherwise, interminable discontent and confusion must ensue.

"Having thus stated the impossibility of commanding a course of human action by the instrumentality of written laws, let me now remind you how infinitely wider is the sphere, and more permeating and constant the influence, of the UNWRITTEN LAW; by which I do not mean *lex non scripta*, the common law of custom, acquiescence, and judicial decisions, but the *great moral law* 'written,' as Coke said, 'with the finger of God on the heart of man.' 'The law of laws, truly and properly to all mankind fundamental, the beginning and the end of all government,' as Milton called it.

"Whatever influence written laws obtain, they gather from the secret forces of nature which have been considered in their framing; and the failure of so many laws passed in disregard of natural laws should instruct us in this great truth.

"Persecutions for opinion's sake have always increased heresy; protection-laws have injured trade; poor-laws have increased poverty, and usury laws have raised the rate of interest. This is common experience. I am sensible of the difficulty of providing a definition for the *unwritten law*, which can not be reduced to formulation or codification. Human government can never be subjected to geometrical exactness, and can only be measured by approximations. Form and method will do only for things of form and method.

"There is, after all, a unanimity of the entire human race in the great rules of duty and the fundamental principles of morals; the general sympathies of mankind flow together and a general judgment is arrived at. There are certain principles to which all nations do homage, and the majesty and authority of virtue are derived from this common consent."

"We need the force of an *unwritten law* to establish in the hearts and minds of the American people a sense of the dignity and the impartiality of the government of the Union; a general and habitual reverence for its justice, and a spirit of proud obedience to its laws, not mere slavish and sullen submission to its power.

"To aid in the establishment of such a sentiment we need the recognition of the equality of the States in our constitutional scheme, a public opinion that shall discourage and prevent assaults upon the credit or good repute of any portion of the Union, and a popular resentment that shall visit any man or body of men exhibiting hostility and malevolence toward his fellow countrymen.

"In other words, we need an invigorated and realizing sense of the value of the Union to the happiness, security, and honor of all its members, so that, perceiving their freedom, they will use it to strengthen the government whose institutions are the source of their freedom, that they may realize the truth of the exclamation of Charles James Fox,

'Liberty is order, Liberty is strength;'

that laws of repression may be regarded with distrust in the knowledge that public virtue owes more to freedom than to jealousy and restraint."

CHAPTER X.

DEFENSE OF THE SOUTH.

The war was fought for the Union. Whatever may have been the hopes or desires of some of the leaders, the people of the North contended for the Union alone. No other motive would have brought them to bear patiently the burdens of such a strife, and to pour out their blood on a hundred fields of battle, but that devotion to the Union which was intensified by the fear of its destruction until love almost became idolatry. And, when they conquered at last, they had a right to the prize they had so dearly won. Not merely justice and consistency, but good policy pointed to the same course. The war had swept a great part of the land with devastation, had wasted the population, paralysed many industries, made bankrupt eleven States, and loaded the rest with debt. The only road to renewed prosperity, north and south, lay in healing the wounds of the past; in such a course of action as would encourage industry, protect thrift, restore confidence, and bring back peace over all the land.

The South, beaten on the field of battle, had accepted in good faith the result of that arbitrament, and was ready to lay new foundations for a new future. All had to be organized anew. Capital was gone, credit almost gone, the labor of years and of generations swept away, and scarce anything left but the soil and the climate.

Their whole system of labor was broken up, and the population of agricultural laborers, deceived by wild reports and false hopes held out to them by designing persons, could not be reorganized. Waiting the time when the lands of their former masters should be divided among them, they flocked to the towns, and there huddled in squalid misery and vice, expectant of the day when an act of Congress or a Presidential proclamation, such as had declared the abolition of slavery, should declare the abolition of the curse of Adam.

Sorely tried, but not despairing, the people set to work to rebuild their fallen fortunes under new conditions. Great estates, no longer manageable, were divided; a system of small farming introduced; capitalists from the North and from abroad, seeing the opportunity, began to invest their money in mines, in mills, in factories, in railroads, and thus to give employment to industry, and develop, as they never had been developed, the resources of the country. For the South, devoted too exclusively to the production of a few great staples, had scarcely touched the treasure of natural wealth with which Providence had so bountifully enriched her. Her mines, of unsurpassed richness, had never been explored. Her raw materials were sent a thousand miles to be worked up, and manufactured articles, which might have been made at home, brought at heavy cost from distant lands. Many of her richest valleys, untapped by railroads or canals, had been almost smothered in the superfluity of abundance for which there was no outlet. With all the drawbacks we have before mentioned, there is no doubt that prosperity would have returned with magical quickness, had things been allowed to take their natural course.

But this prosperity, in which every American had an interest, was only to be had through the renewal of harmony between the States, the reign of peace, order, and law, and the restoration of the Southern States to their equal place in the constitutional Union. Every disadvantage, every disability laid upon those States were so many obstacles to this. And we believe that the sentiment of the whole country, so soon as the excitement left by the war had given place to calm reflection, was strongly in favor of this wise and liberal policy.

But this would by no means have suited the purposes of the radical leaders. A restored Union was the very last thing they wanted. As their party had owed its existence to agitation and sectional hate, so in peace and concord they foresaw its certain death. Destructive in its principles and in its origin, it had no policy to justify its continuance for an hour in a land of peace, order, and equal laws.

For parties, as for individuals, self-preservation is the first law of nature. To perpetuate the radical party, the "old war feeling" must be revived. The Union must not be restored, it must be "reconstructed." And the measures which they devised for this reconstruction were such as deprived all those who had a real interest in the prosperity of the South of any share or influence in the government, and placed all office and power in the hands of negroes, renegades, or unscrupulous adventurers. They did not expect the Southern people to bear these things patiently: they expected and hoped for resistance; and every expression of impatience, every struggle to be rid of this crushing oppression and this plague of unclean and venomous parasites, was seized upon as a pretext for declamation about "renewing the rebellion," "traitorous conspiracies," etc., with the inference that only by continuing the radicals in power could the flames of civil war be kept from bursting out again. The whites must be disarmed, lest they should massacre the negroes; the negroes must be armed and organized to protect themselves against the whites. The "carpet-bag" governments, with their grotesque legislatures, plundered and helped to plunder the States, and, not content with stealing all that there was to steal, by means of fraudulent issues of bonds thrust their rapacious claws into the pockets of unborn generations. At all this carnival of misrule and wrong, the radical leaders rejoiced, because the indignant protests, the inevitable disquiet, could all be turned to profitable account.

Almost the earliest utterance of Mr. Bayard in the Senate was in opposition to these so-called reconstruction acts, on April 9, 1869. In it he thus points out the character and tendencies of this legislation:

"I do not propose to discuss the condition of the people of these three Southern States so called. I could not trust myself to do it, and run through the dreary, wretched catalogue of wrongs to which they have been subjected. It was truly said by the Senator from Oregon [Mr. Williams], in reply to a remark of the Senator from New York [Mr. Conkling], that it was too late upon this floor to talk of good faith to the people of the Southern States. Alas! sir, that is too true; for it would be idle to talk of keeping faith when the lips that profess it have violated it so often toward them.

"What are these communities against which your legislation has been leveled? They are States when you can use them for a party end. You remand them to the condition of conquered provinces when you think they may slip from your grasp and the sentiment of their people stands in defiance to the wishes of your party.

"I do not propose to speak of the effect of this law (if it be worthy of that name) upon the three communities to which it is addressed. Remembering the claims that are made for the progress of mankind, the beneficent influences of Christianity, the peculiar claims for moral and intellectual leadership so exclusively urged by gentlemen representing the dominant majority on the floor of this Senate, one might expect an enunciation of a policy founded upon some recognition of the true qualities which go to make a State. But no, sir. Instead of that, we have from the lips of this party of progress no announcement of a broad, or of a high, or of a Christian character; but there comes the same old stern pagan declaration, *Væ victis!* The history of legislation for the last four years in this country has proven that woe indeed is the portion of the conquered.

"But, sir, I rose to speak more of the effect of this amendment upon the other States, against whom no pretext raised by a condition of war and revolution can be urged. I speak for the State which I have the honor in part to represent on this floor, and I here declare that your proposed submission of the fifteenth amendment to the untrammeled vote of the different States is turned to dust and ashes when you yourselves create the votes that shall overcome the natural majority against you. Congress, by its own terms, usurps the power to cast the votes of three States in the interests of a partisan majority; and that you call a ratification under the Constitution of an amendment to the fundamental law. . . .

"If I know aught of the government under which we live, it is the elective franchise, it is the process of carrying on government by the elective system, that marks it from its first organization to its last act. It is a power that must be, in the very nature of things, the controlling power, because the election is your test of power, of law in every shape and at every stage of your country's government. That power you propose to take from the States and deposit with the federal government; to consolidate the power of all powers, that which underlies and creates all powers; and that you propose to place in the hands of Congress. There never was a graver question, there never was an act which will affect the whole structure and genius of our government to the extent that this must, should it succeed in obtaining the consent of the people of this country.

"It has been demonstrated before this Senate in a manner that could not be and has not been replied to, by my honorable friend, the Senator from Ohio [Mr. Thurman], that by the amendment of the honorable Senator from Indiana [Mr. Morton] you do coerce the choice, not only of the Southern States, which is a barefaced act of simple power, but you coerce the sentiment of every Northern State under your pretended power of governing the Southern States. Talk of the free choice of Indiana, or Ohio, or New York! What is it when a Congress can by law insist that the votes of certain States shall be cast in opposition to it? All freedom is gone. Sir, when Congress adopts such a measure as this, it is doing nothing less than playing with cogged dice. It is the intention therefore, by a measure like this, to destroy, first, all shadow of freedom in the exercise of their opinions by the people of these three States, and next, having destroyed that, to make their votes the instrument whereby you crush out the sentiment of the Northern States. *Per fas aut nefas* seems to me to be the rule by which this amendment is to be forced upon the American people; and the great question will yet come up—it can not be long kept down—how any law, how any amendment obtained by means like this, can be held binding upon the conscience of a people who have either the sense or the manhood to remain free.

"It is, therefore, that I object to the whole of this measure, and I rise here in my place to protest against its passage. While affecting to direct it against those unhappy people whom the fortunes of war have placed in your hands, you use the power so lawlessly held, so ruthlessly exercised, to strike down freedom of choice in the very States which you profess to treat as equals, and entitled equally with yourselves in having a voice in saying how the government shall be conducted.

"And even when this is done, when these States ratify this amendment, giving your party the advantage of having three votes of those States, then what comes? Is the end yet to these people? Are they, even then, States entitled to representation? Not so, sir, for I understand another amendment has been presented and adopted, that again they must present themselves before their captors, again pass beneath their bow and spear, to learn what new terms may yet be exacted before they shall be admitted to representation in the two Houses of Congress. I do not suppose that any opposition of mine, or of those with whom I act in this body, can have any effect upon this vote; but justice to myself, and justice to my State, urged me to say what I have said, and I believe it to be true in respect to this measure now before the Senate, which I aver to be a most dishonest act of legislation." *

* The bill passed the same day: yeas, 44; nays, 9.

In December of the same year a bill was before the Senate "to perfect the reconstruction of Georgia." Georgia had already ratified the fourteenth amendment; but the Legislature had decided that negroes, though entitled to vote, were not eligible as members of its body. Senator Morton, therefore, offered an amendment to the effect that the legislature should be provisional only, until it had ratified the fifteenth amendment also, and members of Congress from Georgia had been admitted to their seats. Mr. Bayard, in reply, argued that the principle that Congress may usurp the powers of State legislatures is as flagrant a wrong and outrage to the Northern as to the Southern people; and that, in view of the continual aggressions of the federal power, they were creating a most dangerous precedent. He then proceeds:

"This whole question of suffrage, whether for negroes or for whites, or for white men or women, is, after all, the great question of our time in this country. It is the question that underlies all others. We have an elective government proceeding upon that principle and doctrine from its first to its last act; and that power is now sought by the fifteenth amendment to be consolidated into the hands of Congress, that the actual government shall obtain the control of the qualification of voters in all the various States. I regard it as most unhappy; I regard it as the most revolutionary measure in its effect that has ever yet been presented for passage to the Congress of the United States, or to the people of the States. If it were an ordinary amendment, my objection to the method by which its adoption is sought to be obtained would apply; but it is an extraordinary amendment—one that will change, in my opinion, the very character of our government. I say that it is monstrous that the people of the various States should not have the fullest and freest expression of their will on the subject. And yet, look at what in substance has been done and what is proposed to be done. It is to turn the question of choice into a mere farce. It is 'your money or your life!' to the Southern States, and the Northern States are to be made the victims of the weakness and inability of the Southern States to maintain themselves and their constitutional rights on this subject.

"Mr. President, I feel most deeply my inability, my want of preparation in the present case, to say what I should like to have the opportunity of saying in opposition to this bill. It is not that I believe that anything that may come from the feeble minority in this body, and I its feeblest member, could have any effect in staying legislation which has been decreed as a party necessity. I would most sincerely desire to have every act of mine and every vote of mine tested by the limitations of the federal Constitution. I would have no questionable measure passed, whether it stood for or against the accident of the hour with which my political affiliations were connected. It is with that reason and following that idea that I have occupied the attention of the Senate for the time I have on this subject.

"It is because I believe that this act is an unfair and an unjust act to the people of the community against which it is directed; it is remanding them back to military power only; it is adding conditions which at that time you had not considered or invented or prescribed for them. Unjust and unwarrantable as is this bill toward them, it tells with equal injustice against the people of other States, whose will is that this constitutional amendment should not be adopted. Therefore it is that I object to the passage of the bill."

The oppressed States were anxious for representation in Congress, where, at least, they might hope for some redress if their voices could be heard. The problem then was how to limit and control this representation in such ways as to exclude, if possible, every man who really represented the people and the interests of the State. The language of the Constitution providing for all the subject of representation was plain beyond the possibility of misunderstanding; but the Constitution had long ceased to be an obstacle in the way of the party in power. In February, 1870, Mississippi being then an applicant for representation, the radical members of both houses, of whom Senator Morton was the acknowledged leader, took the ground that, under that section of the Constitution which guaranteed to every State "a republican form of government," a majority in Congress was entitled to define republican government at their pleasure, and thus to have it in their power to remodel or exclude a State at their will.

To this strange assumption of power Mr. Bayard replied in his speech of February 15. After reviewing the course and the arguments of the opposite side, he proceeds:

"The meaning of the words in a written charter of government is all-important. It includes everything. Give a man power to use words in what meaning he pleases, and you destroy any government and any limitation that was ever devised. First, the senator would construe the word 'guarantee,' and he would claim that to be an unlimited grant of power to create and mold originally the institutions of a State, not a power to fulfill the stipulations of a third party in case of his default, which is what I understand a guarantee to mean. It is a word plainly intended to be used in its natural and restricted sense, but by the senator's advance and his progress of definition is made pregnant with capacities and powers never dreamed of by those who placed it where it stands in the Constitution. Constructions of the Constitution have been strict and liberal, the latter under the doctrine of the implication of powers; but here is proposed something new and far more dangerous—a power to use words in any sense confessedly not intended by those who placed them in the written charter of government, in which, and in which alone, Congress finds the enumeration of its just powers."

After enumerating the various arbitrary conditions imposed by the bill, and showing that, so far from "guaranteeing a republican form of government," they would make such a government absolutely impossible, he continues:

"But, Mr. President, after all, the conditions contained in this bill, these shackles sought to be riveted upon the necks and limbs of the people of Virginia and of Mississippi, are but incidents to the whole system pursued by Congress, and called 'reconstruction.' It has often seemed to me only foolish to be straining at these legislative gnats when camels had gone down the throat of Congress with such apparent ease and frequency. After all, sir, what bald humbugs and wretched shams are your reconstructed governments and your 'resuscitated States,' as they have been termed in the course of this debate! What honest man but must laugh in scorn at these specimens of radical manufacture, set up here as republican States! They are the creations of violence and revolution, based upon the denial of every underlying principle of our original government. They are the products of ruthless military rule, of fraud and force combined. The intelligence and wealth and moral worth of all these communities are utterly proscribed, and ignorance and profligacy exalted to high places of power."

And he closes his remarks:

"The Southern States were overthrown in their struggle for a separate national existence. Heroes of the South gave up their swords to heroes of the North, who received their paroles of honor, which have ever since been kept inviolate. Ghastly and dreadful as were the wounds inflicted in that terrible struggle, yet, at its close, there stood the great *vis medicatrix naturæ* ready and able to draw together the ragged edges, bind up the lacerated parts, and let them heal by 'the first intention.' Time, too, who lessens every human grief, would have covered with his wings much of the natural bitterness engendered in such a strife, and steeped it in oblivion. If a wise and generous policy had in 1865 been proposed and followed by Congress toward those who so lately had confronted them in arms, but who had so fully and wholly surrendered the argument of force, and had freely given the most unmistakable evidence and pledges of their willingness to accept the situation, and conform their former pretensions to the logical demands of events, how easy and how certain would have been the restoration of that Union so dear to the American heart?

"But, senators of the radical party, you prevented this 'consummation so devoutly to be wished,' and did it for party ends. The South was down, and when she was down you struck her. Your blows were foul blows, and were not given in a fair fight. All Christendom cried shame upon you as you inflicted them. You have unnecessarily and wickedly added humiliation to the cup of sorrow the Southern people have been compelled to drink, and drink so deeply. A brave and generous people by the fortunes of war were subjected to your rule. Their hands were stretched out to you and were rejected; their honest pride ingeniously and cruelly wounded; and you have lost that confidence and friendship which, for the sake of your country, you should have cultivated and valued.

"By your course of action the people of the other sections of the Union have been deprived of their natural allies and auxiliaries in bearing their vast burdens of national debt and taxation, and the advancement of our country's prosperity has been greatly retarded. You have placed and kept the people of the South in loathsome subjection to the most debased and worthless classes of their inhabitants, at the cost not only of justice, decency, and good government, but also at an enormous pecuniary expense to the Northern and Western people. And, in order to accomplish all this, it was necessary that you should disregard and violate nearly every limitation imposed upon your power by the federal Constitution, and postpone almost indefinitely the time when the States of the South shall be a source of strength, happiness, and pride to those of the other sections of the Union. Will you be sustained in all this by your people? It is a grave question, which for the sake of the Union of our fathers I trust may soon be answered in the negative."

For years the radicals had unlimited sway in the Southern States. All the apparatus of fraud and engines of violence stood at their disposal; all the machinery of government was in their hands, from Judge Bond on the bench, to Sambo, J. P., at the cross-roads; from Holden sweeping into the capacious pockets of his friends the whole wealth of a State, to the sable legislators at Columbia fighting for ginger-cakes on the floor of the house. The men to plan, the men to justify, the men to execute, were all theirs. Had they desired peace and order they could have had it, but they desired discord and confusion.

One device after another was tried to blind the people of the North to their proceedings, and to explain why that pathetic suspiration of President Grant, " let us have peace," was so hard to realize. The Ku-Klux phantom stood them in good stead for a while, and gave many fine opportunities for laying hands upon hearts and appealing to Heaven. They had collected a body of witnesses of unsurpassable efficiency; visiting committees saw whatever they went to see; until the tragi-comedy culminated in broad farce as honorable members with unequaled power of face stood with upturned eyes beside the couch of Eliza Pinkston.

Grotesque as all this was, it was a matter of terrible moment that men should hold their liberties and lives and whole States their franchises at the mercy of such informers, and those who professed to believe them. Mr. Bayard exposed the whole business, with all its monstrous wrong, in his speech of March 20, 1871. Mr. Sherman had introduced into the Senate the following resolution:

"*Resolved*, That as organized bands of desperate and lawless men, mainly composed of soldiers of the late rebel armies, armed, disciplined, and disguised, and bound by oaths and secret obligations, have, by force, terror, and violence, subverted all civil authority in large parts of the late insurrectionary States, thus utterly overthrowing the safety of person and property, and all those rights which are the primary basis and object of all civil government, and which are expressly guaranteed by the Constitution of the United States to all its citizens; and, as the courts are rendered utterly powerless, by organized perjury, to punish crime, therefore the Judiciary Committee is instructed to report a bill or bills that will enable the President and the courts of the United States to execute the laws, punish such organized violence, and secure to all citizens the rights so guaranteed to them."

Mr. Bayard first protested against the iniquity of drawing a bill of indictment against eleven States upon the strength of evidence collected in one State alone. He showed how so-called confessions were extorted by torture and threats of immediate death; how most of the "outrages" had no political significance, but were merely the struggles of society for self-preservation, in a region where ruffianism was armed and encouraged, where murder, arson, and rape were things of almost daily occurrence, under the beneficent sway of a Holden, who, as was testified, pardoned the offenders before they were inside the penitentiary gate. In such a state of society it would have been a marvel indeed if outrages, aggressive or vindictive, had not occurred; and to this pass had Radical rule brought North Carolina. And these were the things that were offered as a pretext for laying the franchises of all the States in the Union under the feet of a majority in Congress. The speech concludes:

"I appeal to the Senate to rise above mere party views in this case, and remember that we are all Americans, living under this government, and all, I hope, equally attached to our country. The Constitution, which we have invoked, was meant for minorities. The shifting sands of political life may put your party at no late day in a minority, and then, when you appeal to a majority in these halls for every protection which that Constitution entitles you to ask, I and those with whom I act in this body will freely aid you with our votes. The Constitution of our country to-day is imperiled by the demands of party. It never was more directly assailed than by the resolution offered by the Senator from Ohio. He proposes to enter the States, and deprive them of all those police powers unquestionably necessary for their preservation, and to grasp all into the hands of the federal government. The proposed coercive measures, if made for Carolina, must extend to Massachusetts, Connecticut, New York, to Ohio, for we can not have laws unequal in their operation, and applying only to portions of this country. As I hope and believe, political power is about to pass from the party who have held it for the past ten years in this country. I ask, at least, that you shall restore us the Constitution, sorely shattered as it has been by your ten years of administration, without further assaults upon it. There yet remains enough, by an honest subordination to its limitations, to guide us back to a condition of limited government, which the excesses and excitements of the war have in a degree weakened or destroyed. I trust that this measure of violence will not meet the assent of the Senate, and that those who are now in the majority will see the danger of violating the great principles of government in the hope of obtaining temporary partisan advantage."

When in May, 1872, a bill was offered, the effect of which was to give the President absolute and despotic power in every State, authorizing him to suspend the writ of *habeas corpus* at his discretion, Mr. Bayard's voice rose clear and strong in defense of the Constitution and the rights and liberties of citizens. He sifted the whole mass of alleged facts which had been offered in defense of a measure so perilous and revolutionary, showed how false and frivolous were the charges, and what were the characters of the informers and accusers. One of the advocates of the bill had even taunted the Southern people for weeping at the graves of those who fell in the war. Mr. Bayard replied to this unmanly scoff:

"Yes, Mr. President, and, should it ever come to pass that the graves of the Southern dead should be neglected by their kindred, kind Nature herself will take their place, and the Southern earth in which the dead sleep will yield its lilies and its daisies to wreath their places of rest, and the soft winds of the South will gently wave the grass above them, and the dews of her starry nights will keep grass and flower fresh in memory of her brave children who died in defense of the soil which now contains them.

"Why, sir, can it be that a mind can be so darkened by prejudice and party spirit as to forget the very echoes of human nature itself? If these people did not weep over their loved and their lost, they would be something more or less than human; much more likely less than more. Such a speech and such sentiments sound to me like the report of some Russian commander writing from Warsaw to the Czar, followed by an order forbidding the women of Poland to wear mourning for their dead. Is it the feeling or the language of an American senator directed toward those who are his fellow citizens, and who it is the hope of the country will be a source of happiness and strength to our Union? Certainly men can not be won back from error by such sentiments as these, and by such condemnation. They never can be made friends by such processes. . . .

"The law now proposed is an act of assault; it

breathes of violence. It works upon no emotions but those of fear. It will cause hatreds. It will produce no good-will either between citizens or toward the government. It is, as I have tried to show, a plain violation of the limits of our written charter of power, and, even if it were not so, it is unwise and unjust. Cease, then, I beg of you, this maleficent, odious system, so foreign to the genius of American government, called 'reconstruction,' and adopt now and from this time forth the true, the wise, the Christian policy of 'reconciliation' between the States of this Union."

In his strong, though temperate, arraignment of President Grant's policy in his address at Wilmington [October 4, 1872], he makes a noble appeal to the justice, the humanity, and the patriotism of the people:

"General Grant, with all his power, with the great opportunity before him of pacification, has never said one friendly word to the Southern people. There is not, in his messages or in any public paper of his, one kindly, friendly word of encouragement to them, and, as I have said before, not one word of rebuke to those who have acted dishonestly and wrongfully among them. If the rascals have been caught, he has pardoned them. He has never rebuked them. He has never sought to have them punished. When the question came up of abolishing the test oath, which was excluding men from office in the South, although he returned the bill to Congress with his approval, he did so with a sneer and an innuendo against the truthfulness of the Southern people who had been excluded by the oath. Oh, if he had known anything of civil government, if he had known anything of human nature, he would have known that test oaths are useless as to the dishonest, and only tend to exclude the good and true.

"He came into office with a cry upon his lips, that turned out to be a mere catch-word, which did catch for him thousands, nay, tens of thousands of votes which he will never again receive in this country. When he said, 'Let us have peace,' the people thought he meant it; but it seems that he either used the words without meaning, or he has changed his mind most sadly since. Now, discontent, disturbance, unkindness, enmity, are the weapons he seems most to rely upon for his re-election, and he sends his agents off through the country, not to say 'Let us have peace,' but to do what his friend Morton, of Indiana, does, stir anew the old feeling of the war.

"When you look at his work in South Carolina, when you read of the depopulation of those counties, when you read of the reign of terror and the sadness which brood over them, you are reminded of the line of Tacitus who, in speaking of the conquests of the Barbarians, says, 'They make a solitude, and call it peace.' That is the kind of peace that General Grant's policy has produced in the State of South Carolina and wherever else it has been exerted.

"There is a large portion of this audience and a large portion of this community composed of the young men of the country. They are at that period of life when the generous and kindly emotions have most force. Men who are older are more apt to be seared by passion, to be actuated by prejudice, and to have their better feelings almost too much under control. To the young men of this audience, to the young men of this country, I would appeal to see that kind feeling become their rule of action toward their fellow citizens in all portions of this country. The duties of life are now upon them, and the government of this country must, in the course of nature, in a short time pass into their hands.

"If but that feeling can be aroused in their ingenuous breasts, if their feelings of generosity can but be properly touched on this subject, then all will be well. They have power to-day with their votes. They will have all power and control after a few more years have rolled by. To them I address myself, to their emotions of generosity, of kindness, and remind them of the necessity of these qualities in human government.

"I ask you, younger men of the country, untouched by the bitter experiences of life, and by its fiercer passions, to insist that good feeling and union and reconciliation shall be the law of this land between citizens of all parts. See to it that you vote for no man who does not so act as to produce them, but vote now and at all times hereafter in favor of those men who will endeavor again to create a union of feeling that shall indeed make our Union strong and great and perpetual.

"Let your cry be in regard to law, 'Down with the system of coercion. We do not trust lip-service. Up with the spirit of trust; up with the spirit of confidence in our fellow man!' Insist that you will govern him through his better feelings, and not by his fears. Unless this course be adopted there will be no safety.

"I tell you, my friends, the same qualities that affect a family, the same qualities that affect two friends, affect a nation. Why is it that when you pass to the household of your friend, and sit in his family circle, and look into his eyes and the eyes of his family, you feel yourself safe and happy? It is the feeling of human affection that makes you safe and happy, and just as you sit down in friendship either at your own firesides or those of your friends, so the same spirit will gradually extend through a nation. It begins in the little rivulet of individual good feeling and friendship, and it swells into the mighty river of national amity.

"Last fall it was my duty to go into the Southern States upon another committee of investigation, so called. The object of that committee was a plain one. It had been created for the purpose of getting evidence of discontent and disorder, to be brandished before the eyes of the Northern people, and make them approve and accept of further measures of coercion against the South. Strange to say, the Southern white people who had been treated with so much ignominy and unkindness, who had been so disregarded by the administration, did not like them well enough to vote for them. It seemed, in the opinion of the administration, to be a remarkable fact that men did not like those who had used them ill, and did like those who had expressed a desire to serve them. General Grant had it in his power to gain either the good-will or the opposition of the Southern white people. He chose to gain their opposition. He chose it by natural methods. The tree he planted has borne its fruits. General Grant and his party affected surprise at it, and sought some pretext for violence and force against the Southern people, in order to compel them to come into his party. Therefore, a committee was sent down to see what could be picked up of a hostile and unfavorable character to the people of the Southern States, and report it to the people of the North. What they found did not very well suit their purposes, for, although it is published, it is in such bulk that no man in ordinary times could read it, and the number of copies is so restricted as not to admit of general circulation.

"But as I say, on this committee I was placed and served. We went through the Southern States, and heard all that malicious ingenuity could invent against the white people of that section.

"As we came up the Potomac River, having passed through Florida, Georgia, and the Carolinas, to Virginia, and were nearing the city of Washington, I was sitting upon the deck of the steamer, thinking over the intent of this investigation, and the result which was to be reached by it, when I was aroused from my meditation by the tolling of the steamer's bell. I found that we were just opposite Mount Vernon, and that it was the custom of every boat upon that river, by day or by night, to pay the passing tribute of respect to the memory of him who was 'first in war, first in peace,' and still remains, if the truth be told, 'first in the hearts of his countrymen.'

"And how earnestly do I wish the bells tolled in memory of the illustrious dead, who sleeps so calmly by the side of the broad Potomac, could wake an echo now in the breast of every American citizen!

"Will you not recall the impressive words of his farewell address, and let his voice, now from the grave, 'warn you in the most solemn manner against the baneful effects of the spirit of party generally'?

"The paramount and plain issue of the hour is between entrenched and self-aggrandizing power striding over the land, and obliterating in its progress all the wise limitations that our patriot sires sought to place upon our rulers on the one side; on the other, the spirit of civil liberty and the love of that sober-suited freedom which once characterized the American people.

"The present administration and its candidate call

upon their party in the name of party, and for the sake of party power, to endorse and sustain them. We Democrats, truly Democratic, and Republicans truly liberal, call upon all men, not in the name of a party, not for the name of a party, not for the success of a party, but for the sake of our whole country, to join us in arresting the onward and annihilating course of centralizing despotism. Shall personal prejudices or party spirit prevent our success? Shall the counsels of George Washington be in vain?"

We do not propose to recite here the miserable story of Louisiana, how every wrong that could be devised was perpetrated on the unhappy people of that State, by fraud, by open violence, and by both combined, under the rule of those "captains-general of iniquity," Durell, Packard, Kellogg, and the rest, approved and sustained by the administration at Washington. The history of that series of crimes may be read, if nowhere else, in the appeal after appeal made by Senator Bayard to the justice, the humanity, the honor, even the interest, of the majority in 1873, 1874, and 1875.

Nor will we go into the details of the attempt to introduce the Louisiana system of management into Mississippi. It was when he was resisting the latter that he received the only insult ever offered him in the Senate. A senator ventured to insinuate that Mr. Bayard was the secret enemy of the Union. The imputation was repelled with the scorn that it deserved.

"I will simply say, that every drop of blood in my body comes from men and from women who, since this government was established, never harbored a thought or did an act unfaithful or unpatriotic. No man can assert the contrary. The Senator dare not do so. He might attempt it by an innuendo, by classifying me with those whom he terms the enemies of the country; but he knows as well as I that the man who says I ever did an act or uttered a word unfaithful to the integrity of my country's government has lied in his throat. He bids me beware of November. In November the people of this country will submit their candidates for the popular verdict, and then the Senator may repeat his speech where he pleases. Then he may assault men as he pleases. If it shall please a merciful Heaven to give to this country a feeling of fraternity and union, then he and those who think and act with him will be consigned to private life and to an absence from political power. We will go before the people of this country. I expect to go with all the rest as a private citizen, and submit the doctrines of the party with which I act; to submit the measures that we propose for the government of this country to the intelligence, to the candor, to the patriotic sense, of the people of this country. If the verdict shall be against us, it will still be our country, and we shall obey the men whom you have elected just as fully as if we had elected our own candidates. Minorities have no terror for me—none at all. I have not flinched from declaring on any occasion an opinion that might have seemed unpopular at the time.

"Is it to be held up to me that I have tried to make the people of the South feel that this was their country, that this was their government, and that they were bound to come and support it, and find protection as they gave it allegiance? If it be a crime, then am I the greatest sinner on earth. If such feelings, such professions, and such principles shall consign me for ever to a minority, then welcome the shades of private life with the unstained conscience that I shall carry there with it. I would rather have it than all the power that the people of this country can give, for I have something that they did not give, and which they can not deprive me of, and that is my own self-respect."

As he uttered these words, such vehement applause burst from the galleries that the President of the Senate ordered the sergeant-at-arms to place a force there to preserve order. The Senator who had made the assault took the opportunity to slip out of the chamber, and hid himself for awhile from public gaze in the cloak-room.

It was this constant, manly, and fearless struggle for the right that inspired a poet and patriot of Massachusetts to send him a greeting, couched in verse so noble, so trumpet-like in its ring, that our only regret is that we can not reproduce it here. An extract or two, however, may form a fitting close to this chapter.

> "But oh, when Peace resumes its holiest reign
> And hostile brethren might be friends again,
> Say, should the great republic, firmer grown
> By the sharp strife within her—with her own,
> Her own rash children, in the world's applause
> Rebels owned heroes for their ruined cause:
> Lee, dead, heart-broken for the field they lost,
> And stalwart Jackson harnessed at his post;
> Say, should she deal the fallen a needless blow,
> Proclaim VÆ VICTIS—TO THE CONQUERED WOE?—
> Or seize the precious moment to efface
> Of war's foul canker every festering trace?
> Bid prostrate towns revive from ruin's verge,
> See prostrate men to manlier life emerge,
> And freshening fields like gardens deck the wild
> Forlorn where once the burdening harvest smiled.
> Her aliened sons, returning to her side,
> To clasp with more than old maternal pride,

And leagued with brothers on a hostile field
Against a world in arms her spear and shield.

"Such thoughts were thine and theirs, whose generous hope,
Bounded within no party's narrow scope,
Hailed the proud Union to itself restored,
And claimed the grace its greatness dared afford.

. . . .

But, oh! the change when that foul scheming crew,
The pest of nations, to themselves untrue,
The greedy placemen foully set on high,
Through lowest arts that lure the vulgar eye,
In power imperious, and to self so prone
They count the public pocket for their own;
Who heard the whisper of a South restored
Like the low summons to a funeral board;
Sent forth the carpet-bagman's horse-leech brood,
To scatter firebrands—for their country's good;
Made him their tool the soldier who could call
Late foes new friends by Richmond's leaguered wall.

. . . .

Such the long trial, dark with troubled scenes
Of public burdens grinding private means;
Of wild finance, and impotent delay,
Just debts incurred with honest coin to pay;
States crushed beneath the heel of lawless might,
A mongrel rule enforced of black and white;
Veiling base purposes with false pretense,
Alien to nature, truth, and common sense;
Fraudful to use their country's hapless hour
To make perpetual their ill-gotten power;
To keep the great republic's glorious name,
But change its substance for a hollow frame;
To make their factious will the law supreme,
All the old freedom gone—a vanished dream;
A broken Constitution out of date,
One man at length to rule and be the State:
Enough to stir old patriots in their graves,
That their own children's children could be slaves!

. . . .

Mid storms of faction, thine the nobler strife
To wake the bleeding land to fresher life;
To heal the wounds by war's dread struggles made,
To grasp the hand that held a hostile blade;
To make the lowliest as the loftiest feel
Their hope concentred in the common weal,
Once held the just republic's equal scheme,
A glorious vision, if it were a dream!
Leaving to meaner minds their low affairs,
Their false ambitions and degrading cares,
Assured that parts diseased infect the whole,
Thy country's ALL engaged thy statesman's soul.

. . . .

Through this wild turmoil, when vindictive rage
Wrote damning records on our history's page,
Law to uphold, to reassure the right,
And foil each mean device of party spite,
To make the cheat, the force, the mockery plain,
And find, alas! the labor all in vain;
Thy stern rebuke in calm and storm was heard,
And pierced the future like a prophet-word."

CHAPTER XI.

THE BATTLE AGAINST CENTRALIZATION.

"Party" is, after all, a confusing term to the philosopher, to every one in search of the underlying impulses of thought and action. Federal and Republican, Whig and Democrat, Democrat and Republican, when we come to consider these party names in their final analysis, will be found to imply very different things to persons of different temperament and associations. Names very often fail to represent principles, and parties very often are divided against themselves in consequence of the diverse mental constitution and opinions of their leaders. The larger part of mankind take their political principles by inheritance and upon hearsay. Party is with them, in a great degree, a matter of education, of prejudice, so to speak. It is for this reason that it usually happens, when a party leader goes over to the other side, he fails to take his party with him. In 1856 the Conservative-Whig chiefs had nearly all become Democrats, but the mass of the party was Know-Nothing or Republican.

In every state where the people govern themselves, and must think because they are depended upon to regulate their own affairs, there is a natural and inevitable division of parties upon the point of the distribution of power. At bottom, the differences of opinion among men in this respect are due to the temperament and constitution of individuals, but this it is in which parties originate and by which they are kept alive. The construction put upon constitutions, the interpretation of the powers and province of government, vary according to idiosyncrasy, and are, in the last analysis, types of individuality. Of course there are party landmarks, in regard to which character and temperament effect nothing, but it is not wise in considering even the expediencies and temporary contrivances of parties to ignore the influences of idiosyncrasy.

Note, for instance, the differences between Oliver P. Morton and Thomas F. Bayard in this particular. It is not necessary, in a parallel of this sort, to impugn motives or to question the absolute sincerity of any leading statesmen. Both of these two—let us speak in the present tense, for, though Morton is dead, his influence still lives in the Senate—are men of towering intellect, cultivated experience, and distinguished practical ability; both are men of intense and earnest convictions, and men likewise who have weighed and sifted opinions and judgments carefully in order to satisfy themselves that they are rightly held. Both are young, both ardent, both ambitious, both are filled with the consciousness of that sort of force in them which naturally assumes to direct in the national counsels. Yet their courses in the Senate are wide apart as the poles, as different as Sirocco is from Zephyr. Morton's intense individuality asserts itself in the belief that man is the ever-active law for himself; that "definitions advance"; that constitutions and institutions, the work of man's hands, are *ipso facto* not inviolable, but, on the contrary, uncompleted works, ever under the chisel, ever amendable and to be amended. His egoism, his self-sufficiency, his sustained consciousness of and reliance upon his own powers, have given him a disdain for tradition and for established things so great that he can scarcely restrain it within the bounds of politeness and decency. He is ever tempted to blurt out his contempt of the mob, to cry with Horace, *Odi profanum vulgus et arceo.* He insists upon a "strong" government, upon the absolute concentration and accumulation of power in the federal state, in other words, because he despises and has no faith in the capacity of the multitude which he wishes to lead. The "federal state," in his conceit of it, being always a very small "junto," of which he is the active spirit—the steam power of the machine.

Mr. Bayard, on the other hand, over and above his early teachings and traditions, is a Democrat upon instinct. He looks upon "government," not as a force, but as an aggregation of forces. It is not a thing in itself, but a bundle of things. Society is an association of individuals; and the maintenance of the equality and the character of each contributes to the elevation of the whole. The stream can not rise higher than its source; and Morton, who assumes to be the mob's leader, can not dictate thoughts to the mob, but must derive his thoughts from them. Mr. Bayard believes that the people are the fountains of law and government, and that the better their individuality and character are preserved, developed, and stimulated in right directions, the more enlightened will be the law and government which proceed out of them and represent the product and affluence of their thought and their morality. Law is the established rule of government. It does not represent and interpret and stand for merely the "advanced" ideas and opinions of men afloat on the current, but the cooled-off experience of ages. Law is the alternative of force. It enables Mr. Bayard, his neighbors and friends, the whole community, in fact, to live peaceably in the enjoyment of their own thoughts and their own individuality, and without being constrained, under penalty of proscription, to adopt Mr. Morton's ideas, or anybody else's ideas, or to accept their stringent views of government, or some other doctrinaire's looser ones, as the only proper opinions to be held.

Centralization, which was Mr. Morton's hobby, has been Mr. Bayard's aversion from the very beginning of his senatorial career. The feeling was probably intensified at the outset by his experiences of the needs of the minority for better protection than they were able to secure under the application and administration of the rules of the Senate; but Mr. Bayard understands, perhaps, as well as any other senator, the full force of what is meant and implied in the phrase, "the *safeguards* of the Constitution." From the first he has had a peculiar abhorrence and dread of the "legislative anomalies created by the revolution which has accompanied the civil war." The "opportunities" for innovation which this state of things seemed to afford to Senator Morton were especially dreaded by Mr. Bayard, whose principle it is that nothing which is slipped through, because an opportunity affords, can be properly denominated legislation, much less a "reform." Reforms are measures enacted *coram populo*, not simply with the public consent, but upon the public demand, and after mature deliberation. The fact that we had "fallen upon strange times" should make us not more intrepid and hasty, but more reticent and careful in the enactment of laws which were not only to bind us, but future generations also. The Republicans, and Morton particularly, asserted that, because, by processes *ultra vires* of the Constitution, slavery had been abolished and the Union preserved, therefore it was admissible to secure other modifications and "improvements" in the organic law in the same way. But Mr. Bayard held, with Mr. Lincoln, that the fact of one infraction of the Constitution does not excuse another. He held, further than Mr. Lincoln, that the fact that the Constitution had been infringed upon in one instance should make us only the more scrupulous about other encroachments of the same sort. When Mr. Bayard first entered the Senate, he took ground in regard to the co-ordinate powers of government, and looked to the Supreme Court for the redress of grievances created by the usurpations of the executive, and the oppressions contemplated by the legislative license of the day. In his first long speech in the Senate,* Mr. Bayard said, in regard to Mr. Morton's views: "The honorable senator declares, in reply to my friend from Ohio, that that which was a republican form of government in 1787 is not such in 1870; that the lapse of time, the changes in the condition of the country, have destroyed the definition and signification of this word 'republic,' which is older than the language which we speak. . . . Then, sir, if the Congress of the United States, or the majority of that Congress, chose to invade the existing government of a State under the pretense that it was not republican according to their new-fangled ideas of republicanism, that State would have a right to come here or to go into a co-ordinate branch of the government, the judicial authority, and demand that they should be guaranteed in the inviolate possession of the rights they had when they entered the federal Union." "If you once admit," said Mr. Bayard, "that 'definitions advance,'

---

* February 15, 1870. On the representation of Mississippi.

to the four winds of heaven go all your limitations upon legislative power." "The meaning of the words in a written charter of government," he added, "is all-important. It includes everything." In corroboration of his views of this subject, Mr. Bayard quotes the "Federalist," Madison, Jefferson, and Hamilton, and claims with Madison that a State constituted on Morton's plan would realize "the very definition of tyranny."

What is "the underlying principle of a republican form of government?" As Mr. Bayard defines it, "it is that the ultimate sovereignty rests in the mass of the people, and when you would ascertain what is the will of the people you necessarily mean the will of the majority." To restore this Mr. Bayard is willing to make considerable sacrifices. "The power and spoils of party which may attend their political success I shall not envy, nor disturb their enjoyment of. To me, the happiness of seeing my native land once more enjoying that civil and religious freedom which can only exist under a government of laws, under a government of well-defined and limited powers, will more than compensate for the absence of the supposed exultation consequent upon a mere partisan triumph." Mr. Bayard fully believes in the constitutional method of relieving unconstitutional grievances. When the military attempted to exercise civil control, he said: "The framers of the Constitution intended that there should be an armed power which, in cases of necessity, could be called into service by the general government, and used for the purpose of enforcing the laws; but they were very careful to say that Congress should not officer that militia, but that it should be done by the States themselves; and that when you called this force, so organized, into service, then, and not until then, the laws of the Union could be executed by their aid, if it were necessary."

In the very view and expectation of victory at the polls for the party of his love, Mr. Bayard was able and willing to say : *

"I appeal to the Senate to rise above mere party views in this case, and remember that we are all Americans, living under this government, and all, I hope, equally attached to our country. The Constitution, which we have invoked, was meant for minorities. The shifting sands of political life may put your party at no late day in a minority, and then, when you appeal to a majority in these halls for every protection which that Constitution entitles you to ask, I and those with whom I act in this body will freely aid you with our votes."

This prudent and sagacious senator has a very great mistrust of great powers, because, under his own eyes, he has seen them so often and so greatly abused, and always by the influence of the "great men" who hold themselves so much above mere party principle. "All history," said he, in one of his speeches, "shows that the danger to free government is this: that, where you intrust men with powers for the purposes of government, they use those very powers to consolidate power still further in their own hands, and to *use what they have obtained for purposes for which it never was designed.*'

It is in this speech † that Mr. Bayard dwells most emphatically upon his dread of centralization, and gives his reasons most clearly for his fears. It will be remembered that this speech was made in the campaign against ex-President Grant's re-election, not for a third, but for a

---

* Senate, March 20, 1871. Ku-Klux bill.
† Wilmington, October 4, 1872. (Institute Hall.)

second term. Mr. Bayard called attention to the example of Washington, "when he stood at the zenith of his fame and power, . . . that remarkable man," said Mr. Bayard, "when he had achieved victory, when he was crowned with success, when laurels were thickest and his hands most loaded with power, laid all upon the altar of his country, and retired as a private citizen. . . . Why was this act so remarkable?" says Mr. Bayard. "It was because the quality was so rare, that made his act so wonderful. . . . The issue which I tell you has been formed in this country, in one shape or another always asserting itself since the formation of the government, is the issue between the tendencies of power, wherever it is placed, to increase and centralize itself and the corresponding effort under our Constitution to prevent that centralization and insist upon a distribution of power." The men who drew up the Constitution had been the victims of arbitrary power, and sought to screen their descendants from its evil effects. They had been forced to take up arms to relieve themselves, and they wished to defend their successors from any such unhappy expedient or necessity. When, in the hour of victory over these external obstructions, they were summoned to draw up a constitution for the government of the whole country, it was their leading object to limit power, and, to effect this, they were careful in regard to its *distribution*. "The very distribution of power," in Mr. Bayard's words, "was to work its limitation." The tendency, ever active, ever constant, of power, is to steal from the many to the few, and this, if there were no other reason, would account for and excuse the existence of the Democratic party.

"The men who formed this government," in Mr. Bayard's words, "had, as you know, suffered from arbitrary power. They had been coerced by an arbitrary government. They took up arms to relieve themselves, and, under God's providence, were successful. Their sufferings you know; they are part of the history of your country, and I am sure it ought to be a most important lesson for us in all time. Having suffered from arbitrary power, the men who laid the foundations of this government determined that they would put limitations upon power, no matter where that power was deposited. They knew the weakness of the human heart; they knew that if you give a man power he will exercise it for the most advantage to himself and in ways not intended; and they therefore determined that in the Constitution of the government of the United States there should be no grant of power that was not limited, no such thing as an absolute power, no power that was to be without limitation both as to its extent and duration. How did they accomplish that? By distributing powers, by dividing our government into different departments, all of which should be co-ordinate and equal, none of which should be absolute or superior. The national legislature was created with ample power to make laws, but not absolutely, for the President had his right to veto. There was also the check of a written Constitution that those laws should not pass the subjects or the extent of power conferred by its provisions; but, in case they did, there was the other great check upon them, the judicial department. Even if the Congress and the President assented to the law, it was to be subjected to the test whether, in the minds of the judiciary of the country, it was or was not an infringement of the limitations imposed by the written charter."

If we prevent the distribution of power, we prevent

its being limited also. We aid it in becoming consolidated and centralized. The Democratic party, in Mr. Bayard's view, owes its existence and its perpetuity not to the fact that "it contains better men than other parties, not that they are less fallible than their fellow citizens, or more learned, or more wise," but because its membership is "based on the principle of freedom, of opposition to centralized power, and an insistence on the distribution and limitation of powers for the public safety."

The respect which the Democratic party has invariably had for this principle has measurably preserved the rights of the States, and has stood in the way of all sorts of class legislation. This organization, weak in many other respects, has been opposed to imperial grants of land, promiscuous chartering of banks and every other offense against the proper distribution of power. It has upheld the principle of local self-government as distinguished from imperialism, and upon the basis of these issues it has preserved and will continue to maintain its life, in spite of some things, partly constitutional, partly historical, which embarrass its action, and, in a less durable and vigorous organization, would tend to promote dissolution and death. As Mr. Bayard has said: "A party with such a principle underlying it will exist so long as the very forms of freedom are left in this country;" no matter under what name, the party will continue to exist. This non-interference of government with things aside from its proper concern, Mr. Bayard takes to be one main source of our national prosperity. "I believe," said he, "it was for this reason, thus broadly stated, that prosperity, good feeling, and good order existed throughout our land, simply because *no power of the government was urged out of its proper sphere*, and the harmony between federal and State governments was suffered to remain undisturbed, in accordance with the wise system arranged by our forefathers. Nothing but the truth, the actual vitality of this principle that governmental powers, always seeking to aggrandize themselves in one form or another, are steadily to be kept in check by the will of the people over whom they are sought to be exercised, has ever enabled the Democratic party to maintain its existence during all political fluctuations, changes of events and conditions in this country during the whole of the present century."

The men who formed this government wanted the people to exercise it. In Mr. Bayard's own words: "Not only did they mean the people of their generation to be free, but they meant their posterity to be free; that the government was to be preserved by the constant exercise of the principles upon which it was founded; and, therefore, when they distributed power so that centralization should be checked and absolute power made—as far as, humanly, it could be made—impossible, they by that very act gave the people throughout the country the *right and opportunity of local self-government.* What does that mean? It means the school of government; it means the opportunity to learn how to be a citizen of the United States by learning what the functions and duties of a citizen are; and how can you learn unless you practice and try?

"Therefore, I beg you to understand the wisdom of the men who founded this government. They accomplished a double object by distributing powers, insisting upon the State systems and the great rule and principles of local self-government in opposition to centralization. They did that for the purpose of educating the people to become a self-governing nation. The wisdom of all this plan is this: unless the people are practiced in self-government, they will not be fit to govern themselves, and, unless they do govern themselves locally according to their local interests, central power will seize upon them and their liberties, and control them. So that, in order to be free, in this broad land, two things are required: that power shall be diffused throughout the country and not centralized at Washington, and that the people shall exercise their powers in order to fit them to carry on the government."

The opposition of the Democratic party to the fourteenth and fifteenth amendments was chiefly based upon the fact of their tendency to centralize power. It was upon this issue that the Ku-Klux act and all the enforcement bills have been opposed, and this identical and very natural feeling still keeps alive the opposition to enactments providing for the employment of troops and deputy United States marshals and supervisors at the polls. As Mr. Bayard has said: "The opposition that we have to-day to the laws passed by Congress to control our elections, to place our State officials under indictment and punish them for a fair and reasonable execution of the State laws, is all based upon the same reason. It is our opposition to the principle of centralization."

In December, 1870, the Southern Express Company came to Congress to get a charter. Mr. Bayard opposed the bill steadily, because it was a step in the direction of centralization. "This matter," said he,* "of drawing all these powers into the federal net is one great source of our present political complications." It is an entirely modern invention for Congress to set about the granting

* In the Senate, December 16, 1870.

of charters, and there will be no end to the practice if once begun, once permitted. If reason and common sense have anything at all to do with chartering incorporations, they should not be incorporated except in the localities where the individuals who compose them and the property they administer are to be found. "I am a friend to such enterprises as are proposed by this bill," said Mr. Bayard; "but I am not friendly to Congress undertaking to deal with them." Hence, the Senator meant to vote against this bill and all others like it. One very strong reason for opposing all such measures was that they diverted into the United States courts a whole class of actions growing out of this most multifarious branch of business, thus divesting State courts of a very extensive line of jurisdiction previously their own exclusively. The practical operation of the federal election laws is still more objectionable for the same reasons.

Mr. Bayard [*] opposed the scheme for incorporating the Japanese Steam Navigation Company by act of Congress, on exactly the same principle. "Before we can grant any such charters," he said, "we must settle the fact of our authority to do any such thing under this Constitution of ours, of limited, specific, delegated powers." But, even independently of jurisdiction, Mr. Bayard looked upon the practice as impolitic. "I object," said he, "to the practice of the Congress of the United States turning itself into a vast machine for creating corporations. . . . If there was one thing that the founders of this government thought they would prevent, it was the accumulation of vast sums of property in individual hands. Therefore they abolished the rule of primogeniture; they

[*] Senate, February 6, 1871.

provided for the division of fortunes; they proclaimed an easy method of barring all entails; everything that could tend to diffuse and dissipate property was resorted to, and resorted to by them in the fond hope that it would prevent the vast aggregation of fortunes in individual hands. And yet what have we lived to see? So far from having an equality of fortune produced among our people, so far from having but little difference in the amount of means held by men throughout the country, we have lived in the last ten years of our history to find a difference between the fortunes of individuals more vast, more unhealthy, and more unsound than any other government in this world can give example of." This state of things has been mainly caused by the action of government in sophisticating money so as to make it safer for men to do business collectively than individually, and by protecting such gigantic co-operative action by the favors extended to corporations. It would not have been possible, Mr. Bayard thinks, for corporations to attain their present gigantic and unwieldy proportions, but for the illicit powers secured by them from legislatures, State and federal. When the proposition was made to incorporate, under a sort of general act, a system of railroads in the territories,* it was opposed by Mr. Bayard upon the ground that "we have had enough and more than enough of corporation in the United States; its shadows are seen in every legislature in the land, and they are oftentimes seen in the halls of Congress. . . . I would," he said, in reference to this same subject,† "give no corporation the power to live in a State, except at the pleasure of the legislature of that State. The power of revocation is one that ought to be retained in the

* Senate, April 9, 1874.   † April 13, 1874.

sovereignty of the people; the contract to be maintained so long as it is kept in good faith and for public uses. The original grant of this franchise is for public benefit, and, whenever public benefit dictates its revocation, that revocation should take place."

In the cases of the Chicago and Boston fires, Mr. Bayard, with a heart full of sympathy for so much suffering, yet felt himself constrained to set his face sternly against the remissions of customs duties which were proposed. "Hard cases," he said, "make bad precedents. We are rapidly coming down to something like this: When the extent of a calamity warrants it, it is lawful to infringe upon and violate the Constitution; when the casualty is slight, we are not at liberty to indulge our feelings and our sympathies. I hold, on the contrary, that, the more you expand a dangerous principle, the worse it is; and, if you are to infringe the Constitution at all, you had better confine yourself to slight cases. The danger is, in this case, of bringing in the *extent* of this catastrophe *as a reason why this act is in conflict with this provision of the Constitution.*" Any such legislation as this Mr. Bayard considers nothing else than "unjust lavishness."

In this same speech, from which we have previously quoted on "decentralization of power as the issue of the hour," * Mr. Bayard said:

"What will we be, my friends, if we are not to exercise our powers of government in regard to our local concerns? Nay, further, what will become of our local concerns if we who live in the locality are not to have the sole voice in regulating them? If an abuse occurs, who

---

* Wilmington, October 4, 1874.

will know it so well as those who suffer from it? If the shoe pinches, who knows it so well as the man who wears the shoe? If a community is suffering from official robbery, from plunder of any kind, who knows it and suffers from it? The tax-payers and the property-holders. They are the men whose property is taken; they are the men who would seek to apply the remedy. Others at a distance may hear of it, but it will produce no impression upon them. If you take away from a people the control of those matters which are essential to their good government, what will be the result? They will give up all interest in the government, and they will become the supple suppliants at the feet of the central power for any favor that they may get.

"Look for one instant at what was the condition of France. Louis Napoleon Bonaparte was president of the French republic. Powers were given to him to govern that country according to a republican form. He used those powers with base treachery for the purpose of converting a republic into an empire, and he accomplished that end. At the cost of the blood of many of his fellow citizens, he placed himself in the saddle, and his horse's feet upon the neck of the French people. What was the result? Instantly commenced the reign of consolidated power. All over France, the germ of local self-government was destroyed. If any population desired to raise a loan for the purpose of opening streets, beautifying their town, erecting public buildings, or for any other local purpose, all was to be done subject to the sanction of the imperial government in Paris. If they wished to elect a mayor of their city, they had the privilege of selecting a number of names, and out of those names the emperor condescended to choose the man he liked.

"This was the history of French government. What was the result? The people no longer bothered themselves about it. They set to work to attend to their private affairs. They spun their beautiful silks; they made their exquisite velvets. They grew rich; they grew voluptuous; they grew gay. But where was self-government, and where were their liberties? France was never so rich in money, so filled with men, Paris never so gay and beautiful, as when the collision between France and Germany occurred.

"Look, then, at the picture. Napoleon had had just war enough in the Crimea to whet anew the ancient ardor of the French people for military glory. He had the luck to have that war end just at the time when the French fame was highest. Subsequently he had a collision with Austria, and upon the battle-fields of Italy he again had singular good military fortune, which again just ended in good time. The fortune of war had been with him, and the pretext for keeping up enormous military establishments to gratify the vanity of the people and to fortify his own power over them was given to him. But the time of struggle with Germany came—Germany, compact and resolute; taught in the hard school of adversity the true way to success; Germany, who, through long years of humiliation at the hands of France, had learned those lessons that adversity alone can teach men or nations. The French met them in over-confidence; the Germans met the French with resolute energy; and you know the result. .... And can it be, with a pursuance of this system of centralization, that these powers can long remain to us? I ask you to think of it, you men who may be discontented with the nomination of Horace Greeley, you men who may be discontented with the Democratic party or the Liberal Republican party, for they are now one, and acting firmly together.

"So far as the result upon our executive and our legislative departments in the national government is concerned, the Liberal Republicans and the Democrats stand or fall together for the next four years; and what will happen after that it will be time enough for us to know when the issues arise. When they do arise, we will test them by the same principles by which we are testing measures to-day.

"This is my position," said he, in conclusion. "I want it to be your position. I want it to be the position of every man, whether he is of my party or not. I want him to have rights that neither I nor my party can invade, and I want my party and myself to stand equal with him in that respect. And can it be, with a pursuance of this system of centralization, that these powers can long remain to us? I ask you to think of it, you men who may be discontented with nominations. Our people become fit to take part in large matters by being educated in minor matters. A man goes to the county seat to serve as commissioner or assessor, and he learns the order of business: how to levy taxes, how to conduct the affairs of the county, how to provide for the poor, how to provide for the schools, how to provide for the roads, how to provide for the police, and to attend to all the matters necessary for local self-government. After a time, having that knowledge, he expands his attention and his faculties to the government of his State, and after he has learned how to govern his State, and has been so practiced, he is much more fitted then to take part in the government of other States in the general government. That is the natural expansion. It is the natural course of human conduct in regard to our business affairs. We begin by trusting men in a small way. As their capacities are proven and exerted they expand, and as they expand the trust expands, and as the trust expands their experience expands, until they become the valued members of society upon whose judgment and wisdom and good character we all rely for guidance in our daily affairs.

"I beg of you, therefore, do not by your votes destroy the autonomy of your State. Do not consent to act with any party that does so destroy it. It is essential to your liberties and mine. I am speaking as much for you, my Republican fellow-citizens, as for myself, although at this time the immediate effect of your law is to strike down officials who are elected by men who think in politics as I do. But there is no difference to me in that. I would feel as unwilling to see the just powers of a Republican official in the State of Delaware interfered with unduly as I would the just powers of a man of my own party, and I would fly as quickly to the forum here before the people, or go into court to insist upon his rights, as I would upon my own or of a man who belonged to the same political party as myself."

In New England and the West, and in other sections also, where the township system, as yet intact, preserves to every voter the consciousness of local self-government, the force of Mr. Bayard's apprehensions and warnings is naturally much less felt than in communities where the State and county systems have been gradually impaired by federal encroachments. But, if the township system should be left unsupported at last, how can it stand alone? And, if it should fall, would not those who have lived under it so long, and prospered by means of it, lose ten times as much, and feel their losses ten times as acutely, as more Southern communities?

CHAPTER XII.

ECONOMY AND REFORM IN GOVERNMENT.

As the power of the federal government kept steadily increasing at the expense of the rights of the States and of the people, so increased the inefficiency and extravagance of the public service. Offices came to be looked upon as rewards for political services, and were distributed, not among those who could best perform the duties, but those who had most assisted, or would most assist, in winning a political triumph. The higher officials claimed and received their allotments of patronage, which each doled out to the hungry aspirants from his State, county, or district, according to a scale of merits well understood, in which fitness for the duties of the office was the last thing considered (if considered at all).

Naturally, the persons selected for such merits cared much for the continued favor of their patrons, and but little, if at all, for the public service. It was not to be supposed that a clerk in a department, who had received his position as a reward for faithful work at primary meetings or in corner groceries, should expect to have no easier place than the clerk in a bank or store who owed his situation merely to honesty and capacity. If hours of work were made short and pay high, if the men were inefficient or idle, the defect could be made up by employing more; thus widening the area and influence of administrative patronage.

It is not alleged that this state of things existed in all the departments—there have always been honorable exceptions; just as in the vast army of officials there have been many faithful and laborious public servants; but such was the natural tendency of the whole system.

Nor do we lay the existence of this state of things to the charge of the Republican party alone. The seeds of the evil had been sown long before they came into power. But, while it was contrary to the fundamental principles of true Democracy, it was accordant with the Republican idea of aggrandizing federal power and influence; and, inconsequence, under a Republican administration it burgeoned and blossomed with a luxuriance of poisonous growth never before dreamed of, shocking and disgusting the wiser and more patriotic men of that party.

To such a pass had things come by the close of Johnson's presidency that one of the leading thinkers of the North wrote:

"Our present system of appointments to office is not only scandalously wasteful, but is doing more to lower the tone of public morals than all other causes together. It involves every member of Congress in a network of corrupt bargains from which there is no escape. . . . As competence is the last qualification regarded, the very government itself keeps before the people a standing incentive to dishonesty by paying high wages for poor work." *

And when, by dint of hard service, or strong recommendations, the prize of a position in some public office had been won, it was by no means an unalloyed felicity. The free American citizen had riveted a collar about his

---

* Mr. J. R. Lowell, in "North American Review," January, 1869.

neck engraved with the name of the administration, and "Gurth, the born thrall of Cedric the Saxon," would not have envied him his liberty. Whatever his political views might be, on any matter on which he could express an opinion or cast a vote, he was now bound to support the administration through thick and thin. Spies, calling themselves "members of the G. A. R.," or belonging to the peculiar system of delatorship organized by Mr. Boutwell, infested all the departments, listening to every word, and ready to report any want of zeal or independence of thought detected in any employee. Not only this, but they were expected to contribute a percentage of their wages to the administration campaign fund, and they dared not refuse or murmur. Here and there a bold spirit offered resistance to this abject slavery, and was quickly made an example of. Nay, the pretext of voluntary contributions was cast aside, and the spectacle was presented of a United States marshal standing at the pay-table and taking the tax from each salary as it was paid. And this plan was presently replaced by the simpler mode of "docking" the salaries, and filching a corruption fund from the bread of women and children.

The extravagant recklessness and wastefulness of the war had also produced their natural results. The federal government was expected to distribute with a lavish hand the money and the property of the people whenever a sufficient claim to its bounty could be established; and what constituted the sufficiency of a claim can be very well understood. The doctrine of internal improvements took its widest swing, and it became possible to bribe whole States and sections by colossal subsidies or donations. The public lands were given away by Congress with reckless prodigality to great corporations to make railroads which, had they really been needed, could have been better made by private enterprise, and at a fraction of the cost. The Northern Pacific was endowed with lands equal in area to the combined territories of Denmark, Holland, Belgium, Portugal, and Greece; and there were railroad schemes before Congress for appropriating 400,000,000 acres of the public domain. Of course this monstrous extravagance fostered corruption of every kind; schemes fastened themselves like parasites upon other schemes; log-rolling secured concert of action in the raids on the public purse; and that extraordinary culmination of fraud and impudence known as the Credit Mobilier was not so remarkable for its shamelessness as for its exposure.

Of this state of things the writer whom we have just quoted says:

"Congress itself is fast becoming a brokers' board for operators on the treasury. Corporate interests are beginning to be represented there, quite as much as the political opinions of constituencies; and so universal is the want of faith in honest motive that not a measure can pass involving the payment of public money without charges of corruption."

It was fondly hoped by those Republicans in whom party spirit had not overmastered patriotism, that this state of things would be greatly improved, if not entirely reformed, by the election of General Grant. As his military services and success had lifted him to his exalted position, it was believed that he would be able to keep himself independent of the more debasing political influences; his powers of resistance were considered equal to any strain; and the fact that he had been inculpated in no fraudulent act created a natural belief that he was honest and would sustain honesty. It is really pathetic, in the light of subsequent events, to read the glowing anticipations of that time. Never were brighter hopes doomed to more humiliating disappointment. Whether, as his enemies alleged, Grant went into the presidency fully prepared to run the machine in the old corrupt way, and make out of the office the most that he could for himself and his friends; or whether, as his apologists say, he wished to act uprightly, but was forced to surrender to the horde of politicians and office-seekers, it is not our business to decide, nor need the country greatly care. The fact remains that under his administration such a tide of profligacy, extravagance, corruption, and malfeasance, in nearly all branches of the public service, set in, as made previous abuses seem trifling in comparison. This is not a prejudiced Democratic judgment: a well-known Republican writer * says, "It was reserved for the administration of President Grant to descend lower than the worst of its predecessors in the scale of self-degradation." And this censure was passed in October, 1869, before Grant had been in office eight months of his eight years; before the people had begun to measure the extent and fathom the depths of Grantism.

We do not mean to say that President Grant selected his friends chiefly for their dishonesty; but it was his singular infelicity that in so large a number of cases those whom he honored with special confidence, appointed to offices of trust, and stood by despite evil report, damaging disclosures, and even judicial sentence, turned out to be swindlers and thieves. There was "Boss" Shepherd and his crew in the District of Columbia, who, being authorized to expend $4,000,000 in the improvement of

* Mr. Henry Brooks Adams.

streets and general embellishment of Washington city, spent $20,000,000, and raised the debt of the District to $25,000,000. How this was done, one sample may suffice. A contract for a job of grading was taken at $975. The first contractor did a small portion of the work, for which he received $1,450, when he died. The rest of the work was then turned over to another party, who received $18,000 for what he did or did not do. Another man, an adventurer " on the make," received $97,000 for absolutely nothing at all, "without an hour of labor or a penny of responsibility." Does anybody suppose that Shepherd, Mullett, and the rest, went about like the Caliph Haroun Alraschid, bestowing all these purses of gold from the people's hard earnings in mere caprice of bounty, or were they too " on the make "?

The latter was the universal belief, nor was it lessened by that unparalleled and most outrageous attempt, "that crime," as Mr. Bayard called it, " not fit to be mentioned in our own day and time," the safe-burglary conspiracy to convict Mr. Alexander of a felony committed by the conspirators themselves. The plot failed, but all the storm of popular indignation at wrongs known, and others more than suspected, never shook the President's confiding affection for " Boss " Shepherd, any more than for Murphy, or Leet, or Babcock, or scores of others. His blind devotion to his idols seemed to have taken for its motto Moore's passionate couplet:

"I know not, I ask not, if guilt's in that heart;
I but know that I love thee, whatever thou art."

Such was the state of things with which Mr. Bayard and those who felt and acted with him had to contend. But for ten years he was one of a feeble minority, where his voice indeed could be heard, and was heard, clear as a clarion, in the denunciation of wrong and the defense of right, but where it was next to impossible to initiate any measure of reform, and quite impossible to carry it. Revenue bills, moreover, originate in the lower house, so that a senator had but little opportunity for any practical movement in the way of retrenchment. But what he could do, he did. He cast his unavailing vote, and he stripped the masks of patriotism, of morality, of expediency, from selfish, unjust, and unwise legislation. And he brought to the consideration of these questions not only the unswerving integrity, the stainless honor which political foes as well as friends admire in his character, but also that clear practical insight, the gift of his thorough business training, which enabled him to expose the futility of the schemes of crotchety enthusiasts, and disentangle the sophistries of crafty contrivers, and to show the straightforward, practical business way of dealing with the matter.

In March, 1873, a bill was passed by Congress which, owing in part to a misunderstanding of its real operation, excited the public mind to a degree disproportioned to its importance. This was the bill regulating the compensation of members and other public officials, coarsely called the "salary grab." The popular conception of it was that members had agreed to vote themselves a large and unjustifiable increase of pay, at a time when the country could ill bear any additional burden. This, however, was not exactly the case. The bill, so far as members of Congress were concerned, provided for an equalization of the pay by giving each senator, representative, and delegate $7,500 a year in lieu of the $5,000 and mileage before allowed. This, to the members who lived most distant from Washington, would have been lessening of salary: to a large fraction it would have given a trifling increase: and to the rest, an increase more or less considerable. It is possible that, considering the greatly enhanced expenses of living in Washington, and the fact that most of the members had left other profitable avocations, the former salary, in the depreciated currency, may not have been a sufficient compensation. But the most objectionable feature of the bill was a retroactive clause extending the increased payment over the Forty-second Congress then just expiring.

Knowing the opposition that would be raised, the framers of the measure held it back until the very last hours of the Congress, and then brought it forward, when there was no time left for discussion, tacked to the general appropriation bill. It was at midnight of March 3d that the bill was reported from the committee of conference, and the Congress expired at noon of the next day. Mr. Bayard and those who thought with him disapproved the bill, and especially the retroactive feature; but what was to be done? The whole bill had to stand or fall as it was; and the only alternatives were to pass it as it stood, or to defeat it altogether, in which latter case, of course, as there would have been no appropriation to carry on the government, it would have been necessary to assemble Congress the next month, causing directly a heavy pecuniary loss to the country, and indirectly much greater damage in unwise and injurious legislation. Mr. Bayard, without hesitation, took the lesser of the two evils, and voted for the bill in preference to the extra session. The back pay handed to him he returned to the treasury of the United States.

So loud was the expression of popular disapprobation

of this measure, that even its foremost advocates were alarmed at the probable consequences, and in January, 1874, Senator Morton introduced a bill to reduce the salaries of members of Congress to the former rates, and providing for the return to the treasury of the excess already paid. The latter absurd and impracticable proposition was, of course, only a tub to the popular whale; none knew better than the senator that it could not be carried out.

But Mr. Bayard was not the man to be blown around by every real or supposed breath of public opinion. As he had voted for the measure while disapproving it, because he saw that by doing so he was serving the public interest, so now he had the courage to face the storm and tell the public that it was in error. While the introducer of the bill was, or pretended to be, tremulously eager to undo his own work, Mr. Bayard stood boldly forward to insist that equity and reason should govern their action, and that two wrongs would not make a right. He showed that the plan to compel members to refund the excess of pay by a tax on their future salaries, even if constitutional, would operate unequally, and would be impracticable in many cases, such as that of Mr. Casserly, who had resigned his seat.

The Houses of Congress had the power to fix the compensation of their own members; there was no question of that; and in determining it they should be guided by justice alone—justice to the public and justice to themselves. It should be liberal enough for a reasonable and comfortable maintenance, and no more; not so high as to make the salary the chief object of ambition, nor so low as to tempt members to eke it out by indirect means, or to add another to the causes, already too numerous, which rendered men of high ability and character reluctant to seek public office. On this point he says, in his speech of January 7, 1874:

"Mr. President, in my opinion one of the chief dangers of our day and country is the devotion of citizens to their private pursuits, to the neglect of their public duties. If this federal Constitution shall go down, if this experiment for human self-government shall fail, there will be few more to blame than those intelligent men who have grown rich in their private pursuits, and allowed places of high public trust and honor to be filled by men less worthy and able than themselves, but who were willing at least to give their time to public service. Who does not know of the frequent advice to young men of talent and character: 'Keep out of politics; stick to your business, to your profession, to your ledger, to your office, to your studio; keep out of politics'? This is the common cry which is accepted as wise, as just, as commendable, in a country which must depend for the elevation and the continuance of its government upon the best efforts of its most intelligent, its most able, its most conscientious men.

"What is the consequence of all this un-American, worldly-wise advice to the youth of our country, too often followed by them? They have sought to make the name of politician discreditable. They have sought to make attention to public duties suspicious. And what has been the result, senators? Has it not been a lower tone of public service? Has it not been a degraded tone of public service? I say that to a certain degree it has; for I believe if there should be an increase in honorable competition between men of intellect and character for public position, it would tend largely to the elevation of the tone of our service and to the benefit of the whole country. This government is not an automatic machine. It is not to run itself. It calls for the efforts constantly, and often times the self-sacrificing efforts of the ablest and the purest and the bravest, to guide it on in the right direction, and to keep it in the paths of honor and safety.

"Now, senators, if a large pay would of itselfe scure really the best men, if it would really fill Congress with statesmen worthy of the name, what measure of economy would be so beneficent to the whole people? The benefit to the people of even one pure-minded, clear-headed, patriotic man in the Congress of the United States, in either house, is not to be weighed in money, and scarce any sum in reason but would wisely be paid if that alone would secure it. I do not say that it would; I do not believe that by money alone such things are to be accomplished. The thing is for us to consider, upon a question so broad as this, what is the just medium that will tend to secure the presence here of proper men capable of rendering valuable service to the country? A proper, respectable maintenance ought to be secured—no more. The Representatives should not be harassed and embarrassed by constant pecuniary needs. A man is not to come here to save or make money by his office and position; such a man is unfit for the place, and falls far below a proper comprehension of its duties and responsibility."

His proposition, in view of the general public distress, and the urgent necessity for economy, was that the pay of members of the houses should be replaced at what it was before the change, without any attempt to compel restitution of the sums already paid. The increased salaries of heads of departments and officers and employees of Congress, he thought, should remain as they had been fixed. His speech concludes thus: "I am perfectly aware that there is a great deal more that is important in this subject of compensation for public service. Certain it is that I am not in favor of illegitimate appropriations for expenditures; and, as I am opposed to illegitimate expenditure, I wish to prevent that by a reasonable, legitimate appropriation. You have seen already how a habit has grown into the executive departments of allowances of a questionable nature for those conveniences which are essential to the prompt transaction of public business, and scandal has been created by it; but I think the best way to avoid these things is to make a reasonable appropriation, that shall not drive officials, high or low, into illegitimate methods of eking out an insufficient income.

"Mr. President, I think it of the last importance to the people of this country that they should have confidence in the integrity, the home-bred pecuniary honesty, of their representatives and of their rulers. It is the duty of every man to do what he can to establish that. It is his duty equally, in establishing confidence, to strike down in any place, high or low, dishonesty and peculation in officials. I rejoice, sir, that the public eye is turned in such criticism. It has not turned too soon; it can not be turned too often or too closely; and I hope the day will come when any public official of the United States who is found engaging, directly or indirectly, in abuses of the privileges of his office by small peculations, by indirect and illegitimate gains, will be rebuked by a wholesome public sentiment of the country, and that no man in office will be found to sustain such conduct. And it is from high officials that the example can come with best effect, and the public service surely needs it.

"Sir, I hope public attention and displeasure have been

aroused. I hope they will not slumber until these abuses shall have been remedied. But, depend upon it, the people, who from a sense of honesty demand these reforms, are too just to ask for a sacrifice that is unnatural, and which can not be performed except at a loss to the public service."

The singular lack of wisdom of the ruling party in all matters of political economy and finance—next to their theories of currency, for a parallel to which we must go back to the days of John Law—was chiefly displayed in their schemes of tariff and excise. Instead of adjusting the burden of taxation so as to make it press as equally as possible, some industries were pampered and others crushed with extortionate imposts. Caprice, or sentiment, or even less excusable motives, seemed so to govern their measures that they succeeded in combining the greatest possible inconvenience and distress with the least proportionate net income to the public purse. They seemed not to know that in all matters of this kind there is a point which it is futile to attempt to pass, because men will take the chances of breaking or evading the law rather than pay the excessive tax; and, let coast-guardsmen and excisemen be multiplied as you will, for one smuggler or illicit manufacturer that is caught, ten go free. As for the pernicious effect of enlisting the feelings of the community in favor of law-breakers and against the law, we will not speak of that, though one would have thought it worthy of consideration by those who claimed a monopoly of "high moral ideas."

One of these futile and vexatious measures was the tax and tariff bill of 1875, the true character of which, and indeed of the most of this crotchety and tentative legislation, was well shown by Mr. Bayard in his comments upon it:

"It is simply a revenue bill, and I have but this comment to make upon it: that, in accordance with almost every bill which has been framed under the present administration and those which preceded it for twelve or fifteen years past, it has not been so much a bill to provide revenue to the treasury as it has been to create unequal burdens and to protect favored and special classes. . . . I trust this is the last bill which under the false pretense of raising revenue is only a bill to continue that unequal system of raising taxes which shall bring little revenue compared with the tax and cost to the public, while benefit flows to favored and special classes. . . .

"When will senators learn that an over-stringent law defeats itself? Laws to be successful must be reasonable; they must be proportioned to the power of the government to collect without that great excess of inquisitorial power and of annoyance to those who are to be subjected to the tax. Besides, it seems to me that in this matter of taxing distilled spirits there runs that fine vein of morality combined with many views which seems to me so false and so absurd. I do not object to the system, for I think it a true one, of levying your tax upon leading articles, and allowing the tax to rest there until by its stability it shall extend itself over all those who consume, and thereby produce equality of taxation; but many are voting this high tax upon whiskey, as it is termed, for the purpose of inflicting a high moral punishment at the same time that you exact large sums of money. Such a system of mingling morals and politics is absurd and unsound. It is property which you are taxing, and you ought to view it solely in a commercial sense if you wish to treat it with reason and justice."

Mr. Bayard's sound, business-like way of looking at questions of this sort, to which we have already adverted, is well shown again in his remarks on the reduction of the tax on tobacco (February 17, 1879):

"I have sometimes thought, in the last ten years of my life, that there runs through many of our laws a fine spirit of moral instruction designed to punish whatever of immorality may lurk in the personal habits of men, to give them a fine lesson, and at the same time to extort from them heavy pecuniary tribute. I do not believe that legislation should be a matter of sentiment; but I think it should be enacted with reference to the characters, the habits, the capacities, the prejudices of the population over whom it is to be extended. I have witnessed in our tariff laws, and in their administration, such a tone of reprobation and rebuke toward the merchants from whose commerce we were drawing mighty revenues as was scarcely consistent with the dignity of a government addressing a respectable and responsible body of its own citizens. And so, in all their multifarious laws and regulations in regard to the imposition and collection of taxes upon tobacco and distilled spirits, a great deal of the same feeling seems to have prevailed. The citizen who is to pay the tax seems scarcely regarded as a co-operative integer in his country's government, but rather as one who intends dishonesty from the start, and who is not simply called upon to pay tribute as one of the class selected for taxation, but who is to perform his duty to the government under a certain sentiment of reprobation and puritanic feeling which persists in giving him high moral lessons, while at the same time it takes the largest sum of money possible out of his pocket.

"I believe in laying wise taxes, adjusting them, as far

as justice to all classes will permit, upon such commodities as universal use, universal production, will lead you to believe will bring you the greatest revenue with the least individual or class oppression and discomfort; and everywhere and in every way that I could secure the co-operation of the tax-payer in the full payment of the revenue, I should feel that I was achieving a great success in the painful art of taxation."

In the sentence we have just quoted there is, perhaps, a more statesmanlike statement of the fundamental principles of sound and reasonable revenue taxation than can be found anywhere else in as few words. To lay the tax upon "articles of universal use and universal production," so that the burden may, as quickly as possible, be distributed as equally as possible—there is the sound political economy of the subject. To obtain the willing co-operation of the tax-payer—there are the true ethics of the subject.

The practice that has prevailed has been a compound of the "Donnybrook fair" principle—"wherever you see a thing, tax it," regardless whether it can bear taxation, or will yield any revenue worth the trouble—and of a mixture of short-sighted selfishness and silly sentimentality, that selected some articles for pampering, and others for vindictive prosecution, the result of which, as was said before, was to combine the greatest amount of inequality, oppression, and irritation, the strongest temptation to break the law, and the greatest difficulty in enforcing it, with the least proportionate gain to the revenue.*

---

* At the time when the preposterous Morrill tariff, with its encyclopædic lists of dutiable articles, was crippling business here, the whole customs revenue of Great Britain and Ireland was raised on nine commodities, and

But, while dealing with practical questions in a practical way, he did not ignore that broader philosophy which should form the foundation of all sound political economy. To check extravagance, to spend with wisdom, to distribute equally the public burdens, these were the applications of a science, the basis of which he has given in an address to a body of young men just entering into active life.* After adverting to the war and its result, he continues:

"When I refer to the past, it is not idly to mourn over it and the changes wrought in so much we held in close affection and just value, but here to aver my belief that, whatever may be the present condition of our government, its forces and tendencies, we of this day have our only hope for that happiness, individual and national, that security to person and property, that social, political, and religious freedom which were the objects for which our forefathers instituted this government, in the revival and constant exercise of the simple virtues practiced by the founders of the republic, which the growth of wealth and luxury, and a period of civil war, with its necessary accompaniment of public demoralization, have done so much to lessen in public as well as private use.

"The men of our first Revolution were truthful, honest, constant, frugal, industrious, and brave. Adversity had been their nurse, and these virtues were the rugged texts of her instruction. When they came to lay the foundations of a government, they naturally based their organic laws on these principles, so that they became its motive power, the inspiring sentiment of the entire scheme.

the entire list, with the scale of duties and accruing revenue, was printed on a card the size of an ordinary visiting-card.

* Speech before the Literary Societies of the University of Virginia, July 2, 1873.

"Throughout the written charter of carefully enumerated and limited powers, with which they intrusted their official rulers and representatives, everywhere are to be found evidences of this. It was because they were possessed of the virtues I have named that they founded the government they did. It was the natural result of such possession. The government was designed for a people like themselves; it was totally unfit for a people unlike them. And we may be sure that attempts to engraft upon it a government having a different class of ideas and principles for its basis can be but the commencement of a career of loss and sorrow, with certain failure as the final result.

"If the federal Constitution should have been so invaded and overthrown that it shall never again be restored in the beauty and beneficence in which the eyes of our fathers beheld it, it has been because the virtues which gave it birth have fallen into disuse, and the hands and brains which have destroyed it have been those of men whose hatred was stronger than their love of justice, whose love of gain overcame their love of truth, and whose fear of local and temporary discontent overcame the courage necessary to enable them to stand by their duty."

And after adverting to abuses such as we have already touched upon, and showing how fraud, falsehood, and the palliation of wrong-doing were corrupting the morals of public life, he lays his finger upon the very heart of the evil, and points out the remedy:

"Properly considered, no one virtue is more absolutely and practically necessary in human society than simple truth, the essential basis of that good faith upon the preservation of which the honor of men and of nations alone can safely depend. Surely no social crime is more dangerous than a lie, and the man who utters it, or palters with the truth, should be considered a public enemy, unworthy of any post of honor or profit. SIMPLE TRUTH is an essential, a prime necessity, in human intercourse. The safety of nations as well as of individuals requires its close observance. Truth in the historian, truth in the ruler and legislator, truth in the manifold affairs of men in public or private life—this is the keystone; strike it from the arch, and the greatest edifice of man's toil and skill and ambition tumbles to certain and deserved ruin. We need everywhere the MAN 'who speaketh the truth in his heart. . . . Who sweareth to his own hurt and changeth not.' . . .

"All public laws that lead to or tend in any way to the commission of falsehood should meet disapproval. Take, for instance, the whole system of political test oaths, the inventions of a dark, distant, and deluded period of government, unhappily revived of late years in this country. Does any man doubt that they were productive only of weak and mean falsehood, and of the exclusion and injury of men whose conscience and personal honor would have afforded the most certain and cheapest protection to the government that sought it? Slowly sensible of the demoralizing effects of arraying self-interest against truth, propositions were made at the last session of Congress for the abolition of the entire system of custom-house oaths, and the substitution of declarations made on honor. Experience had amply shown that custom-house oaths, under the present system of excessive tariff duties, were almost universally held, however solemn in their form, to have no binding effect, and to be of no protection to the government which exacted them. And I am warranted in saying that no prosecution for such frequent perjury has yet been recorded. Might it not be suggested that men should not thus be tempted to commit wrong, and that wise rulers should so frame their laws as to make the inducements to deceive as slight as possible? Wise recognition of and condescension to the frailties of humanity are surely important elements in legislative judgment."

Happy would it have been for this country if its rulers and legislators of late years had heard and heeded in their youth such admonitions as these; happier still if their counsels had been guided by such clear-sighted wisdom, broad love of country, and simple integrity as were his who uttered them.

CHAPTER XIII.

THE ELECTORAL COMMISSION.

The session of Congress from December, 1876, to March, 1877, was one of the most exciting and deeply important in the annals of our government. It was truly a "time that tried men's souls," as much as they were tried in 1776. It is to the steadfast moral courage of certain of the Democratic leaders in the two Houses of Congress that the honor is due of preventing the United States from being converted from a government of laws into a government of force.

Mr. Bayard was a conspicuous and important actor in those scenes. Certain ill-advised and unscrupulous persons have made the attempt to misstate history, mislead the public mind, and create unworthy prejudice by suggesting that in some way, not distinctly stated, the counsel and desires of Mr. Tilden were not heeded in creating the Electoral Commission, and that he and his more intimate friends were not in accord with the efforts which produced the law for it. The contrary is the fact.

The history of the Electoral Commission has yet to be written, and the historian in the next generation who undertakes it will be embarrassed by the circumstance that a vital portion of the crude material for his narrative is in cipher. In the mean time, however, it is eminently due to Mr. Bayard that some of the facts bearing upon his part in that great drama should be set out in the public view. It is believed that a portion of these facts are not as well known as they should be, and that those which are known have been warped, garbled, and distorted very much out of their actual semblance.

Mr. Bayard cordially endorsed the nomination of Tilden and Hendricks, and threw himself into the canvass that ensued with an ardor which threatened seriously to impair his health. "I made a hole in my lungs in that campaign," he has been heard to say, "which it took me eighteen months to patch up." He spoke throughout the canvass, in a great many different places, from the first ratification meeting in Philadelphia, at Horticultural Hall, to the last speeches in Baltimore and Princess Anne, Maryland, on the eve of election.* There is evidence that Mr. Tilden knew how to value and to appreciate such devoted services. June 30, 1876, Mr. Bayard had telegraphed to him from Washington as follows: "I take the first hour since my return from Mississippi to assure you that my fervent support will not be wanting to elect you to the presidency, where your services are so much needed by the American people," and Mr. Tilden replied at once and the same day: "Cordial thanks for your telegram. *You already know you have my highest appreciation and full confidence.*"

The election took place duly on November 7, 1876. Tilden and Hendricks were elected by a majority of the popular vote, and by a majority of all the electoral votes. But the Republicans were in power at Washington, and they had Grant there intrenched. Chandler, chairman

---

* To vast audiences in Brooklyn and New York city, in Trenton and Newark, New Jersey; in Chicago, Indianapolis, Terre Haute, and a dozen other places in Indiana.

of the Republican committee, had "returned" Hayes and Wheeler elected, and he would not suffer any one to go behind his returns. The Republicans determined to "hold the fort." They had all the machinery necessary to enable them to do it. They had the President and Cabinet, the Senate, the army and navy, and the treasury. They had 100,000 office-holders at their beck and nod, so long as "hold fast" was the avowed policy. They had any number of "visiting statesmen," sensational ready-writers, and Eliza Pinkstons at their disposal. More than all, they owned, body and soul, the returning-boards in the disputed States, and Mr. Chandler felt confident of being able to dictate, from his head-quarters in Washington, the operations of these notorious organizations for giving the semblance of legality to wholesale fraud. The "outrage mill" had still some grist left for grinding over, and then and there were American politics and the American vocabulary enriched with the word "bulldozing."

The Democrats blustered and threatened, but were in sad lack of guidance. The "literary bureau" in New York had ceased its labors with the day of election. The voice of command in Gramercy Park had sunk into a whisper. All the time that the Republicans were organizing, drilling, arranging, dominating, controlling the wires and the press, the Democratic leaders seemed to be doing nothing except more and more relaxing their grip. There was no organization, no defiance. The consciousness of a righteous cause seemed to give no strength, no backbone to its adherents. The bigness of the prize they had won appalled them, and they let it roll away out of their reach, as babies sometimes will do with their big apples. In all this time really nothing was done except to gather some conclusive evidence, which could not be used when it was needed, and is worthless now because of subsequent revelations. If anything was said, it was said in the language of cryptograms. The great Democratic party, winning its first success since 1856, stood dumb as a stock-fish while the prize was filched away. The paralysis at the top seemed to have invaded all its members. We remember but one production of that painful and astonishing interval which seemed to emanate from a Democratic source, and this was a reference book, giving an historical review of how Congresses in the past had been in the habit of counting the electoral vote. This excellent handy volume was published by the Appletons,* and it was whispered about that the publication had Mr. Tilden's sanction.

In the midst of all this doubt and uncertainty, Congress met in December. The Democratic members instantly discovered that if they wanted guidance in such a dire emergency they would have to supply it themselves. They had elected a president, but they had missed to supply their party with a general. By this time even the whispers from New York had become inaudible.

Yet something must be done, and done promptly. For the Democratic senators and representatives found that there was at Washington a party still in control and power, which was elaborately preparing to resist and overcome the outbreaks and disturbances which they hoped would be provoked by the uncertainties of the times. It is simply God's mercy to this republic that the railroad and labor riots of 1877 did not break out sooner and in connection with the unsettled presidential election of 1876. Had that happened, it is not likely there would be any third-term agitation to-day. We repeat it, Grant

---

* But not until January, 1877.

was prepared in 1876–'77 to meet and put down a "Democratic rebellion" on account of the disputed succession, and he looked for such a state of affairs as would compel him to "hold over." The real question, in case of a non-settlement of the presidential controversy, in other words, was not between Tilden and Hayes, but between the republic and Grant.

Senators and representatives knew this state of affairs, and in both parties they dreaded results. There were plenty of people who favored the idea of Grant's holding over, the more especially as Hayes was understood (by those who maligned him to his political associates) to be a reformer. Mr. Bayard confesses that he and all his friends were filled with apprehension at what they saw and heard and knew. It was not the bluster of Chandler and his committee men which appalled them, nor the snuffles and whines of the visiting statesmen, nor the purse-panic of capitalists and money-lenders in the great cities. It was the silence, the secrecy, the thoroughness of the military preparations at the White House and in the departments. There was more than intimidation or necessary precaution in these. A battalion of artillery was called in from one point, but only the arrival of a section of a battery was announced. When a regiment came, only a company was announced. When a brigade was assembled, no more than a regiment was officially stated to be present. Before the day came for the meeting of the two houses in joint convention, more than half the entire army of the United States was collected in Washington. It was openly boasted that they were present here to do in the House of Representatives what they had already done in Louisiana, nor was the boast an idle one.

At least something must be done in such an emergency, since nothing could be gained, while everything might be lost, by drifting on a helmless way. It is a fallacy to say that nothing need have been done; that the House of Representatives had all the necessary powers, and could have proceeded to elect a president according to the forms of the Constitution. What would really have happened would have been this: the Republican Senate and the Democratic House would have disagreed as soon as the vote of Florida came to be counted; the Senate would have retired to its own chamber, and would have been followed there by the Republican members of the House, leaving the Hall of Representatives to the Democratic "rump" and the "Confederate brigadiers." Tilden and Hayes would both have been declared president, and we should have had a disputed and divided succession, with the purse and the sword and the bench and all the machinery and property of government in the hands of the usurper. What then? Would Mr. Tilden have resisted, and demanded and asserted his rights? The result would have been civil war. If he had not done so (and few who know Mr. Tilden believe that he would), we should stand pretty much where we now are, except that Mr. Hayes, while practically president, would have no color of valid title to his office. Such a situation would unquestionably have intensified, in a very serious degree, the condition of affairs during the railroad riots of 1877. The very contemplation of such a situation, however, was intolerable to every patriotic member of Congress, and a means of preventing it was sought with zeal and earnestness. The result of these endeavors was the Electoral Commission. The deliberations of that body did not, indeed, secure the presidency to the man who was really elected, but they secured the peace and dignity of the republic, and vindicated, in a signal manner, the capacity of the American people for self-government under the most trying circumstances.

It is to be added that the system for counting the electoral votes was so imperfect, and led to so many grave and perilous difficulties in 1865 and 1873, that Republicans and Democrats united in seeing the necessity for improvements; the difficulty being that nobody's plan for amendment was quite acceptable, each side seeming to mistrust the other, and to suspect a " Trojan horse " in propositions emanating from it. In this way, while many bills for counting the electoral vote were introduced into Senate and House, none succeeded in getting the approval of a majority. The adjustment of this delicate matter had been advocated by Senator Morton, of Indiana, during several sessions, but without success. He had secured the reference of the subject to a special committee, of which he was chairman, but even the committee would not agree as to what they should recommend. Mr. Bayard was fully alive to the importance of taking steps to obtain relief, and on January 19, 1876, he introduced a resolution in the following words :

" *Resolved by the Senate (the House of Representative concurring)*, That the Committee on Rules of the Senate and House of Representatives be, and they are hereby, instructed to examine, and, after conference, to report, what amendments, if any, should be made in the present joint rules of the two houses; and also whether any, and what, legislation is expedient in regard to the matters considered in the present twenty-second joint rule."

On the 25th of January, he endeavored to have it considered in the Senate, but was thwarted by the action of Frelinghuysen, Conkling, Hamlin, and Morton. In earnest language he besought the Senate to adopt some plan by which the result of the coming presidential election should be honestly ascertained and faithfully accepted. He said:

"I will merely say that there is no time more favorable for the discussion of this rule than the present. There has been no time for the last twelve years when the discussion of the subjects embraced by the twenty-second joint rule could be more favorably had than the present. There are few subjects of more critical interest to be settled rightfully than the matters embraced by that rule, and I think the sooner we bring it to the calm consideration of the Committee on Rules of the two houses, the better for us all, and the better for the country. The longer this is delayed, the nearer we drift to one of those periodical contests under our form of government; and, the sooner we settle in a calm, high spirit these questions which may involve great differences of opinion and interest, the better for us all.

"In view of the suggestion of the Senator from New Jersey, I shall not press the consideration of this resolution in the absence of the Senator from Vermont, although my impression is quite distinct that the Senator from Vermont concurred in the resolution as I presented it. The Senator from New York asked that it might lie over, and it was at his request continued. I meant to bring it up, and I shall bring it up again, when it is the pleasure of the Senate to consider it. I think it important that it should be settled as speedily as possible, if it can be. If the two houses can be brought to agreement on this subject with the present condition of party matters between the two houses, I think it will be a guarantee that the result will be satisfactory to the people of the country. Not only is it important to us that the election should take place with all proper guards, but the great matter is that, after it is over, all the people should come together as one people to support whoever may be the persons chosen by the majority."

But Mr. Bayard was unassisted by his own side of the Senate, and obstructed by the other, and no action was ever taken on his proposition. The Republican majority were unwilling to commit themselves to any but their own partisan plans.

But time passed; the election had been held; and now Congress felt compelled to do something, face to face as they were with a vital issue that admitted of no delay. A joint committee of seven senators and seven representatives was proposed, with instructions to prepare without delay such a measure, either legislative or constitutional, as might be best calculated to count the vote authoritatively, and declare the result by a tribunal whose decision would be generally accepted as final. The proposition came from the House; it was accepted by the Senate, the joint committee was appointed; it matured and reported the bill for counting the vote by the Electoral Commission. The bill was accepted by both houses by an overwhelming majority, and the machinery was thus at last provided for escaping a revolution or a disputed succession.

During the preparation of the measure the sessions of the committee were secret, and the plans of the House committee and those of the Senate committee had been separately matured. The joint committee then met for the first time, and the two communicated to each other the several plans they had respectively prepared. From the mingled features of these plans the Electoral Commission bill was framed.

Mr. Hewitt, of New York city, was a member of the committee, and gave Mr. Tilden instant and full information of the proposed plan of the *joint* committee, as he had previously of the action of the committee on the part of the House. Mr. Hewitt had been selected on Mr. Tilden's nomination as chairman of the National Democratic Committee, and had zealously conducted the political campaign under the personal supervision and advice of Mr. Tilden himself. Thus, throughout the whole proceeding, Mr. Tilden's able and trusted lieutenant, known to be in his closest confidence, was in hearty co-operation with his Democratic associates and constant communication with their chief. The report that accompanied the bill was signed by every one of the fourteen members, excepting Oliver P. Morton, who refused. Those members of the Senate and House who were known to hold the closest and most confidential relations to Mr. Tilden were open and earnest advocates of the measure at every stage. In the House, conspicuous were David Dudley Field and Hewitt, of New York; Randall, of Pennsylvania; Springer, of Illinois; Waterson, of Kentucky; and Money, of Mississippi. In the Senate, Barnum, of Connecticut, and Kernan, of New York (who subsequently became a member of the Electoral Commission). The same spirit which had allowed the minority party in each house to elect its representatives in the joint committee prevailed in both houses in election of members of the Electoral Commission. But how marked the contrast between the action of the two parties! The Democrats, in a spirit of good faith, selected known friends of the measure to carry it into execution; but the Republicans placed Morton and Garfield upon the Commission, knowing they had bitterly denounced and opposed the passage of the act;

had denied in debate its constitutional warrant, and yet took an oath to execute it. By such selections the honest execution of the law was prevented by the Republican majority in the Senate, and the honorable settlement it had been ordained to procure was shamefully defeated. It is also true that, in December, 1876, before the committee had taken any action, Mr. Bayard, in compliance with the request of Mr. Tilden, had gone to New York, to receive his counsel and instruction. He spent an entire evening with Mr. Tilden, by appointment, at the house of a mutual friend, and the following day, accompanied by Mr. Lamar, of Mississippi, went to again see Mr. Tilden at his house, and held an interview, lasting four hours, in the effort to ascertain his views and wishes, or, as Mr. Bayard himself once phrased it, "*to sit at his feet and gather his instruction.*" Mr. Tilden, however, gave no intimation whatever of his intentions, nor any light upon the grave subjects under consideration. The compilation of congressional precedent, then in course of preparation by Mr. Bigelow, was exhibited and referred to, but no plan of action was indicated, and the two gentlemen returned to Washington uninformed and uninstructed by their party chieftain of his intended action, and from that time forth were left to their own resources and responsibilities, to meet the grave emergency whose shadow covered the whole land.

Mr. Bayard did not intend this country should be "Mexicanized," but addressed all his energies to the preparation of a remedy in the form of law, which should vindicate the results of popular election, preserve the faith of our people in their government, and keep the country from falling into such a condition of confusion as would give a pretext to the military conspirators to seize the reins of power, and leave us not a vestige of civil and constitutional liberty. The electoral bill passed the Senate on January 24, 1877, by a vote of 47 to 17. Every Democrat in the Senate voted for the measure, with a single exception, in which a want of constitutional power was stated as the reason. In opposition were found the crew of carpet-baggers—Dorsey, Clayton, Patterson, Bruce, Hamilton, Conover, and West—combining with Morton, Sargent, and Blaine—the most "stalwart" of the radicals. It passed the House of Representatives, then strongly Democratic, by a vote of *191 to 86*, and in this minority were found but 18 Democratic votes.*

Mr. Hendricks, the Vice-President elect, had at once, upon the bill being reported, made public expression of his gratification and of his warm approval of the measure.

The report accompanying the bill, which was not drawn by Mr. Bayard, though it was amended in some details at his suggestion, embodied a very strong argument for its adoption. It said:

"We have applied the utmost practicable study and deliberation to the subject, and believe that the bill now reported is the best attainable disposition of the difficult problems and disputed theories arising out of the late election. It must be obvious to every person conversant with the history of the country, and with the formation and interpretation of the Constitution, that a wide diversity of views and opinions touching the subject, not wholly coincident with the bias or wishes of the members of political parties, would naturally exist. We have in this state of things chosen, therefore, not to deal with abstract questions, save so far as they are necessarily involved in

---

* In this majority were included all the Democratic members well known as friends to Mr. Tilden and his election.

the legislation proposed. It is, of course, plain that the report of the bill implies that in our opinion legislation may be had on the subject in accordance with the Constitution, but we think that the law proposed is inconsistent with few of the principal theories upon the subject. The Constitution requires that the electoral votes shall be counted on a particular occasion. All will agree that the votes named in the Constitution are the constitutional votes of the States, and not other; and, when they have been found and identified, there is nothing left to be disputed or decided: all the rest is the mere clerical work of summing up the numbers, which being done, the Constitution itself declares the consequence.

"This bill, then, is only directed to ascertaining, for the purpose and in aid of the counting, what are the constitutional votes of the respective States; and, whatever jurisdiction exists for such purpose, the bill only regulates the method of exercising it. The Constitution, our great instrument and security for liberty and order, speaks in the amplest language for all such cases, in whatever aspect they may be presented. It declares that the Congress shall have power 'to make all laws which shall be necessary and proper for carrying into execution the foregoing powers, and all other powers vested by this Constitution in the government of the United States or in any department or officer thereof.' The committee therefore think that the law proposed can not be justly assailed as unconstitutional by any one, and for this reason we think it unnecessary, whatever may be our individual views, to discuss any of the theories referred to. Our fidelity to the Constitution is observed when we find that the law we recommend is consistent with that instrument.

"The matter, then, being a proper subject for legislation, the fitness of the means proposed becomes the next subject for consideration. Upon this we beg leave to submit a few brief observations.

"In all just governments, both public and private rights must be defined and determined by the law. This is essential to the very idea of such a government, and is the characteristic distinction between free and despotic systems. However important it may be, whether one citizen or another shall be the Chief Magistrate for a prescribed period, upon just theories of civil institutions, it is of far greater moment that the will of the people, lawfully expressed in the choice of that officer, shall be ascertained and carried into effect in a lawful way. It is true that in every operation of a government of laws, from the most trivial to the most important, there will always be the possibility that the result reached will not be the true one. The executive officer may not wisely perform his duty, the courts may not truly declare the law, and the legislative body may not enact the best laws; but, in either case, to resist the act of the executive, the courts, or the legislature, acting constitutionally and lawfully within their sphere, would be to set up anarchy in the place of government. We think, then, that to provide a clear and lawful means of performing a great and necessary function of government, in a time of much public dispute, is of far greater importance than the particular advantage that any man or party may in the course of events possibly obtain. But we have still endeavored to provide such lawful agencies of decision in the present case as shall be the most fair and impartial possible under the circumstances. Each of the branches of the legislature and the judiciary is represented in the tribunal in equal proportions. The composition of the judicial part of the Commission looks to a selection from different parts of the republic, while it is thought to be free from any preponderance of supposable bias; and the addition of the necessary constituent part of the whole Commission, in order to obtain an uneven number, is left to an agency the farthest removed from prejudice of any existing attainable one. If would be difficult, if not impossible, we think, to establish a tribunal that could be less the subject of party criticism than such a one. The principle of its constitution is so absolutely fair that we are unable to perceive how the most extreme partisan can assail it, unless he prefers to embark his wishes upon the stormy sea of unregulated procedure, hot disputes, and dangerous results, that can neither be measured nor defined, rather than upon the fixed and regular course of law that insures peace and the order of society, whatever party may be disappointed in its hopes."

When this bill came up for discussion in the Senate, Mr. Bayard advocated it in one of his best and most earnest speeches, delivered Wednesday, January 24, 1877. He said: "There is for every man in a matter of such importance his own measure of responsibility, and that measure I desire to assume. . . . The period of advocacy of either candidate has passed, and the time for judgment has almost come. How shall we who propose to make laws for others do better than to exhibit our own reverence for law, and set the example here of subordination to the spirit of law?" After a very full and lucid discussion of the bill, Mr. Bayard concluded with the following peroration, one of the finest which ever came even from his lips:

"Mr. President, in the course of my duty here as a representative of the rights of others, as a chosen and sworn public servant, I feel that I have no right to give my individual wishes, prejudices, interests, undue influence over my public action. To do so would be to commit a breach of trust in the powers confided to me. It is true I was chosen a senator by a majority only, but not *for* a majority only. I was chosen *by* a party, but not for *a* party. I represent *all* the good people of the State which has sent me here. In my office as a senator I recognize no claim upon my action in the name and for the sake of party. The oath I have taken is to support the Constitution of my country's government, not the *fiat* of any political organization, even could its will be ascertained. In sessions preceding the present I have adverted to the difficulty attending the settlement of this great question, and have urgently besought action in advance at a time when the measure adopted could not serve to predicate its results to either party. My failure then gave me great uneasiness, and filled me with anxiety; and yet I can now comprehend the wisdom concealed in my disappointment, for in the very emergency of this hour, in the shadow of the danger that has drawn so nigh to us, has been begotten in the hearts of American senators and representatives and the American people a spirit worthy of the occasion—born to meet these difficulties, to cope with them, and, God willing, *to conquer them.*

"Animated by this spirit, the partisan is enlarged into the patriot. Before it the lines of party sink into hazy obscurity; and the horizon which bounds our view reaches on every side to the uttermost verge of the great republic. It is a spirit that exalts humanity, and, imbued with it, the souls of men soar into the pure air of unselfish devotion to the public welfare. It lighted with a smile the cheek of Curtius as he rode into the gulf; it guided the hand of Aristides as he sadly wrote upon the shell the sentence of his own banishment; it dwelt in the frozen earthworks of Valley Forge; and from time to time it has been an inmate of these halls of legislation. I believe it is here to-day, and that the present measure was born under its influence."

Mr. Bayard's remarks in the course of the deliberations of the tribunal show that, no matter what others felt, he considered himself a judge upon a very supreme bench. We happen to know something about Mr. Bayard's conception of the duties of a judge. In 1876, at a meeting of the bar of Wilmington, he was called on to speak of the death of Chief Justice Edward W. Gilpin, of Delaware. "The profession of the law," said Mr. Bayard on that occasion, "is elevating; its business is to mete out justice between man and man. It requires a delicate and sensitive honor. The administration of justice should be controlled by upright men, having a high sense of conscientious responsibility, always recognizing fairness and fair play as the jewel of our profession. The law is grounded upon truth, and the lawyer is the professor of that truth. In it he is bound to attain his right position. Favor can not make or break him, or keep him down. The position of judge requires sound sense and sound morality; both are essential."

It was in this spirit that Mr. Bayard went to his work on the Electoral Commission. In speaking of the Florida case, he said: "I can only say that while I feel a just and natural distrust in my powers to deal competently with such issues, yet I am at least conscious that I approach the duties imposed upon me by the oaths I have taken, both as a senator of the United States and a member of this Commission, in a spirit deeply solicitous to act worthily in my place." This he did. In the course of the debates on the South Carolina case, the effort was made by Senator Frelinghuysen to accuse Mr. Bayard of inconsistency by contrasting his line of argument with his speech on Morton's bill for counting the electoral vote made in the Senate, February 25, 1875. "I am very glad," Mr. Bayard retorted, "that this extract from my former speech has been thus brought to my attention, because I am aware that it has been furnished before now to members of this Commission, although I will not suggest that the object in bringing it now to my notice is to impale me upon a supposed inconsistency between my views as expressed in 1875 and now. To the doctrine, however, contained in these remarks I can only give my renewed approval and assent, although I must frankly admit that within the two years which have elapsed I have had a better opportunity for the study and attention of this subject which had been denied me then, and which has given to my mind information and light not obtained before. I trust the time will never come when I shall cling obstinately to an error which can only grow into a wrong by becoming willful, nor do I believe that I shall be found to lack the courage to retract an opinion when I am convinced that it is erroneous."

In regard, however, to the subject matter of the issue attempted to be made, his mind was perfectly clear. "Such a proposition as was stated by me," he said, "in the debate referred to, was applicable only to the admitted election of a State. The presence of fraud and its effect in qualifying every proposition was not then considered. The most solemn judgments and decrees of courts, pardons by kings and rulers, every treaty or compact between nations or individuals, alike lose every quality of obligation when touched by fraud. I know of no human contract more irrevocable and binding upon the parties than that of Christian marriage, in which civil and religious obligation combine to secure its performance. The sanction under which marriage is entered into is the most solemn known to civilized men; yet who ever denied that the tie could be and ought to be dissolved upon proof of fraud by one of the parties in obtaining the marriage? *Fraud is a universal solvent, and destroys whatever it touches, and it ought to be hunted down and crushed whenever possible, in order to protect human society.* Every proposition as to legal or moral obligation must be considered as made in the absence of fraud, because fraud admitted as an element displaces all the reasoning which guides men in the ordinary conduct of life or in the administration of human laws and justice."

This admirable doctrine did not meet with as much deference from the tribunal as they would probably pay to it now if their work was to do over again, and they were aware of the condemnation with which their performance has been met. In discussing the case of Louisiana, Mr. Bayard showed that he was aware of the verdict which the people would pronounce should the tribunal decline to meet the real equities of the case before them. "I have felt very deeply," he said, "the necessity of not only deciding this case according to law and justice, but also of satisfying the moral sense of our fellow countrymen. Montesquieu has told us that, as honor is of vital essence to a monarchy, so is morality to a republic. I am perfectly aware of the real condition of the State of Louisiana. I am aware that what they are pleased to term 'the rights of the State of Louisiana' have been most loudly proclaimed, and sought to be protected in argument before this Commission, against the slightest invasion, by many who view with complacency her government and her people to-day in absolute subjection to the army of the United States and its official head. I recognize fully the abnormal condition of affairs that grew out of and has succeeded a period of civil war and widespread revolution. I have had no object so near to my heart, and none which has drawn from me more of my energies, than the restoration of all parts and sections of this country to their former harmonious and normal relations to each other and to their common government. I can not shut my eyes to the fact that the disorder and crime of all grades which mark the history of the last few years in Louisiana, and yet which I believe have been shockingly and shamelessly exaggerated for political purposes, have been chiefly, almost wholly, the result of the destruction of local self-government in that State by the constant interference of federal power, invariably in favor of that one of the political parties of that State whose interest it has thus been made to produce disorder in order to procure that armed assistance without the aid of which it would long since have disappeared. The eyes of the American people must not be closed to the fact that if the voting material of a community is corruptible, it will be corrupted; if it is purchasable, it will be bought; if ignorant, it will be deceived; and, if timid, it will be intimidated. If elections are put up at auction by placing their control in vile hands, whom will you blame? Those who have created such an order of things; surely not those who seek to abolish it. On the one hand, you see property seeking protection from plunder in the garb of law, and on the other, plunderers in the garb of law offering to sell their official powers; and thus property seeks to buy immunity from plunder by bribing men in office, or, impoverished and despairing, strikes down the robbers with fierce blow."

The history of the Electoral Commission, so far as Mr. Bayard's connection with it is concerned, has been presented here frankly and freely. He is quite willing to be judged by it and upon it before the American people. He can hardly lose in their esteem for having not only acted uprightly himself, but assuming, in the essential nobility of his nature, that other men would be actuated by the same motives as those which compelled him to do what he did.

His feelings are well portrayed in his own language, when the decision of the tribunal in the case of Louisiana was ratified by the Senate. He then said:

"Mr. President, as a member of the Electoral Commission, I have given all that I could give of earnest, patient, steady labor and devotion to secure the just execution of the law under which I was appointed. I could not now, even if I would, repeat here the arguments made by me during the consultations of the Commission in opposition to the result arrived at by eight of my associates. Hereafter, those debates may be given to the public. My labors and my efforts have been crowned only by failure. Deep, indeed, is my sorrow, and poignant my disappointment. I mourn my failure for my country's sake; for it seems to me that not only does this decision of these eight members destroy and level in the dust the essential safeguards of the Constitution, intended to surround and protect the election of the Chief Magistrate of this Union, but it announces to the people of this land that truth and justice, honesty and morality, are no longer the essential bases of their political power."

We submit the case, without further argument, to the public, who are judge and jury in such matters. But, no matter what their verdict, it will not affect Mr. Bayard's consciousness of having acted not only rightly, but in a spirit of exalted patriotism in everything connected with this period of difficulty and danger.

CHAPTER XIV.

MR. BAYARD IN THE SENATE.

On Saturday, March 20, 1875, Mr. Bayard delivered one of his longest, most elaborate, and most effective speeches in the Senate, against executive interference with the government of the State of Louisiana. The occasion was momentous, and Mr. Bayard felt its full force. A resolution had been introduced by Grant's supporters approving his illegal invasion of Louisiana. It was a caucus measure, and the Republican senators, with some exceptions, supported it solidly and stolidly. It was brought in at an extra session of the Senate, ostensibly convened for other and executive business. It was an attempt to "whitewash," to slaver over a bold and glaring usurpation of power, dangerous, if justified, to our institutions, and to the perpetrator, if condemned. In France or Mexico a military commander who had ventured so far would have been compelled to resort to a *coup d'état* in order to save his head. The resolution was both unwarranted and unprecedented; not to oppose it was to accept Grant as an "authorized interferer and agitator in the affairs of the States, and constitution maker for all the States."

Every feeling of Mr. Bayard's, all his convictions, bristled against any such conclusion, which seemed to him to imply the definitive and final winding up of constitutional government in this country, and he spoke against the fact and spirit of the whole proposition with intense force and earnestness. His argument was profound and conclusive, but the tincture of strong and deep feeling which pervaded it was unusual, even for so earnest and positive a man as he. In his peroration to this speech there are frank declarations in regard to himself which we do not encounter elsewhere in any of his speeches, and which it would be impossible to elicit from so reserved and modest a public man in his calmer moments. These golden words embody a confession which ought to be engraved in a conspicuous place among the recorded speeches of American statesmen. They are the declaration of faith of a Senator of the United States in these turbulent, self-seeking, corrupt times.

"Mr. President," said Mr. Bayard, "in 1869 I came to the Senate of the United States, never having been a member of any public assembly prior to that time. My pursuits were congenial; the reward obtained was sufficent to give me a pecuniary independence. Those from whom I drew my blood, whose name I bear, had been too long in public life not to have become poor; and, if my personal interests had been consulted, I should have continued to seek those rewards that industry and fair intelligence will bring to any man in a profession for which he is at all adapted. I had but one object, and that I believe I have steadily pursued. The country that I love had been rent by discord, and the hearts of its people had been alienated far, far from each other. I had no other object in coming here than to bring my fellow countrymen into accord with each other, and I am not conscious since I came that a word has been uttered by me or a vote cast tinged with unfriendliness to any portion of my country, North or South, or East or West. And now, sir, if I lift my voice in favor of a measure or in opposition, I have long ago been taught it will not be efficient in this assembly, but may be heard elsewhere, and even from me, if what comes is truth, there is a God of truth who shall make it efficient in his own good time."

These are words which should be pondered carefully. They were uttered in a moment of intense feeling, with the utmost sincerity. They are exactly and literally truthful. They represent the standard by which the life of at least one public man has been regulated and guided throughout; and how many of Mr. Bayard's fellows in the Senate could utter them as ingenuously?

Only the other day, in repelling the insinuation of Mr. Blaine, that Kellogg, of Louisiana, could not be unseated because he was seated in pursuance of a bargain by which the Democrats gained a member, Mr. Bayard indignantly said that he would sooner have resigned his seat and abandoned his position as senator than consent to any such arrangement. This, in courtlier phrase, was the repetition of his declaration that, if he were left only the alternative of violating his conscience or retaining his honorable post, he could still " take my hat and go home." These things are quoted again in this place because they illustrate the character of Thomas Francis Bayard as a senator. They show that at the root of his consistency, which is too sincere, too vital, too much awake to living and contemporary issues and needs, to deserve the reproachful epithet of Bourbonism, and at the root also of his intense individuality, which is distinctive and forceful enough to have enabled him to tower aloft in any station, there are the big, warm heart and the sane mind in the sound body of an honest man of good proportions perfectly and orderly developed.

This character goes for its full worth in the Senate. Mr. Bayard is understood and appreciated there as in the outer world. Many hate him, for there are mean men, supple knaves, and fawning hypocrites there as elsewhere, and Mr. Bayard's frank scorn of pretense, his ready resentment of misrepresentation, and quick detection and exposure of fraud in intent and in act, have pricked many a bubble reputation, and torn away the veils of many a job; but those who do not love him still can not withhold from him their respect. He has not many intimates, yet his relations with all are courteous and kindly. The admiration which his natural powers and robust, incisive thought command is supplemented by the instinctive deference accorded to his pure and blameless integrity of life, his sincere and devoted earnestness of purpose. He is impulsive, warm-hearted, ingenuous as a boy, and his reserve is not of manner, nor does it create any suspicion of rusé policy. A rapid, untiring talker, you can not be with him ten minutes without noticing his alert curiosity of intellect, the wide range of topics of deep modern interest and vital purport to which his thoughts are constantly directing themselves, the exact co-ordination of his ideas with logical forms and firm-rooted principles, and his versatility, richness and correctness of diction, which is more striking, because less severely pruned, in his conversation than in his orations. You find him to be a simple-hearted, courteous gentleman, richly endowed with original thought and fine expression, robust in mind and body, straightforward, unaffected, earnest, a hearty and thoroughly modern American, in the fullest sympathy with democratic institutions and ideas—the very type and exemplar of a virile American hickory in the vigor of its maturing growth, strong, symmetrical, columnar, with its top toward the blue sky and its shaft unbending to wooing zephyr or to assailing storm. And, what you find Mr. Bayard to be in ten minutes, his associates in the Senate have known him to be for ten years. He has ripened, but he has not changed. He has grown, but always from the same roots, always upward!

He is tall, with a large frame, square, broad shoulders, massive joints, long limbs, spare but not thin in flesh. His clean-shaven face looks younger than his iron-gray hair, and his calm, cool, expressive gray eyes have the mobility and firmness of youth. But the pent-house arch of heavy eyebrows above them—eyebrows of prodigious flexibility and an unusually wide arc of motion—is that of the man who has earned his seat in the house of the elders. Those eyebrows, the well-lined mouth, and large, strong nose, give to Mr. Bayard's face traits enough of decision and faculty for leadership and command. But the forehead, high and white, and the general effect of the countenance are to create the impression of the thinker in active life, the philosophic athlete, who does not forget the academy while doing his duties and winning laurels in the palæstra. Mr. Bayard dresses with the simplicity and good taste of a man of the world whose duties are social as well as political. In talking with him you perceive the outcome of his active energy of thought and earnestness of purpose in a slight nervousness of manner that comports agreeably with his flexible, sonorous voice, so clear in enunciation and so equable in volume. He twirls a watch-key, he twists and untwists a bit of paper, he emphasizes his remarks with a lead pencil in his fingers, his mobile eyebrows rise and fall like a portcullis to a tower of strength; finally, he leaves his seat; he leans back, with his elbows upon a mantel or other piece of furniture, he sits astride another chair, his arms folded across its back, and, at last, when fully warmed up, he walks the room with long steps, his hands planted deep in his pockets, his chin raised, and his eyes now fixed upon some point above their level, now upon the carpet in deep concentration of thought, while the well-balanced sentences never cease to flow out from the large, expressive mouth.

Mr. Bayard's manner of discharging his duties as senator reflects a good deal of his individuality and his idiosyncrasies. He works well and works hard, but he selects his work, and, except on particular occasions, confines himself to it. He is not perpetually on the *qui vive* for words and phrases, for something to suspect or to quirk and carp at, like the captious and sardonic Edmunds. He loves business better than the sound of his voice, and has not Thurman's untiring joy in fence, which leads that pugnacious senator not only to take up every challenge, but also to keep tossing his own gauntlet into the ring, as if ever spoiling for a fight. He does not envy Blaine's "bounce" nor his reputation as a "free lance," nor does he lie in wait, like Conkling, for chances to make "hits" such as will please the galleries. He attends to the duties of a senator, and is too much occupied with the solid part of these duties to have either time or taste for their frippery and fribbles.

There are two classes of senators: those who do real work, and those who do nothing, or simply pretend to work. Mr. Bayard is of the former class. But this class must again be subdivided into other two classes: those who work for the public service, and those who work for their own private ends or to serve their selfish ambitions. Mr. Bayard is of the first class again; but these, in a still minuter classification, must be separated into the species of those who like details and routine work, and those who prefer broader fields and larger and more general matter to deal with and accomplish—just as lawers are case-lawyers and principle-lawyers, attorneys and counselors. Mr. Bayard's large, synthetic mind inclines him naturally to consort with those who act upon the broader field, and survey the affairs of the Senate from the wider point of vision. He does not neglect detail, but does not seek it. He is not a minimizer upon preference. His is a constructive intellect, rather than an anatomizing one. He is a statesman with a mind better adapted to grouping together large things than for picking small ones to pieces.

Mr. Bayard, like every other senator, is of course constrained to select the subjects of legislation to which to give his particular attention from the wide and multifarious range of matters coming before the Senate, and his choice is characteristic. He is alert upon all questions bearing upon the powers of the Constitution and the interpretation of that instrument. All questions interest him which affect in any way the functions and the harmonious reciprocal action of the co-ordinate branches of government; which involve the interpretation of, not so much this or that particular law, as *the law* itself, that *corpus juris* which rises towering, like a decorous and stately trunk, out of a bed of humus formed by the decay of particular leaves and branches from time immemorial. All questions are his which bear upon men's artificial relations in society—education, finance, political economy. His mind seems to have formed a distinct and definite conception of the ideal state that the founders of this republic had in view when they framed the Constitution as the ligament which should bind the States together in one harmonious whole. He defends this conception by holding himself armed cap-a-pie to resist every assault made upon it, and by toiling to repeal and lop away every excrescence which has grown upon it, and by trampling down every abortion that seeks to secure legitimacy by assuming its name and parodying its shape. The great leading and guiding principles of the tariff, the currency, the transportation service, the exchanges, he has mastered thoroughly and effectively ; he has gone into our foreign relations as far as they affect the national welfare and the national honor, and understands the principles of appropriation and the details and the rationale of the " Book of Estimates " as well as any man.

But omniscience is not Senator Bayard's foible. He does not air his opinions and his phrases *ad captandum*. He does not speak for buncombe. He does not speak at all unless the occasion demands it. Nor does he dabble a little here and dibble a little there day after day in the Senate, for the sake of saying something with each revolving sun. He does not feel called upon to support or object to every little bill that comes up from the committees. If his mind is made up, he votes. If he doubts, he asks for information. If it is satisfactory, he acquiesces. If he is not pleased, he states his objections simply and courteously, and then has done. All this makes him a pleasant senator to the whole body, and he never wrangles, never is assailed, unless, as we have shown, now and then in such cases as we have already described. This habitual abstention, this simple way, conjoined with his earnestness and zeal, make Mr. Bayard a very strong and powerful debater, and give great weight to his arguments when he does choose to speak. He speaks not for the sake of talking, but to convince or to persuade, and he has often done both. He gives a striking instance of this power of his, in his Phi Beta Kappa oration, from which we have already made some quotations. He was illustrating his views of the force of " unwritten laws."

"I wish," he said, "I could bring to the minds of those who hear me now the spirit and meaning of a scene which took place two or three years ago in one of the Southern States, whither I had gone to urge in friendly counsel the rejection of some false and dangerous suggestions in relation to our national finance, which were being introduced and recommended disingenuously and mischievously by political agents from other parts of the country. In the utter impoverishment of an agricultural people, suffering from a disorganized system of labor, prostration of industries, and an abolition of the only banking facilities upon which they had been accustomed to rely, it is scarcely to be wondered that any promise of immediate relief, even the shallow and mocking cry of 'More money,' should have been hailed with delight. It seemed to me then to be my duty to warn those fellow countrymen of ours, not only against the false economies of such doctrines, but to develop the danger to our national credit, and the assault upon the government itself, that lay concealed within the propositions of renewed 'inflation' and 'convertible bonds.'"

"One evening, after a pleasant dinner, and in all the freedom of social assembly, these topics were debated in a room filled with men of whom I was almost the only one who had not 'worn the gray' from 1861 to 1865.

"The discussion was vigorous—first, the economic, and,

finally, the patriotic side of the question—and to my appeals on this point there was but a chilly response; for it was in the days when military menace unhappily still survived as a political force of administration in the affairs of some of the States.

"Finally I said, 'Gentlemen, you are all very positive, and unwilling to accept my views, but I think I know how to control you, and, despite your strong language, can find means to obtain your submission.'

"There was no response for a moment; an atmosphere of resistance seemed to fill the room, and in the eyes around me shone a light of defiance. Then one of the party asked, with some severity of manner, 'Pray, sir, *how* do you propose to manage us so easily and compel our submission?'

"*I said, 'I would give you power to do right, and then I would defy you to betray the trust. You yourselves should be your conquerors.*'

"There were few men in that room who had not faced death in battle, and many bore the scars of conflict on their persons; but, as I looked around, the angry light of resentment had passed from their eyes, which were not unmoistened by a generous emotion, and I was left the victor on that field."

That was true eloquence, satisfactory to even the most exigent definition of the great mysterious power. Mr. Bayard has often exercised this force in the Senate; he always makes it felt on the stump. There, on great occasions (he never speaks on small ones), and in the open air, or in crowded assemblies, his attractive, judicious style warms up with a new glow; his clear, sounding voice, always well and skillfully modulated, rings with a new fervor; passion runs hand in hand with argument and reason, and the engrossing subject, the tremendous occasion, the inspiring presence, fill him with a fire that sets all his hearers aflame. His elaborate speeches are models of forensic skill and scholarly elocution, masculine, rapid, full of spirit, full of thought, illustrative of his captivating manners and bright, incisive intellect. He always commands attention, and, as has been neatly said, "His most trifling utterances derive force and dignity from the earnestness and sincerity pervading them." His winning courtesy is most charming, and inspires him always with the happiest "hits," and his hearers with a personal warmth of feeling for him. Thus, in opening a campaign speech at Baltimore, in 1875, he said: "Even to-night a man whose heart is in the cause asked me why I came to Maryland when there was more debatable ground elsewhere. A soldier feels that he must go where he is ordered, but even to him there must come a choice of duties, and I could not resist the wish to address the people of Maryland. *Elsewhere, I can ask and hope for a welcome; here, I am sure of it.*" So, likewise, when he spoke at the Georgia State fair in the same year, he said, in acknowledging the welcome extended to him, that it had been so general that he could not believe that it was restrained by party ties. Burns, one of the sweetest of native poets, had said that, when called upon to enter the great, unknown future, he could wish no better reception than "just a Highland welcome." "I," said the Senator, "could wish nothing better, after passing an ordeal of any kind, than just a Georgia welcome." More pleasant still was his compliment to scholarship, when addressing the literary societies of the University of Virginia in 1873. "Specialists," he said, "undoubtedly have their high uses, and far be it from me to suggest a want of respect for their recondite and highly meritorious labors. But to such I do not presume to speak. How should I, heated and dusty, and not a little weary with the march and struggle of active life, address myself to such a professor as that German, celebrated for a life-long devotion to the Greek article, and who, when dying, whispered to a friend, 'My life has been a great mistake!' and, when asked what so troubled his last moments, feebly and feelingly replied, 'I have attempted too much; I should have confined myself to the dative case.'"

But this velvet covers steel, as we have shown in the way in which Mr. Bayard retorted upon Mr. Boutwell. In his earliest speech upon the currency question,* Mr. Bayard found it necessary to retaliate upon the late Vice-President Wilson for some of his flings at the Democratic party, and the rebuke was full of a very lofty scorn:

"The other day," he said, "the Senator from Massachusetts took occasion, in the plenitude of his power, and from that elevation which the vast majority of his party in this body gave him, to throw taunts and slurs upon the Democratic party. His mouth was filled with phrases from Scripture. He stood knee-deep in his own praises of himself and his party. He referred us to the Bible for his commission, and announced himself one of the vicegerents of Almighty God. There was a parable in that good book, with which he affected to have much familiarity, which it seemed to me he had overlooked. It was that of a certain Pharisee who went up into the temple to make his prayer, and made such a one as we heard here a few days ago from the honorable Senator. The value of that prayer we have nothing less than divine estimate for. We know how it was compared with that

* Funding Bill, March 7, 1870.

other and humbler prayer that came from a man who had at least begun his Christianity by the necessary virtue of humility.

"As I listened to the honorable Senator, there were some readings of my earlier days that came back to me, and among them I remember when one of the purest-minded and sweetest poets of our language had been similarly assailed for his alleged irreverence. It was Tom Hood, who dedicated an ode to one Mr. Wilson of his day, when, in his absence from his native country, he was assailed by that gentleman. There is a portion of it which, it strikes me, it might be well to recall, to see whether there can be found in it any application to our own time. Hood's ode to that Mr. Wilson ran as follows:

> 'Shun pride, O Rea! whatever sort beside
> You take in lieu, shun spiritual pride.
> A pride there is of rank, a pride of birth,
>   A pride of learning, and a pride of purse,
> A London pride—in short, there be on earth
>   A host of prides, some better and some worse.
> But of all prides since Lucifer's attaint
> The proudest swells a self-elected saint.'

"The moral of the lecture which we received from that honorable Senator was that we should shun principles that led us into minorities; that when a man's political principles became unpopular, they should therefore be abandoned. He did not seem to understand how a man can go cheerfully into a minority rather than surrender his convictions of right. It has been the standing by those convictions that has brought the Democratic party into the minority in which they stand on this floor."

In the course of Mr. Bayard's speech in the Louisiana

Returning Board*—fruitful theme! he was rudely assailed by J. Rodman West, carpet-bag senator from that State. Mr. Bayard's reply was brief: "Mr. President," said he, "one word. Perhaps the rules of order of this body might have been invoked when any Senator was charged with having by his precept and his example led to lawlessness and outrage. Such was the language in effect used by the Senator who has just taken his seat in regard to me. But I do not invoke the protection of the rules. It seems to me that it might have been wiser for him to have abstained from such remarks; *for on the one side stands the record of my debate in this chamber, and stands the record of my personal life, and on the other side stands the charge. I leave them there to those who know both.*"

His scorn of action for buncombe, of neglecting obvious duty in the pursuit of cheap popularity, broke out finely when the amendment for abolishing the franking privilege was before the Senate.† In casting his vote against it, Mr. Bayard said: "I think it pretty certain that an equal amount of humbuggery has never connected itself with any matter that ever came before Congress as is connected with this proposed abolition of the franking privilege. It has been a joke pretty much for the last hour in the Senate, perhaps a serious one for the people of the country. In order that the Senate may take time to consider this matter a little more discreetly, I move that the Senate do now adjourn."

His power of irony is capitally illustrated in his speech on the admission of Mississippi.‡

"Mr. President, yesterday I listened with much interest and pleasure to the very able and eloquent speech of the

---

* Senate, December 15, 1876. † January 22, 1873.
‡ Senate, February 15, 1870.

honorable Senator from Wisconsin [Mr. Carpenter], and
I regret that I had not the opportunity of reading it before
I submitted these remarks to the Senate. It contained
a very novel and ingenious method for dissolving
the Union, by all the States, by means of conventions
called for that purpose, going back into their territorial
condition by what might be termed a universal solvent
for melting away government. If the honorable Senator
applies for a patent, I trust it will not be granted to him;
the invention is too fraught with danger. In other respects
his speech struck me as containing much that was
sound in doctrine, and to much that he said I would give
a warm approval. But it is so now that a man can not
make in this body a sound, constitutional argument without
being instantly accused of tending to the Democratic
party. This is the great bogie with whose name radical
nurses frighten their unruly children into quiescence. The
honorable Senator seemed disturbed in his mind—his prophetic
mind—inasmuch as it was to his vision quite possible
that for the sins of the Radical party Providence
might permit the Democratic party again to come into
power. This, to my mind, would be only another proof
of Almighty beneficence, that after all the crimes of this
Radical party, committed through so long a time and so
often, such mercy should still be extended to them; and,
believing in that beneficent spirit, I do not doubt that we
shall soon, and at no very distant day, see this precise exhibition
indicated by the Senator of the forgiveness and
care which a kind Providence extends to sinful men even
in the midst of their wickedness."

On another occasion, also, Mr. Bayard sent a shaft at
Mr. Carpenter, which must have found its way through
the joints of that senator's harness. This was in his

speech on Louisiana, on February 27, 1873, delivered about 6 A. M., toward the close of a stormy, continuous session, in which the conservative members had resorted to every parliamentary device to prevent what they knew to be an unconstitutional measure from being adopted. "No other senator," said Mr. Bayard, "than he who has just spent an entire day in demonstrating with force and brilliancy the utter falsity of a proposition, and ended his debate by recording his vote in its favor, could have been capable of the coolness, not to say effrontery or audacity, which has just been exhibited by the Senator from Wisconsin, in turning to Democratic members of this body, and seeking to place upon their shoulders the responsibility for the defeat of a measure which the Senator has just aided in loading down with an amendment, reciting facts proven by himself to be false, and including results full of outrage, injustice, and usurpation of control in the affairs of the unhappy people of Louisiana."

Senator Logan was treated to a touch of this same sort in Mr. Bayard's speech* on the army bill:

"Why, sir, what is the object and intent of such language as was used by the Senator from Illinois the other day when, in the midst of very audible denunciation, he warned us in his most tragic tones, and with the aid of his elaborated manuscript, in such words as these:

"'Let Democrats of the South and their northern allies beware the storm they are raising. The spirit of retaliation once raised, sir, will only be appeased by the most radical assurances of future quiet. If the disease upon our body-politic again requires the knife, they may rest assured the surgeon will "cut beyond the wound to make the cure complete."'

"This simile may be termed one of surgery; to many

* April 21, 1879.

it will be more suggestive of butchery. I do not propose to exchange warnings, much less threats, either with the Senator or his party; but to my fellow countrymen I suggest that the knife, the use of which is to be restricted only 'by the most radical assurances of future quiet,' may indeed 'cut beyond the wound,' and reach the life of the patient."

In this speech Mr. Bayard's quickness in repartee was illustrated at Mr. Blaine's expense. There had been a little "spat" between them, of the sort which Mr. Blaine is ever provoking, in regard to some "precedents" for military violence at the polls. The dialogue closed in this way:

"Mr. BLAINE. Will the Senator yield to me a moment?

Mr. BAYARD. With pleasure.

Mr. BLAINE. In regard to the Senator's direction as to my wisdom, of course I will take care of that myself. The Senator began the interruption which I made by palpably misquoting what I had said.

Mr. BAYARD. I accepted the Senator's correction.

Mr. BLAINE. Then the Senator comes back now, and gives me monition as to my lack of wisdom in making an assertion which he had put in my mouth, and which had no foundation whatever in fact. That is all to which I desire to call attention.

Mr. BAYARD. *The Senator does me injustice. His lack of wisdom I shall never attempt to supply.*"

Mr. Bayard's indignant resentment against Sheridan's infamous "banditti" dispatch to Belknap, dated January 5, 1875, burst forth in the Senate three days later, and the Senator's words should be pondered by those jaunty politicians of the day—the ephemera of a very transient sunshine—who would "go with a light heart" to Grant and a third term. After quoting the dispatch, and Belknap's reply to it of the 7th,* Mr. Bayard said: "Ah, Mr. President, if there was the tone that under other administrations animated the executive of this country, he would never sign his name again as Lieutenant-General of the United States army. Is this the language of an American officer toward his fellow countrymen? Why, sir, if he were in a hostile country among the sick and wretched Piegan Indians, had he been in the service of Mexico, there could not have been a more ruthless, a darker, or more bloody threat than is contained in the closing lines of this dispatch to the Secretary of War. This is language relating to the citizens of three States of this Union. Is it the language that is due from an officer of the army of the United States, wearing that honorable uniform, the protector, the guard, the glory of his people, without distinction of party; or is it not the language of some captain of a band of janizaries, asking orders from an Oriental despot in regard to his ruthless extermination of those whom he may deem the foes of power? This man, educated with one of his text-books the Constitution of his country, asks that Congress shall pass an *ex post facto* law, making that a crime which was not a crime at the time of the commission of the alleged offense, and creating new punishments to make the penalty still more severe. He asks for military commissions, in these times of peace, to try men neither in the land nor naval service of the United States. He asks for drum-head courts-martial to try citizens over whom there is no pretense that the authority of the army or of the

---

* "Your telegrams all received. The President and *all of us* have full confidence, and thoroughly approve your course." How many of "all of us" shared in the post-tradership profits?

navy is extended. What is the dark and bloody threat at the close of his dispatch for, Senators? What did he mean when he asked the President to issue a proclamation declaring these citizens banditti, and that then no further action need be taken *except that which would devolve upon him?*

"I confess to you as I read this dispatch my blood curdled in my veins. If it had been sent in the midst of strife by a man heated by the excitement of combat, there might have been palliation for it, because a cooling time would have come when his better reason would operate, when 'Philip sober' would have answered this 'Philip drunk.' But this dispatch was penned in safety; it was penned in quiet; it was penned where there was nothing that threatened him, and without anything to cause him excitement except the apprehended loss of political power to the chief whom he was sent there to represent.

"What character does this officer seek to assume? There was Tristan l'Hermite, the provost-marshal of the royal household, whom the genius of Scott has painted until he is familiar in every household. It seems to me that this officer has modeled himself much upon the morals and conduct of this hangman of royalty of days gone by.

"Sir, I say that in a proper condition of sentiment with those in power he would not have been suffered to remain for five minutes in command at New Orleans. He has no one quality that fits him properly for the duties of command there now. His first requisite should be good-will and kindness to the people, strict impartiality; no threats of force, careful obedience to civil rule. This was the example he should have set as a high official, honored by his country, and invested with high discretionary powers; and, as this example does not seem to originate with him, I want it now taught him, and taught so that not alone he will not forget, but that every other officer of the army and navy of the United States will learn and know that it is in the affections, in the respect of their fellow countrymen, and not in their fears, that they are to find their place of honor and of safety."

In the same vein are the denunciations of Major Merrill, and many another passage of fiery scorn or fierce indignation in Mr. Bayard's speeches. Mr. Bayard's speech on the Civil Rights Bill, in the Senate, on February 26, 1875, contains a masterly example of the *reductio ad absurdum*. The question being upon the bill to protect all citizens in their civil and legal rights in pursuance of the new amendments to the Constitution, the Senator, after showing in a strong legal argument that the Supreme Court had decided these ordinances to be mandatory upon the States, and not upon the individuals in the States, he proceeded to call attention to the impracticability of enforcing the proposed regulations and prohibition in the manner suggested. "Now, does it not appear too absurd, almost impossible, to imagine Congress gravely proposing that the grave federal government of our Union shall be attending to the duties of an hotel clerk; that we shall be examining into the relative advantages and condition of the bedrooms of an inn, or deliberating upon the measure of duty of the head waiter at an hotel, legislating so that equal enjoyment at the *table d'hôte* is given to the guests, or supervising the railway conductor, and taking care by law that he assigns equally good seats to all the passengers, or, assuming the functions of the theatre manager or his usher, shall insist that he have always present in his mind the dignity and power of the great government of the United States. No other illustration is needed to exhibit the absurdity of this bill than the mere suggestion to assign duties of such a nature to such a government. It seems to me that when the Supreme Court of the United States shall be found sitting in grave judgment whether A or B have had equal seats or equal comforts, or equal enjoyment at a hotel, or in their transportation, or at some theatre where their idleness and pleasure may have led them, then the position will be so absurd that the case will be laughed out of court, even if there was no other way to get rid of it."

Illustrating here, as we try to do, rather the form and quality of his elocution than the body and texture of his thought and feeling, it is not needed to do more than refer to those many pages in his speeches in which his deep and sedate reflection overflows in sententious paragraphs of gnomic thought, in comprehensive statements of fundamental principles and universal law, and in fine original summaries of complex conditions in public affairs. The philosophy of government is often and luminously expounded in these discursive moments, which seem to have a peculiar charm for his grave and earnest intellect. Even in active and exciting debate he will fling out a philosophical period such as distills the very essence of a situation. One of the finest and most characteristic of these may be found in Mr. Bayard's speech on the Louisiana Returning Board, when, in replying to Mr. Sherman's long tirades about atrocities to the negroes and the need for further "protection" to them, he said:

"The laws of the land have given all that human laws can give. They have given to the colored people—

EQUALITY OF OPPORTUNITY. Now, that being given, how are you, upon the basis of equal rights, to undertake to supply the deficiencies and differences with which the Almighty has seen fit to mark his creatures, both as races and as individuals? We all know that men start in the race of life equipped perhaps with equal opportunities of information; it is so at the bar; it is so in every pursuit; but we start, how? We start with the natural gifts which are not created or bestowed by statute law. They did not come from man, and by him they are not to be controlled. You might as well tell me that you could dwarf the intellect of a Webster to the stature of that of some half idiot, and say that because these grand and almost God-like gifts had raised the one to a position of weight where his counsel and thought swayed nations and senates, therefore the weak and the ignorant could, by some poor statute law or amendment to the Constitution, be raised to the level of the gifted and the strong. No, Mr. President, it can not be and it never will be. All that we can do is to give a fair chance, to give, as I said before, equality of opportunity to the people of this country, to the poor boy equally with the rich man's son, to the black man who comes from his hovel, or the rich man who emerges from his palace. They must take their chances in this battle of life, and, if they be deficient and defective, do not suppose that an act of Congress can undertake to remedy the fact. It will not be so."

The equality of opportunity, let it be noted, is the limit. Republican government can not go any further in that direction, for the next step is communism, which requires the state to destroy the uses of opportunity by creating and maintaining the equality of *condition*. Mr. Bayard said some noteworthy things in this connection in his speech on the Pacific railroads* and their relation to the government. After remarking with surprise the indifference of the people to these great land and money grants, and comparing it with the excitement about the salaries bill, Mr. Bayard said:

"Mr. President, these great debts, which are being piled upon the toiling masses of this country in total disregard of the sufferings which are causing one universal groan to arise all over the land, are greatly to be deplored and dreaded in their results—but still more formidable is the question of the inroads upon and the overthrow of *the great republican idea of disintegration and distribution of power*. The possession of irresponsible power never failed in human history to corrupt its possessor. Well did our forefathers know it. They knew that power, like jealousy, grew with what it fed upon, and in many modes in building up this government they sought to check its growth.

"They did not intend that the individual should wither, but by encouraging individuality they sought to encourage the growth of men. They sought, not strength by massing weakness, that atom might protect atom, but, by creating the greatest number of vigorous integers, to make the state strong. Out of individuality grows competition; out of consolidation grows monopoly. Hence their political institutions, the abolition of rank and title, abolition of the rule of primogeniture, an equal division of estates without regard to sex, the subjection of lands to the payment of debts, the equality of all men before the law, widespread suffrage, destruction of entailed estates, limitation upon devises, all tending to facilitate the distribution of wealth, and power and to prevent per-

* Senate, April 5, 1878.

petuities. And yet the doctrine and practice of incorporation was suffered to creep in, destroying as it does individuality, consolidating as it does all power and making its owners morally irresponsible, creating artificial beings who never die and whose estates are never to be distributed, but are perpetual.

"Mr. President, the consequences of this may be remote, but to my eye they are certain. It is the creation of power without moral and legal responsibility, and that is fatal to any form of government under which it shall be encouraged or permitted to exist."

We have already spoken of Mr. Bayard's eloquence. Let us close this chapter with another instance or two to illustrate its quality. In his speech on the Ku-Klux act (May 21, 1872), Mr. Bayard was referring to the need for brotherhood between North and South, and the ease with which it could be brought about, and related the following to the listening Senate:

"When the war closed in the spring of 1865 an officer of the Southern army found himself, like thousands of his compatriots, without a dollar, on his way to his home and family. Not far from Atlanta he found his aged mother and family, people whom in 1861 he had left in affluence, surrounded by all the luxury and refinement that inherited wealth and cultivation for generations in the same family can alone produce. He threw himself from his weary horse and entered the door of his dwelling. The aged mother, the wife, sisters, little children, were all there. Death, which had held his harvest among the brave men on the field of battle and in the Northern prisons, had spared the weaker ones. Their suffering had been to live. They had seen not only the luxuries which their mode of living had made habitual swept away by the breath of war, but even the necessaries of a frugal life had gone, and when my informant found these ladies and children, once so tenderly cared for, they had been living for ten days upon dried okra and salt. This had been their sole subsistence. Unable to relieve their desperate condition, he remounted his horse and rode back to the town of Atlanta, to solicit food to keep his family alive.

"I am credibly informed there was not a head of horned cattle, a sheep, a pig, or chicken in that county out of the camp of the United States army. On his way to Atlanta he met a colonel of the United States army who, without knowing him personally, mentioned his name (historic in Georgia and Carolina), and inquired the way to his residence. My informant disclosed himself to the officer, and, finding his purpose, told him of his condition, and accepted such a loan of money as enabled him to purchase from the United States commissary at Atlanta the necessaries of life for his family. I will not recount how, with energy and courage, he struggled with varying success to make a living for those who were dependent on him, but the election of Bullock and the appointment of his State officials forced him to abandon the practice of law, where merit and ability could not compete with corrupt favoritism.

"About this time he wrote to a friend in the North a letter descriptive of the condition of Southern men like himself, honestly endeavoring to act as faithful citizens of the government of the United States, and finding no confidence exhibited in their good intentions, but, on the other hand, rebuff and discredit, while thieves, camp-followers, and ignorant and vicious negroes were placed in power over them. This letter found its way into print in some of the Northern papers, among others, I believe, in the 'New York Tribune.' A few weeks after the letter was written my informant received by mail a letter postmarked Boston, Massachusetts. He opened it, and found inclosed a check for $1,000 and a few lines from the writer, stating he had seen the letter referred to, and desired, as a Northern man, to aid a fellow citizen in a distant State struggling in such bitter adversity. The writer's name was totally unknown to him, and he thought it must be a mistake or a cruel hoax. He submitted the check to a banker, who at once informed him it was good for its full amount. He, however, considering there must be some mistake, wrote to Boston, stating the arrival of the letter with the check, but his fear that his motive in writing which drew forth the remittance had been misunderstood; that he might have been supposed to be what was known as a 'Union man' in the Southern acceptation of that term, or a repentant rebel disposed to gain favor with the successful party by condemning his own past course. He told him that he was neither; that he had been an original and conscientious believer in the right and duty of secession in 1861, and had no regrets, except for his failure; but that he accepted his fate and was ready to keep faith with the government which had conquered.

"A reply from Boston to this letter assured him that the writer had earnestly advocated the prosecution of the war, and during the war would have held him an enemy, but that peace had come, and he now sought to make him a friend, and took this as a natural mode of doing it, and begged him to keep and use the money. I need not say how much the heart of this Southerner was touched, but he was a man of honor, and, though sorely pressed for money, felt in looking over the entire field of his affairs that even with the $1,000 he was greatly in debt, and, in fact, insolvent. He felt it was his duty, as it was his right, to avail himself of the bankrupt law of the United States, and start afresh, after giving up all he possessed, which consisted chiefly of the farm and homestead which sheltered his family. He therefore wrote again to the good man in Boston, telling him these facts, and declining his proffered loan under the circumstances. The mail soon brought a request to know the precise condition of his affairs. He made it out in exact detail, and his statement disclosed debts several thousand dollars in excess of his assets.

"In prompt return of mail a letter reached him, with a check for the amount of his needs in full. His debts were paid, his energies restored, his family retained in their home, the day of his adversity had passed, and prosperity met him with pleasant smile and open hands. The money so lent by the Boston merchant to a total stranger in a Southern State, one whose face he had never seen, whose opinions, social and political, he had ever opposed, has been returned; but this is the least part of the transaction. There is a debt which will never be paid so long as life-blood warms that Southerner's heart—the debt of love, of gratitude, of friendship, which binds him and his kindred with ties stronger than iron to that Boston merchant, and all who bear his name or are of his kindred. The name of the Northern man is borne by the son of the Southern man. It will be a household name that shall couple those two families in true ties of friendship while their names shall last. Should danger or trouble assail the man of the North or his kindred, he can count upon the ready hand of his Southern brother to defend him—a defense rendered without money and without price; the cheap defense that human love gives without reckoning, never so glad as when giving it.

"Why should not these two families of Massachusetts and Georgia be allowed to typify the relations of the Northern and the Southern people? You may be sure, Senators, that like causes will produce like effects. It is in your power. Shall it be done? In justice to his State and to the people of all America, I am called upon to give the name of the Boston man who set this wise and noble example to his fellow countrymen. It was Daniel Denny, the Boston merchant, whose wisdom of the heart knew how to conquer men more effectually than he who has won the bloodiest garland gained in battle. He overcame enmity by kindness—the great law of love, whose divine Expositor was born on earth eighteen hundred and seventy-two years ago, but whose teachings seem so little heeded in these latter days.

"Within a few weeks Mr. Denny has gone to his honored grave, but his good name shall not be forgotten.

> 'Only the actions of the just
> Smell sweet and blossom in the dust.'

"I saw and felt in my personal intercourse in Georgia the kindly influences which his trust in human nature had created.

"I remember well this gentleman telling me of a meeting of those who had been Confederate officers shortly after the occurrence which I have related. They were impoverished; they were sore with many things that had visited them in the way of domestic and political affliction. They had much to condemn and little to praise. In the North they found but little to praise, and little, apparently, to thank the government for. While they were relating instances of their hardships, this gentleman arose and told this story in simplicity and truth; and he told me that among these angry and sore men, who had breasted battle many a time and bore upon their persons the scars of conflict, there were tears soft as woman's shed at this one touch of human kindness:

'What can war but endless wars still breed?'"

In a still finer strain than this, to our thinking, is the peroration to Mr. Bayard's recent speech in favor of restoring Fitz-John Porter to his place in the army.* "Something," he remarked, "has been said about his receiving the pay and allowances of his rank. Upon my soul, I think it is scarcely worth mentioning. It seems to me that the great act is the act of restoration, and that this incident, the payment of money that was due to him fairly under the law, should go with it. If it be true, and who can doubt it is true, that for fifteen years this man has sat with a crushed and aching heart asking for justice at the hands of his government, what money can compensate him? Who among us would for money's sake stand for one week with that dreadful, slow, unmoving finger of scorn pointed at us, conscious all the while of its cruel and bitter injustice? If you unbolted your treasury and poured its contents at his feet, it would be nothing to him as compared to that which he has suffered. It really seems to me this point is insignificant and small beyond notice.

"In the course of this debate I have heard it said, 'Wait until you hear from the people on this subject.' Well, Mr. President, I hope we will hear from the people; but before we hear from the people I want them to hear from me. I am not waiting for the echo of popular applause or condemnation. I think no greater insult can

* March 8, 1880.

be offered to the people of America than to tell them that you suppose they will condemn a public man who tells the truth and endeavors to do justice. Is it service to the people to distrust them and conceal from them your real judgments? Oh, sir, there rang out in the ages long ago from the lips of the aged patriarch in the depth of his sorrows, 'Though he slay me, yet will I trust in him'; and shall not we trust in those we profess to serve? Shall we not trust in those who we say are virtuous, honest, and intelligent? Shall we not vote and speak according to the conscience that has been placed in the breast of every man among us? This country of ours is one of the leading nations of the world, and little minds are not fit to govern it. If this government should fail and go down amid the tears of those who love constitutional liberty and republican freedom, close to the root of its cause of failure will be found the fact that her representative and public men disguised their honest opinions and failed to tell the people the truth, as they knew it to exist."

This sort of speaking can not help but be effective, and we know that it is so. A narrative is extant of the impression made by a speech of Mr. Bayard's, at a small town in Eastern Maryland, in the last days of the campaign of 1876. "We can not pretend," says the imperfect account, "to give an extended synopsis of even that address, but we can not forbear to print one great utterance that fell from his lips. In words so simple and calm he said it, too, that the audience sat hushed and still. 'When I look at the way in which unprincipled men,' he said, 'have outraged the laws, the trust of the great American people, the confidence of the better men of their own party, it does not make me angry, but it makes me sad, *so sad*.' This was said with a pathos and a sudden overclouding of his face that was lighted all up with energy but a moment before. He looked tired of the contest, and the people could not break the spell with applauding. The spell that fell on the audience was the outgrowth of that mesmeric influence that emanates from some men born to lead. . . . For a moment after he had taken his seat the spell remained, and then it was broken, and pent-up feelings found utterance in a deafening greeting."

This is eloquence, and the naïve honesty of the imperfect description makes one regret he had not heard it with his own ears. It seems more fitting to conclude this brief outline of Mr. Bayard's public life with this little narrative than to prolong it with eulogies not to his taste or parallels which might reflect upon political rivals. Such as the man is, his works, and, in some measure, his ways, have been frankly and fully presented. It is such a character as must give all intelligent persons new confidence in the stability and permanence of our institutions when they reflect that Mr. Bayard is one of our foremost statesmen, and a man upon whom the hopes of very many are concentrated, that he may become in the near future the leader of the republic backward from perilous paths to the better ways of old.

THE END.

www.ingramcontent.com/pod-product-compliance
Lightning Source LLC
Chambersburg PA
CBHW022051230426
43672CB00008B/1139